LETTERS FROM
THE VOYAGES OF
ST. FRANCES CABRINI

Letters From the Voyages of
St. Frances Cabrini

Catholic Treehouse, Columbus, Ohio 2024

Letters From the Voyages of St. Frances Cabrini

ISBN 979-8-9855509-8-6

This work has been prayerfully entrusted to the patronage of St. Francis de Sales.

Dedicated to all missionaries who, like Mother Cabrini, bravely devote their lives to bringing the light of Christ to those living in spiritual darkness and physical hardship.

Santa
Francesca Saverio Cabrini

BEATIFICATION
NOVEMBER 13-1938

CANONIZATION
JULY 7-1946

Born in Sant'Angelo Italy
July 15-1850

Died in Chicago
December 22-1917

Table of Contents

Preface i

Editor's Note iii

Forward 3

Introduction 9

1. Second Voyage to New York, April, 1890 19

2. New York to Havre, August 1890 35

3. Havre to New York, September, 1891 43

4. New York to Nicaragua, October, 1891 59

5. Genoa to New York, September, 1894 83

6. New Orleans to Panama, May, 1895 109

7. Panama down the Pacific and across the Andes to
    Buenos Aires, October, 1895 145

8. Buenos Aires to Barcelona, August, 1896 189

9. Liverpool to New York, November, 1898 207

10. New York to Havre, September, 1899 235

11. Genoa to Buenos Aires, December, 1900 247

12. Buenos Aires to Genoa, August, 1901 265

13. London to New York, August, 1902 271

14. On the Occasion of the Inauguration of
    the House in Denver, November, 1902 285

15. Letter to the Students of the Teachers' College
    in Rome, May, 1904 297

16. Letter to the Students of the Teachers' College
    in Rome, May, 1905 311

17. Letter to the Students of the Teachers' College
    in Rome, February, 1906 321

Epilogue: Mother Cabrini and Her Work 347

Selected Prayers 353

Preface

During the course of history, there are unique souls whose lives illuminate for us examples of compassion, service, resilience, and unwavering faith. Among these radiant individuals is St. Frances Xavier Cabrini, a true beacon of hope whose legacy continues to echo through time. As the first American citizen to be canonized as a saint, her life embodies the triumph of dedication, love, and service in the name of the Sacred Heart of Jesus. She came as a missionary to our country and now she is forever remembered as America's first saint.

Within the pages of her letters we are not merely presented with historical remarks and facts; we embark on an inspiring profound journey alongside a woman whose unwavering devotion to God's work transformed lives —especially the poor and forgotten—and thus impacted this very country.

St. Cabrini's letters are a gift to all who read them. They are more than mere correspondence–they are windows into the heart and mind of a saint. Mother Cabrini's journey is one of courage, conviction, and tireless commitment to aiding the marginalized and forgotten, especially women and children of Catholic immigrants. Her words, penned with an invincible spirit, resonate even today, and invite us to join her in her mission of love and compassion. She knew and believed that, like St. Paul, "with God, all things are possible." These letters offer us a glimpse into the past and an opportunity to encounter hope among the pages. As you will read, life was not easy for Mother Cabrini, but with Christ, she was able to bring meaning and purpose to each day of her life.

As you delve into these invaluable letters, allow yourself to be guided by the wisdom and grace of Mother Cabrini. May her words inspire you to cultivate a deeper understanding of her extraordinary life, guide you toward a deeper spiritual life, and inspire you to want to grow in virtue and grace.

May the Sacred Heart of Jesus touch our hearts and guide us each day!

Emily Jaminet
Executive Director, Sacred Heart Enthronement Network

Editor's Note

When I first ran across the letters of St. Frances Cabrini, I was immediately struck by them and captivated by their charm, eloquence, and the way she captured the moments of her travels with such vivid detail. Her letters breathe with the life of a tireless voyager, describing what it was like to travel by sea, train, and donkey around the turn of the 20th Century. Her words paint shimmering seascapes and landscapes, and recount anecdotes that range from humorous to heartwarming to harrowing. Woven throughout, one also finds radiant depictions of her faith life: her love for the Eucharist, her devotion to the Sacred Heart of Jesus, and her passionate zeal for the salvation of every soul. Indeed, these letters are a window into the heart and soul of a missionary saint.

I tried to find a print copy of the book, but even the used booksellers had nothing. I felt that Mother Cabrini's letters were too amazing to be so inaccessible, so I began work on re-typesetting them from the original; the work you hold in your hands is the result of that effort. Every attempt was made to keep the language of the original translation intact. In a few instances the spelling has been modernized and the punctuation set in modern style, but otherwise the text is identical to the original translation. Several of the letters are incomplete, and are noted as such.

Most of Mother Cabrini's letters included herein were sent to the Missionary Sisters of the Sacred Heart, the order she founded, to whom she affectionately called her "dear Daughters". The others were sent to the students at the Teacher's College in Rome. When you read her letters and see her relationship with the sisters, you will see clearly that the title "Mother" is appropriate when referring to this amazing woman of faith.

Now, let us begin our journeys with Mother Cabrini.

In Corde Jesu,
Michael A. LaMorte
Editor

The English translation of Mother Cabrini's travels, printed in London twenty years ago, lacks much of the classic beauty of the original Italian. Though the Blessed Foundress wrote exclusively for her "Daughters", without any attempt to literary style, the original letters, penned *tra un'onda e l'altra*, are gems of literature.

This new edition is printed to satisfy the numerous requests of Mother Cabrini's clients. A more faithful and better translation will be published as soon as circumstances permit. No letters of Mother Cabrini's first voyage were found among her manuscripts. This volume begins with her second voyage to New York.

We are grateful to His Excellency, the Most Reverend Amleto Giovanni Cicognani, D.D. for his kind permission to preface these letters with the biographical sketch from his book *Sanctity in America*.

The Missionary Sisters of The Sacred Heart Of Jesus, 1944

Foreward

by The Most Reverend Amleto Giovanni Cicognani, D.D.
Apostolic Delegate to the United States

Frances Xavier Cabrini was born at Sant'Angelo di Lodi (Lombardy), Italy, on July 15, 1850, the youngest of a family of thirteen children. Even as a child she learned to love prayer, following the splendid example of her parents, her brothers and sisters. At the age of seven she was confirmed and at ten received her First Holy Communion.

Frances, who possessed a ready intelligence and an unselfish disposition, was fired with enthusiasm upon reading the Annals of the Society for the Propagation of the Faith. Although she was but a child, the missionary ideal was beginning to fasten itself in her heart–only half understood perhaps, but nonetheless real. In her child's play, she would gather violets and, placing them in tiny paper boats, send them away on the waters of the country brooks, dreaming the while of herself making long voyages to distant lands to carry on the work of converting pagans. When she was thirteen she revealed her desire to her sister Rose, fifteen years older than she. "You who are so small and not yet educated dare to dream of becoming a missionary!" was the comment she received. But Frances kept her radiant dream in her heart and waited patiently. In the meantime she continued her studies, and at the age of eighteen obtained her teacher's certificate. A year later her parents died.

Frances then definitely considered the question of her vocation. She sought to enter two religious communities, and in each case was rejected on account of her delicate constitution and poor health. Thus apparently unable to follow her heart's desire, the young girl nevertheless gave her leisure to works of charity and religion. At the request of the parish priest she taught catechism to children and visited the poor; when she was twenty-two (1872), she distinguished herself in assisting the victims of an epidemic of smallpox.

For two years Frances now taught in the public school of the nearby town of Vidardo, and became known even to the civil authorities for her ability and her kindness. In 1874 she accepted the position of directress of a school for orphans at Codogno–always, however, keeping the missionary ideal before her. In 1880 the Most Reverend Dominic Gelmini, Bishop of Lodi, who had learned of the extraordinary intellectual and moral qualities of the superior of the orphanage, summoned her and said: "You wish to become a missionary, the time is ripe; I do not know a community of missionary Sisters, you must found one." Frances, as an obedient daughter, answered humbly and confidently: "I shall seek a house." On November 14, 1880, with a few companions she took up residence in an abandoned monastery, formerly the property of the Franciscans of Codogno. The new home was soon surmounted by a statue of the Sacred Heart, and on the door was placed an inscription that is now known throughout the world: "Institute of the Missionary Sisters of the Sacred Heart."

The new Institute grew rapidly, and in a few years there were houses in many parts of Lombardy and Italy. In 1887 Mother Cabrini went to Rome to request the approval of the Rule by the Holy See, and to found a house in the Eternal City. The Cardinal Vicar answered her: "A Community founded only seven years ago wishes to establish itself in Rome and to be approved? This is too much! In Rome there are already many such Communities. And then, the funds? Do you have at least 150,000 *lire* ($30,000) to build a house? Return, return to Codogno: we will talk about it some other time." This answer was a deep disappointment, but Mother Cabrini, undaunted, comforted her weeping companion: "Be calm, the Lord will soon change his heart." God rewarded her faith, for a few days later she was again received by the Cardinal Vicar. "Are you ready to obey?" he asked. "Well then, found two houses instead of one." And shortly afterward, the decree of approval was given to the Institute.

During her residence in Rome, Mother Frances Xavier had occasion to make the acquaintance of the Most Reverend John B. Scalabrini, Bishop of Piacenza and founder of the Missionaries of St. Charles Borromeo for Italian Emigrants. It was this holy bishop who first informed her of the conditions existing among the Italians in America, and requested her to send some Sisters to cooperate in the work that the Scalabrinians had already begun in New York. Mother Cabrini had always earnestly desired to go among the infidels of China, and she would not even now have changed her plan had it not been for the advice given her by Pope Leo XIII. "Not to the East, but to the West," said the aged Pontiff; and Frances no longer had any doubts or regrets. She was provided with letters of recommendation from the Secretariat of State of His Holiness and from the Sacred Congregation of the Propagation of the Faith; and in just two weeks, she was on her way to the United States with six companions.

She landed in America on March 31, 1889. Immediately there were difficulties, but she was able to overcome them by her spirit of faith and fortitude, in the knowledge that she was fulfilling the mission entrusted to her by the Vicar of Jesus Christ. The condition of the Italian immigrants socially, economically and religiously was then very poor. The work of an apostle was urgently needed among them to help them combat the constant danger of loss of faith. Mother Cabrini began and extended her work for them with an energy that at times seemed rash. Taking for herself the motto of the Apostle, "*Omnia possum in eo qui me confortat*"—"I can do all things in Him Who strengtheneth me" (Phil. 4:13)—she opened schools, colleges, kindergartens, hospitals and free clinics in New York, New Orleans, Chicago, Seattle, Denver and Philadelphia. She did not confine her work to the United States but extended it to Nicaragua, South America, Spain, France and England. Her program was to follow the multitudes of Italians who had gone abroad from their native land, to keep alive and renew the faith of the adults and to care for the new generations. Unsparingly, she undertook long and repeated journeys with the daring of a fearless explorer. Her health, never strong, had become worse and often she burned with a fever for months at a time; yet she went without hesitation to whatever place offered a new field for the charity of herself and her Sisters.

Mother Cabrini studied the advisability of purchasing new properties, drew up contracts and directed construction of buildings with an insight that seemed inspired. "She constructed islands of rest, havens against germs, cold, hunger and death, restful houses of prayer and schools ventilated with fresh air as if by the very breath of Jesus; and by all those buildings she put in circulation the wealth of the rich for the benefit of the poor. Mother Cabrini placed the education of the learned at the disposal of the uneducated, turned kindness to the relief of misery, and brought fresh air and sunlight for the destruction of typhoid and tuberculosis. She was a swift and determined agent of the Heart of Christ."[1] Her work did not destroy in her the great tranquility of one who entrusts all to God Omnipotent; in the midst of her feverish activity "she seemed a portrait of peace."[2]

If we can say that Mother Cabrini favored one field of endeavor rather than another, it was the United States of America. She lived and worked here about twenty years. She came to know and love this country, and she saw in it the path of opportunity for her fellow countrymen and their children. Because of her attachment to the United States, as well as to develop her enterprises better and to unite her institutions to the country more securely, she obtained American citizenship in Seattle, Washington, in the year 1909. Mother Cabrini understood the great future reserved to the Church in the United States. She founded here many of her community's most elaborate institutions. She understood the American mentality, and, in turn, Americans, in their admiration for the complete dedication of the "little Sister" to the work of God, assisted her generously. After 1912, Mother Cabrini spent five consecutive years in the United States; that is, until the day of her death, which occurred in Chicago on December 22, 1917. Her body now rests in New York beneath the high altar of the chapel of the Mother Cabrini High School, 701 Fort Washington Avenue; and large numbers of the faithful go there to venerate Blessed Frances Xavier Cabrini and to ask for blessings and grace.

Beatification and Steps Toward Canonization

The death of Mother Cabrini caused both mourning and lively hope. Those who had been the objects of her charity soon began to experience her efficacious protection from heaven. The tomb of the "Mother of the Emigrants" became the goal of pious pilgrimages and the fame of her sanctity grew not only in Italy and in America but wherever the Sisters of the Institute carried on their works of charity and faith. The study of the Cause of beatification began soon after her death. The ordinary process was opened on August 3, 1928 at Chicago, and closed at Lodi, Italy, on April 5, 1929. The apostolic process began at Lodi on April 3, 1933, and was terminated at Chicago on September 27 of the same year. On October 3, 1933, in the presence of the Apostolic Delegate to the United States, the recognition of the body took place at West Park, New York, and it was then transported to the Chapel of the Mother Cabrini High School in the city of New York.

There seemed to be but one difficulty in the processes of beatification. Francis Xavier Cabrini had died only sixteen years before, and Canon 2101 of the Code of Canon Law prescribes that fifty years must elapse after the death of a Servant of God before the examination into the heroism of his virtues is begun.

At this point in the process, on May 8, 1935, the writer of these pages, as Apostolic Delegate to the United States of America, humbly implored the Supreme Pontiff, Pius XI, to deign to dispense from the prescriptions of Canon 2101 for the cause of Mother Cabrini, and to give, as far as possible, precedence to the Causes of beatification from the United States, especially those of Mother Seton and Catherine Tekakwitha. The August Pontiff, who had known Mother Cabrini personally, summoned Monsignor Natucci, Promoter General of the Faith, granted the dispensation and expressed the desire that the above-mentioned Causes proceed rapidly, "in view," as he said, "of the need of great spiritual currents." On November 21, 1937, Frances Xavier Cabrini was declared Venerable and on November 13, 1938, she shone in triumph in the Basilica of St. Peter, the first citizen of the United States officially pronounced Blessed in heaven. The Pontifical Mass in the Vatican Basilica was celebrated by His Eminence George Cardinal Mundelein, the late Archbishop of Chicago, who twenty-one years before had celebrated Mother Cabrini's funeral Mass.

The Cause of Canonization was resumed the following year, with the decree of the Sacred Congregation of Rites, dated June 21, 1939. The new miracles proposed were approved June 20, 1943 and the final decree of Canonization of Mother Frances Xavier Cabrini was signed on February 27, 1944. Such rapid progress is becoming in the case of one who in her lifetime saw the rise through her own instrumentality, of sixty-seven houses of the religious institute she had founded.

From Sanctity in America, *St. Anthony Guild Press, Paterson, N. J.*

1. "La Madre Cabrini in America," by Igino Giordani, in *L'Osservatore Romano,* November 13, 1938, p. 3.

2. *Parole Sparse della Beata Cabrini,* by Don Giuseppe De Luca, Istituto Graflco Tiberino, Roma, 1938, p. xlvi.

Introduction

The first cry heard in these pages is the voice of an apostle, who yearns to win souls for the Heart of Jesus. They are letters that breathe flames of love. One seems to hear Saint Francis Xavier again repeating in his letters, "Oh, that I could visit all the universities of Europe, especially that of Paris," where he had studied and taught, "and say to those who have more learning than charity, how many souls are lost in India through their fault. I should like to write to the professors and tell them how many thousands of pagans are eternally lost for want of laborers; that gold and diamonds are sought with more fervor than the missionary seeks souls which cost Jesus Christ much more than gold or diamonds, His Precious Blood and His Life."

In like manner, Mother Cabrini wrote long letters to the University Students, and to the other students of the House in Rome, echoing the words of Saint Francis Xavier, and telling them that innumerable souls, especially those of poor Italian emigrants who go to the two Americas, were miserably lost through ignorance of religion, the source of every other calamity, as Benedict XV, and Pius X. often stated. She saw the Indians of Albuquerque without the light of the true faith, and, in consequence, suffered with the sorrow of the Apostle. Albeit, she had led to America up to the year 1906 more than 400 Missionary Sisters. Love is, says the Holy Spirit, like unto fire and so is never satisfied, and longs for new victories, investing all with its warmth. Just as Saint Francis Xavier made the conversion of China the chief object of his desire, so did Mother Cabrini make it her own most ardent wish. But Saint Francis Xavier died at Sancian, at the entrance of China, without being able to enter it, and our Missionary Sister died before she was able to conduct any of her children thither. But as Saint Francis Xavier in Heaven obtained for his brethren their entrance and Apostolate in the vast Chinese Empire, so Mother Cabrini, having become more powerful in Heaven, has opened this new field to the indomitable zeal of the Missionary Sisters of the Sacred Heart of Jesus. Even "Darkest Africa," once so fruitful in Fathers, Doctors and Martyrs of the Church, seemed to her destined to provide many a hero of the Faith. Women, indeed, are called by God to be really helpful to the African Missionaries!

We are touched when we see in her letters how she reproached the steamers which did not move fast enough to satisfy her zeal! She wept when she met entire populations, still uncivilized, groping yet in the darkness of error. She hastened to make a vow to go where the missionary had not yet reached. She shuddered when she saw how Protestants fearlessly travelled to imbue people with their false doctrines, and to earn the large salary which the Bible Society of London and U.S.A. offers. How she lamented and reproached, with womanly eloquence, the pusillanimity of so many Catholics. She envied those who spoke English and Spanish, and she made an effort to say a few words, but her tongue could not do justice to the ardent aspirations of her heart, for she wanted to tell of the beauty of the Catholic Religion and the attraction of the Sacred Heart. Secretly she mourned whilst voyaging on one occasion with 1,300 Italian emigrants from Italy and Switzerland, who were so poor and crowded in the third-class cabins, that in the New World they were called Barbarians, and she sorrowed more at the fact that these unfortunate people had no one to speak to them of God. How sublime was that apostolic exclamation:

"Oh, if I could build a steamer for myself to traverse all these seas! I should call it 'Christopher,' i.e., the bearer of Christ to the people."

One might ask on taking this book in hand, "How could a Missionary Nun, who, in thirty-five years, crossed the ocean thirty times, climbed the awe-inspiring Cordilleras, and traversed the immense Pampas which extends from Mendoza to Rio de la Plata, and founded hundreds of schools and institutes of Charity, write such long accounts of her voyages?" She wrote on the decks of the steamers. How great must have been her power of quiet concentration! What control of self was required! And, though she always suffered poor health, she was always anxious for the health of her spiritual daughters, who suffered during these voyages, and for the government of the many communities of her Institute. It was a spectacle worthy of angels and of men. Where others well inured to traveling would succumb to fatigue, this woman remained calm and serene.

She relates that in one of her voyages she was obliged to change steamers nine times in twelve days, the ships being unable to continue. She was obliged to walk on a plank for four hours under a downpour of rain with no place of shelter near. She watched over her spiritual daughters who succumbed to the hardships of the storm-tossed voyage, and would spend hours in their cabins, encouraging them and trying to make them happy.

It is delightful to read her ever kindly comments on the sea-woes of her dear companions. As things improved, she would gather them around her on deck to perform their devotions as if in the Convent. They had lectures, meditations, examination of conscience, as prescribed by the Rules. They made novenas for the Feasts of Our Lord, Our Lady and the Saints. They sang the Litanies, *Ave Maris Stella,* and the voices of the Sisters blended with the waves of the ocean. At times a crowd of astonished voyagers took part in these reunions. If on the steamer a priest was present, she rejoiced to be able to hear Mass, to receive Holy Communion, to have the usual ceremonies, and would tactfully make arrangements for the priest to preach to the people. How she would grieve when on board there was no Holy Communion, no Holy Mass celebrated! On arrival at some port where the steamer stopped for a short time, she would make every effort to get on shore to assist at the Holy Sacrifice. When from the steamers she perceived the steeple of some church, her thoughts would fly to the Tabernacle, and she would invite her children to make a Spiritual Communion.

Whence did this Missionary Sister draw so much calmness of spirit? Did she not feel and fear the difficulties and see the dangers? Yes, she felt them and feared them! She instinctively feared the sea, for at seven years of age she accidentally fell into a swift stream, and was all but carried away by the turbulent current. She was saved almost miraculously, but her constitution, already delicate, ever felt the consequences. If it were not the voice of the Holy Father that consigned to her the American Missions of the Italian emigrants, she would never have dared to cross the ocean. But Holy Obedience and her Apostolic aim had almost transformed her nature. She looked serenely at the roaring waves and blessed them with a lithe statue of the Savior. Everyone advised her not to attempt to traverse the Cordilleras of the Andes; but nothing could frighten her indomitable heart, neither the terrific heights, nor volcanoes, nor snow eight meters deep, nor lakes, nor the incredible distances. Confident in Our Lady, Saint Rose and Saint Philomena, she crossed these mountains on mules to reach Buenos Aires, where she was to found schools for all classes. As her Patron Saint used to say, so she repeated, "I am afraid only of want of confidence in God my Protector." After her first voyage to New York, which was in 1889, she was wont to write: "My secure boat is the Sacred Heart, my Star of the sea is Mary, and my Protector is Saint Francis Xavier, the wonder worker."

The pages of these letters are very attractive in many ways, but everything else yields to the fragrance of their religious spirit. Her letters indicate the free up-soaring of her soul, and she did not learn all this in the school of rhetoric, but from the Holy Spirit during her daily communications with God. To see in her voyages the beauty of nature, of art, particularly of the cities she visited, was, as it were, for her to raise herself on the wings of love from visible things to the invisible. In the immensity and depths of the ocean she contemplated the Majesty of God, in the tempests she saw His divine displeasure provoked by the crimes of men, She painted the storms with the brush of a great artist, and so vividly, that one shudders as page unfolds page. The transparent azure sea was, as it were, for her the Heaven of a soul possessed of God. The works of Jesus in the souls united to Him she describes in such detailed mystic psychology that one would think she spoke of her own personal experiences. If, in such matters, she emulates Saint Teresa, when dealing with the Sacred Heart, she recalls to our minds Saint Gertrude. The Christian Feasts which occurred during her voyages were passed in sublime and practical contemplation, the like of which I have never read of in other books.

She lived always in the midst of her loving daughters, and by her letters she encouraged them to seek that religious perfection required by the glorious title of Missionary of the Sacred Heart. She thinks of all her daughters scattered in her many Houses, though many of them are 4,000 or 6,000 miles away. With those who are with her, she forms one heart and one soul with them in the heart of Jesus, conversing, singing, working with and amusing them. There are perhaps fifteen Sisters with her on a voyage, and she makes each Sister represent a Mystery of the Rosary. To them she is the Mother rather than the Superior; she charms them, and does what she likes with them in order to give them Jesus Christ.

At a tender age she consecrated her genius, her heart, her time and even her very life. Death suddenly snatched her from us in the Hospital of Chicago, founded by her, while she was preparing Christmas presents for five hundred children. The poor emigrants, especially the sick, were her favorites. For them she founded several Hospitals of New York, Chicago and Seattle, where many thousands of Italians find refuge and health. In these letters of hers are found counsels for the solution of the Emigration problem; she is full of compassion for the emigrants, who are often deceived by those who hypocritically pretend to act as their protectors, cloaking their unjust intentions with the mantle of philanthropy and patriotism. The fate of many Italians would have been dreadful if they had not had help from the Missionary Sisters of the

Sacred Heart. Who would have consoled them in prison, visited their unfortunate families, fed their orphans, defended their cases even in civil courts and obtained reductions of their penalties? And especially can we read of the lamentable condition of the Italians working in the coal mines, buried alive away from their families and hearing little or nothing about God. Mother Cabrini had the gift of being all to all in order to bring them to God. One reads of this in the two long letters addressed to the students of Rome who were preparing themselves for public teaching. They are typical letters, rich with interesting news, written spontaneously, yet in how perfect a style! In them you may recognize the teacher of natural history, literature, pedagogy. They are two masterpieces of their class, wherein are blended sound piety and sound erudition. Associating utility and sweetness, she raises the mind of young girls from earth to Heaven, describing the elevation of woman through Mary Immaculate, whom she represents as a cloud illumined by the sun or by the rainbow announcing clear weather. Without any effort she gives them a catechetical lesson, and speaks of religious culture as if she were a Bishop... She shows the need of discipline to form the character, and, speaking with full conviction, she declares it to be the only guarantee of success for private individuals and public institutions. She closes her two letters to her dear students, calming their fears for their coming exams, which are the torment and bugbear of youth, showing them the secret of success.

We must not suppose that the foundations of Mother Cabrini always enjoyed a favorable wind. It is certain, however, as is seen in these accounts, that when the strong woman encountered difficulty in her foundations, she felt more courage and hoped, like Abraham, against hope. The reason is sublime and derived from her evangelical meditations. "Instead of fearing, I felt more encouraged, and I seemed to rejoice when my work began with a cross, which is the seal of all good enterprises." She always depended on the local Bishops, and never began anything without their approbation. Read what happened in Paris, as narrated of that foundation.

Her strong will and indomitable courage appear in her letters. Read the account of the expulsion of her daughters from Nicaragua. She was always true to herself, always well-balanced in mind and heart, having the grand program of St. Ignatius before her. *"Ad majorem Dei gloriam et ad animarum salutem."* This was the program of Our Savior Himself. These sublime ideals permeate her account of her transactions with Presidents of Republics, with Bishops, captains of ships and public administrators, for the foundations of Houses.

"The style of writing reveals the man." This is true where the writings are simple, and these letters reflect, faithfully, humility, strength, patience, perseverance, constancy in enterprise, contempt of the world, the holy freedom of the love of God, candor of the soul, the most fragrant zeal for the glory of the Sacred Heart and for the salvation of souls, which so enriched the heart of Mother Cabrini.

In reading these letters I felt better, and thank the Author of all good. For my apostolic life, I learned salutary truths.

The comfort I derived from the reading of these letters I wish to all other readers of them, but in double measure.

Ottavio Turchi, SJ.

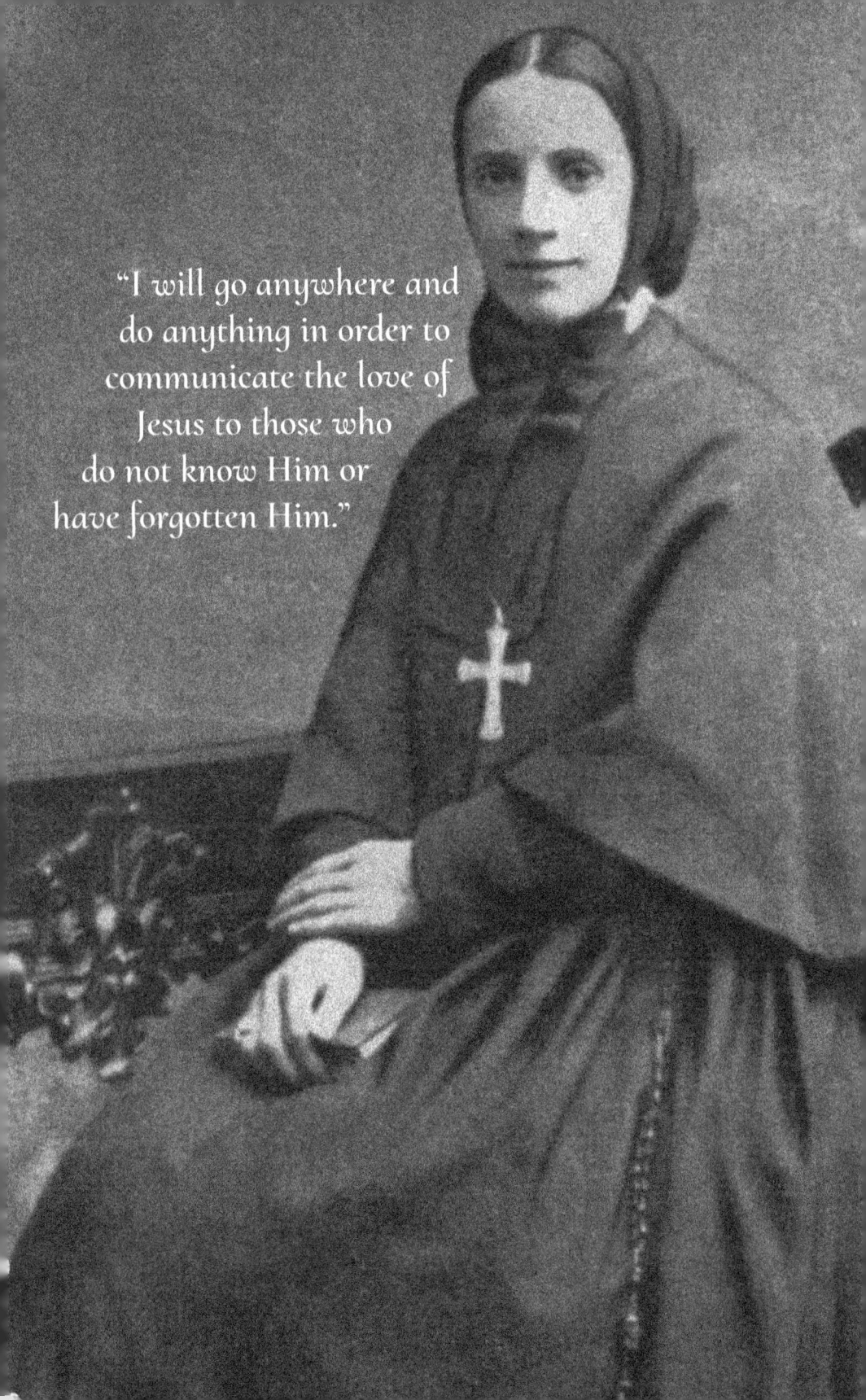

"I will go anywhere and do anything in order to communicate the love of Jesus to those who do not know Him or have forgotten Him."

1. Second Voyage to New York
April, 1890

Friday, April 18, 1890

My dear Daughters:

When I left you, last Wednesday, I tried to think that I was only going as far as Milan, and would therefore remain near you; but in Milan, when I was about to undertake such a long journey across the ocean and leave you for a long time, I felt overwhelmed. Relief came when I remembered the promises, made by each one of you, to study to become true brides of Christ and worthy Missionaries of His Sacred Heart.

How much this thought, my daughters, softens every pain! It makes me find sweetness in all labors and crosses, should I have any, and gives me great joy. If we reflect well, for us there are no distances: the Missionaries of the Sacred Heart of Jesus must participate in the immensity of this Divine Heart, Who embraces all, comprehends all, animates all, unites all in Himself. It is He Who sustains us in these temporary separations, Who makes us share in His strength, Who communicates to us every grace. He is our true Treasure, love Him with all your hearts, serve Him faithfully, encourage all souls to be detached from creatures, from all things, even from themselves, that they may succeed in possessing His perfect love, which is an anticipation of Heaven. Let all your affections, my daughters, be centered in this beautiful Heart, and you will always be happy; but if, instead, you foster private affections that tie you to self, or to creatures, you will always have annoyances, hours of disgust and melancholy. Free yourselves, and put on wings, I pray you, in order that you may rise above the earth.

Arrival at Paris

The journey has been very happy. While we were passing through those high chains of mountains, and admiring so many beauties of nature created by God just to give pleasure to His creatures, our souls felt raised to sublime meditation. It was beautiful to notice the sweet impression the many various sights they saw made on the minds and in the hearts of the Sisters, for this was the first time they had made this journey.

About 2 a.m. someone opened the door of the compartment and asked us to alight, but we did not obey, because we had been told it was a through train to Paris. Three minutes later they returned and begged us again to leave the compartment, but they received no satisfaction, because I did not understand what they were saying. Sister Ignatius, half-asleep, contented herself with answering, "Close the door." To bring us to our senses, the station-master, accompanied by several porters, told us that the carriage in which we were had broken down. At last we understood and left the compartment in haste. Quicker than I could tell, our luggage was transferred to another compartment, where we remained very comfortable until we arrived in Paris. We then thanked our dear Spouse for the great love He had shown us in preserving us. We made a very fervent Spiritual Communion, and went to sleep again!

We arrived in Paris an hour and a half behind time on account of the accident, nevertheless we found Mrs. Gabin awaiting us. At once she conducted us to the Church of Our Lady of Victories, where we all received Holy Communion, to the great joy of our souls. This being our first visit to this Sanctuary, it left a great impression on me. The most holy Virgin, our loving Mother, invited me, maybe, because I have placed our Institute and each one of you in a special manner under her protection, and through her, in the Heart of the Child Jesus. What beautiful graces will shower down upon us, for our sanctification, for the good of the Institute and for the salvation of souls! We spent a few hours, accompanied by a lady who was our guide, in viewing the principal streets and sights of importance. A little after midday we took train for Havre, and arrived there about 5 o'clock in the afternoon.

Saturday, 19th

This morning we went to visit and pay our respects to the Captain and Commissioner. They listened with great courtesy, and offered their help in all our needs. These persons did not know us, but they were so kind to us. From this we can learn to appreciate the great love the Heart of Jesus has for His Spouses. He heaps upon us benefits and favors we do not merit. Let us be ever grateful, so that gratitude may obtain for us greater graces. This morning we went on deck, saluted the sea, the image of the immensity of God, then we recited our prayers, which, without effort, came fervently from our souls. We then recited the *Ave Maris Stella*. We did not sing because we were afraid of disturbing the other passengers on board, but the Most Holy Virgin, who had blessed our departure, listened to the melody of the affections of her devout daughters, if not the melody of their voices.

At 9 a.m. we left the port, and in a short time we were soon on the open sea and had lost sight of land. It was raining a little, but the passengers said we should have a good voyage. We did not feel anxious about this, because we knew we were in the Hands of God, enclosed in the Most

Sacred Heart of Jesus, and this thought rendered us secure and tranquil in every event. As soon as Sister Battistina saw the boat move, she said she felt a dizziness in her head. Half-an-hour later she was very sick, and one after the other followed her example. I was the only one who remained unaffected. I wished the boat were steady, so that I might go on with my work, but I found I had to give up all idea of this. However, I continued to feel much better, and by degrees I felt I could breathe more freely. This, too, helped me to raise my soul to God, and I could almost say in all seriousness what I said jocularly a few days ago, that if the Sacred Heart would give me the means I would construct a boat called "The House of Cristoforo" ("Bearer of Christ") to traverse with one Community, little or big, so as to carry the Name of Christ to all people, to those who as yet do not know Him, and also to those who have forgotten Him. But these are futile thoughts, and I do not permit them to occupy my mind, but they serve for a little recreation.

At half-past ten the bell rang for breakfast; they all found courage to come to table with me, but could not take anything, and they soon left one after the other. Sister Ignatius tried to force herself to eat and keep herself strong, but half through the meal she also had to follow the others. I remained alone and stayed until breakfast was over.

Sunday, April 20th

Yesterday, at dinner, all the Sisters came to table and took a little refreshment. Then we all went on deck to inhale the air and revive and refresh our lungs. At half-past seven we returned to our cabins. We stayed a little time and said prayers. Towards nine o'clock we went to bed and slept all night. The sea was very calm. Sister Assunta thought she heard a hurricane, but it was only a little rain beating against the windows. You should see poor Sister Assunta! She looks so woe-begone. How would she be if the sea were at all rough?

However, she laughs heartily when asked what is worrying her and making her look so miserable.

This morning the sea is still very calm. I have never seen it so calm. It is literally like a lake. The boat goes so quickly, and we don't feel the motion at all. The sun shines beautifully, and the air is good. There is no odor in the cabin whatsoever. The boat is so well-built and well-ventilated, we seem to be having a journey on land. For all that, all the Sisters were not able to be present at breakfast, and the few that came were not able to stay. I soon found myself alone as yesterday. The steward, who is near us at table, gave orders to the waiters to bring something special for the Sisters who were sick. Poor Sisters! At every movement of the boat they think we are in a great storm. Sister Eletta would like to have the boat stopped, at least during meals. I told the steward this just to make him laugh; he is so kind, he looks like a Saint Francis de Sales.

How many beautiful thoughts the calmness of the sea suggests. We see in it the happiness of a soul that lives in the tranquility of the grace of God. In such a fortunate soul all is calm, peace undisturbed; it has the capacity of raising itself to the sublimity of the Divine mysteries. This gives us a vision of the immensity of the power of God, Who commands this endless sea, which could rise in whirling billows, while on the contrary it remains calm and tranquil. God commands, the sea obeys. If also in Religion every Sister would obey her Superior, with perfect submission that is, without relying on her own judgment, what calmness, what tranquillity, what a sweetness of Paradise would be hers! My daughters! Act in this way, be obedient, be most humble, not having your own judgment, submitting with great peace and simplicity to your Superiors, and there will be in your Houses a true anticipated Paradise which will precede the eternal one which awaits you. It seems as if Jesus

Himself has said to the sea, "Peace be with you." Hence this is a figure of a pure soul, without wrath, who leaves all, and is united exclusively with her beloved and Divine Spouse, reposing on His left arm while with the right He caresses her. My dear daughters, be purely disinterested, be detached from all things and all persons, and also from yourselves, from your desires and inclinations, and thus be like a true sea of peace. You will become like a great ocean, because the pure soul is capable of great things, and the mind is thus able to wander in the immensity of God. The soul full of earthly ties, full of attachments, is always narrow, very small, understands little, pusillanimous, frequently dejected, and is never able to throw itself into the immensity of Divine Service. I don't want any such souls among my daughters, nor among my friends. I want you all to have wings and fly swiftly and repose in that blessed peace possessed by a soul that is all for God. Therefore I desire to be likewise. Then pray, my daughters, pray for me; I have many desires, but all are barren. If these desires were talents, oh, how badly off I should still be, because I should be obliged to multiply them, even now they lie hidden and bear no fruit. The thought that we can always humble ourselves and obtain pardon from God is a consolation for me. Yes, my daughters, let us always humble ourselves before God in every instant of our life, and we shall be, by God's merciful condescension, raised above our pettiness, and we shall be admitted to a foretaste of the peace and tranquility of which the sea I am crossing is an image.

Monday, 21st

Here we are, the see-saw has started, moved by almighty hand of God: willy nilly we have to play the game. Yesterday about five o'clock in the afternoon the sea began to be a real sea. It was not possible to stand on your feet without leaning on something for support. Already five hours have elapsed since Sister Eletta began to pray God to calm the sea. But now, seeing such a frightful spectacle, she is lost for words, and thinks the best thing to do is to go to bed as the other Sisters have done. I remain firm and always keep on deck. I made them laugh so much that Sister Eletta said she felt almost better. After supper, about six o'clock, I wanted to see the other good Sisters, and, following their example, I began to feel seasick. Patience! Twice I was obliged to resign myself to their company. Sister Assunta looks like a soul full of thoughts and weariness. Sister Giovannina is always laughing, even when she is very sick. Sister Agostina also smiles. Sister Bernardina is just like one dead, so is Sister Battistina! Sister Ignatius tries to endeavor to follow my example, but after a time she has to run for her life, or else stay in the cabin so as not to fall. Of all the passengers on board, both men and women, only six or seven come to the table. It is dreadful if we do not try to resist this sickness, the best plan is to stay on deck; even if it rains, it is better to remain in the open. Last night, I stayed until after midnight, partly dressed (because I believed a storm was threatening), so as to be ready to save myself and all; but the good God is continually watching over His Spouses. The great swing subsided though the gale beat all around us. I rose early this morning to go on deck to view the wonderful spectacle. Oh! how beautiful is the sea in its great motion! How the waves swell and foam! Enchanting! The wind is, however, favorable, and the boat goes so quickly, it seems to fly. If you could only see the waves! None of us could stay at the stern because the waves swept over the vessel at every moment. At the bows it is not so bad, and, stretched in an armchair, I can write fairly well. A single wave could submerge all, but He Who has created the sea and has commanded it to rise like mountains, would not permit His beloved creatures to be drowned, much less His loving Spouses. God loved us before He created the sea; nay, He created the sea itself for our use and pleasure. He has chosen us for His Spouses, and we have answered His call, attracted by His infinite lovableness. Let us remain, my daughters, entirely subject to Him, conquered by His love; and let us run swiftly in His footsteps. The good

God has perpetually loved us with the love of predilection, so let us love Him and serve Him with joy during the few days of our life. If you were all here with me, dear daughters, to cross the immense ocean, you would exclaim, "Oh, how great and loving is God in all His works!" But the ocean of graces, oh, my daughters, that the good Jesus pours down upon us, in every instant of our life, is immensely superior to anything in nature. All natural splendors are eclipsed by the abundance of riches which God showers upon His beloved Spouses. Let us venerate and love, then, our excellent state, and let us examine ourselves frequently and remove all defects that are unbecoming the Virgins of Christ, so that our Beloved may quickly introduce us into the Holy of Holies and plant charity in our souls.

Tuesday, 22nd April

Today I am writing a few lines only, because I am tired out after what we have gone through. Yesterday evening the movement of the boat increased. It dipped at the stern to such an extent that we thought every moment it would capsize. Then they increased the speed of the engines so much that about midnight we felt a terrible shock, and the boat stopped suddenly. The engine was broken. The blowing of the horn, a bell and a bugle called all the sailors up. A great noise was heard, but no one knew what it was except that we realized the ship was at a standstill. I got up in order to secure a life belt in case it was necessary. As soon as I was dressed I went to see all the Sisters. Sister Eletta ran to me first– she was terrified, and asked if I had heard anything. I laughed heartily in order to make her laugh so as to chase away her fears. In her cabin all were alarmed, while in the next all were sleeping as if nothing had happened. I thought it better to leave them there because they were all sleeping soundly. Meantime we went to see what was wrong. They told me we should be obliged to stay here until the engine was repaired; however the sea became tranquil, and the boat rocked gently. The voyage was impeded from about midnight until eleven next morning, when, while we were at table for breakfast, the boat renewed its course. Now we are swiftly sailing towards New York on a calm sea, as if nothing had happened. In the meantime, when the boat was at a halt, all the Sisters got up, and now I am pleased to see them all with me on deck. Sister Agostina, Sister Battistina and Sister Assunta are still half-bewildered. They don't feel able to take anything, although it is nice to see them smiling and always resigned to the dear and holy Will of God. Having lost my sleep last night, I am very tired. Nevertheless I walk about, I eat; I am with you in spirit. Tonight I will sleep, if the good God does not wish otherwise. Often we take pleasure in seeing the beautiful seagulls, at one moment flying in the air and at another frolicking on the water. They seem to be the image of our Guardian Angels, or of the many dear young Virgins that come to our Institute to become Missionaries. This is the first time I have seen seagulls.

Wednesday, 23rd April

We are near the shore of Newfoundland, and, as usual at this spot, the boat has an extraordinary movement indeed, which makes everyone feel uncomfortable. All the Sisters are again ill, or, rather, half-dead, except Sister Eletta and Sister Giovannina, who are now quite used to the sea and keep me company. Sister Eletta is our amusement with her geographical difficulties. She does not understand how the pilot of our ship is so ignorant as to keep in mid-ocean, while other boats from time to time in the distance always sail on the horizon, and therefore she thinks they are nearer the land and more secure than we are. And she marvels to see how the great circle is always at the same distance. Today they have prepared the list of passengers to be given to the Officer of New York as soon as we enter the bay. Our names along with the others were stamped on a most beautiful card, and given to each first-class passenger. Sister Giovannina was from the beginning named Sister

Giovannona. The points of meditation we have always ready, at the sight of the sea many beautiful thoughts and feelings arise within one. The sky is blue and the horizon is vast. It is the image of the love of God when it takes possession of a soul and makes it capable of an immensity of holy deeds. Yes! Grace is an infinite treasure of God and those who receive it, and make good use of it, are truly partakers of the friendship of God. Is it not precious for the immense increase which at every hour it makes in our souls? It is true, then, that the ocean is a beautiful image of grace. Let us try, oh, my daughters, to attract the grace of God to our souls, by perfect detachment of all and from all, even from our most ardent desires that may disturb the peace and quietness of soul, which are the fruits of grace.

Thursday, 24th April

I write after having assisted at a spectacle quite new to myself and also new to some of the sailors. About eleven o'clock we saw ourselves surrounded by enormous masses of ice. At first they appeared to be things of no importance, like white doves resting on the water, but afterward, little by little, they grew much larger. They took enormous proportions, and when we got nearer to them we saw that they were about twelve times larger than our ship. The Captain reduced the speed of the engines and took a different route to avoid them, but for all that at one moment we were only a distance of about sixty yards from them. Now we see some of them in the distance. We feel afraid of the coming night. Perhaps, then, there will be danger, but we leave ourselves in the Hands of the good Jesus.

A gentleman who already had made twenty-one ocean voyages had never seen a spectacle like this before; this has precisely been reserved for us. These icebergs are similar to great fortresses with their cutting notches. The sea today is very tranquil. All the Sisters are well except

Sister Agostina, who still looks nearly half-dead. First one thing and then another delays our arrival. According to our calculations we shall not arrive before Tuesday. Imagine! We thought we should arrive in time to keep the Feast of the Patronage of Saint Joseph, instead we shall have to pass the Feast on sea and without Holy Communion. We are beginning to feel gravely the austerity of this painful fast. Oh, yes! when we arrive on land we shall look for a priest at once, in order that we may communicate, as we did a year ago. The marvelous spectacle, which is continually present to our vision, offers us a good preparation for Holy Communion, as we all see this is the work of Him, Whom we so ardently desire to welcome in the small Sanctuary of our souls.

Friday, 25th April

Today it is very hot, just like July. The sea is very beautiful, but the motion of the boat is very marked. The chairs will not stand in their places, and the waiters have a lot to do in order to keep them fastened, so that we may be comfortable and able to stay in the open. However, all the Sisters are well. They have had breakfast with me, to my great delight.

The ladies were late in getting up this morning, and we have been able to say the prayers and Office of the Sacred Heart on deck. We also made a little meditation on the beautiful lesson of Saint Bernard, wherein he speaks of the force and power of the love of God in a soul, and how the possession of this love enables a soul not to feel further the weight of any cross, which rather becomes a great pleasure and delight. Oh, happy the soul that lives in the true love of Christ! My daughters, detach yourselves from all persons and all things, and you will have a foretaste of the Paradise of true, solid and Heavenly love.

Before we went to rest last night we were thinking of you making the Holy Hour perhaps for us. We united with you in spirit and tasted with you the Paradise of holy union with God. Every day we invoke the Star of the Sea with the *Ave Maris Stella,* in honor of our loving Mother who truly protects us. Only yesterday we escaped a collision with those enormous masses of ice that were threatening our ruin. We owe this to our dear and powerful Mother. We are fairly happy. It seems that the passengers share our happiness, for first one and then another comes to stay and favor us with their company.

Saturday, 26th April

Yesterday, about three o'clock, a heavy fog set in. So dense was it that we could only see a distance of a few yards. Fogs are always a source of great danger, more so on sea than on land. Our fear increased, for again we saw blocks of ice floating all around the boat. The engine was stopped for fear of striking against some of these masses of ice, but before evening the fog cleared, and we could see the horizon clearly. So the night will be calm. For fear of the ice the boat diverted its route. Whilst at other times the route is more northern towards the Banks of Terranova, this time it is more towards the south. Meantime the heat is like summer. For three days I look like Bacchus. My forehead is very red, even purple, and this redness is spreading all over my face. At first I thought it was erysipelas. I did not like the prospect, for I should have had to retire from the open, and fresh air is life to me. Happily, however, the doctor said the redness was the effect of the air and of the water which was spraying on my face. I did not want to run away directly it began to rain and deprive myself of the air.

Today the skin has begun to peel off my forehead and nose. I am changing like a serpent. God wants me to change my life and be converted; to confirm this, my dearest daughters, pray. The Sacred Heart of Jesus will always hear favorably the prayers of children for their Mother. Pray! Pray! I am in need of your intercession. When I am converted and begin to lead a good life, it is certain that this will obtain many beautiful graces for the Institute. However, I am happy to think you have been so good. While in the midst of many dangers, especially those enormous masses of ice, we did not fall into the sea. Continue to be good, more generous and sacrificing, humble and meek on all occasions, especially in the moments when you feel self-love.

A Protestant gentleman last night came and asked me to go with all the Sisters to a concert. I told him we could not accept the invitation, as Religious did not go to secular entertainments or amusements. He wanted to stay with us. He presented us with six tickets of a lottery worth half-a-dollar each, and he promised to be on the alert when the tickets were being drawn. I am sorry I do not understand, as this gentleman is a very good man. I like his frankness and the manner in which he speaks of our Holy Religion. Patience! Pray to the Sacred Heart and Our Lady for his salvation. He is an Englishman who has lived for five years in New York. He promised to come and bring his wife with him to see our Orphanage; his wife is a Catholic. This gentleman thinks we have undertaken a very difficult mission, which offers little probability of success–that of the Italians; but hearing that it was just for this reason we undertook it, and will at any cost work for it, he has more esteem for us than ever, and is willing to give us help. Also another passenger, a certain De Pedro, Milanese, is traveling with us. At first he did not make himself known as an Italian, but when he saw everybody coming to us and making friends, he came also and declared his friendship, saying how happy he was to know us. Now he delights in speaking Milanese with all his power. He admires also the success we have achieved in a few months, while he, for fifteen years, so he says, found nothing but sorrows and disappointments numerous enough to fill a volume. The poor man does not know Jesus and the goodness of His Heart. He trusts only to his talents. Thus his days cannot be happy.

Sunday, 27th April

Today is the beautiful Feast of the Patronage of Saint Joseph. If we could find a priest on board, we should at least be able to hear Holy Mass; instead, this is the second Sunday that 1,300 persons are without Mass. There are on board 900 poor emigrants of the third-class, 700 Italians and 200 Swiss. Poor things! I hope at least they will arrive in a town or village where there will be someone who will break for them the bread of the Word of God. But God alone knows what will happen to the greater part of them! Perhaps they will become associated with their poor brothers of the New World, called Barbarians, because they have forgotten the noble principles of the Religion they were brought up in. For, unfortunately, they have amongst them a rabid anarchist, who often gathers them around him and, like Belial, incites them to revolt against authority and order in such a manner that the officers of the boat have to interfere. This is a small picture of many European nations, whose sons have lost the true sense of patriotism, at the mercy of their disorderly passions and of civil wars. They go rapidly towards their last ruin, the just punishment of God upon those who have forgotten that the Catholic Religion of their country constitutes their principal nobility and security.

Oh, let us pray, my daughters, let us pray for so many of our brethren, and let their blindness be a good lesson and teach us to be more faithful in the observance of our Holy Rules, in order to console the afflicted Heart of Jesus, and obtain from Him blessings in great abundance for ourselves and for our neighbors. Their mistake will induce us to remain very humble in order that we may be enlightened and never allow our intellect to be darkened. God resists and confounds the proud, whereas He reveals Himself to the humble, and draws them nearer to Him and caresses them. I don't want any among the Missionaries of the Sacred Heart to be attached to her own judgment, to cherish her own reasons, to receive badly any corrections from whomsoever it is given, or to submit with a bad will to this or that Superior. Each one must consider it a duty, rather, feel it a necessity, to be under subjection to all. The Religious who acts in this way will be a true jewel of our Institute and an object of complacency to the most Sacred Heart of Jesus. She will move Him to pour forth upon us many great treasures. Are you, then, humble, my daughters? Do you like the last place? Are you pleased to be despised, forgotten, and to be made of no account? The one who feels in this disposition, oh, let her pray for me! She is a real gem presented to me by my dearest Jesus; through her I will obtain all. Last evening the Commissioner of the boat presented me with six tickets for the lottery and another gentleman six more—now we have fifteen. Today the drawing is to take place; we shall see who is successful.

Monday, 28th April

Today we shall see land about three in the afternoon, but perhaps we shall not arrive in port until late in the evening, and we shall have to sleep again on sea. Our poor Sisters will be equally impatient to see us as we are to embrace them. We have been greatly delayed, but here we are now, and it is our duty to thank the Most Sacred Heart of Jesus. We were alarmed on the day the engine broke down, but now we know that the delay was a great grace, because without this delay the meeting with the icebergs would have happened during the night and been fraught with great danger. Yesterday we were presented with other tickets for the lottery, in all nearly a hundred *lire* worth. They invited me to view the exhibition. I found nothing of any use to us. Even if we win, it will matter very little, because they are all useless things. I hope to have a greater gain of a more important kind–that of converting, with the help of the Most Sacred Heart of Jesus, the Protestant gentleman who presented me first with the tickets. Yesterday we had a discussion, and he ended by saying I was right. He loves the Pope very much and feels a profound veneration for him. He also has a great esteem for our holy

Religion, but he does not wish to embrace it because he has seen so many priests without the true spirit; but also on this point he understood well when I told him the reason. You should see with what patience he listens to me when I speak. The Sisters tell him in English what he has not understood from me. He is very intelligent, and from the expression on my face he understands what I intend to say. He asks me to speak English as well as I can, and he helps me with some French words, saying he can understand. Sister Bernardina is going to make a novena for me to obtain the grace to speak English, and assures me she will obtain it. What do you think of it? I fear the day of judgment will arrive before I learn English. Notwithstanding, I trust in my good Jesus, and if He wants me to bring to His Heart any souls, He will also give me the grace to speak the language of the country I shall visit.

A lady of New York never leaves us. She is very frank and active. She always speaks, in the presence of everybody, of the work of the Sisters, and persuades all regarding the advantages and benefits of our little Mission. Now I leave you with this little news, though badly connected, which I have been able to write between one wave and another. You must accompany me always with the practice of the most beautiful virtues, and especially of those you know I desire from each of you,

May Jesus bless you and enclose you in His beautiful Heart, where we shall find a true Paradise on earth, and may He make you always most fervent in spirit, in the perfect abnegation of yourselves, and in the detachment from all creatures and from all pleasures.

The Sisters salute you dearly.

Your Affectionate Mother in the SS. C. J.,

Frances Saveria Cabrini

2. New York to Havre

August, 1890

My beloved Daughters,

Peace be with you and accompany you always and everywhere.

August 17th, 1890

Having lost the previous night's sleep, yesterday I was unable to work, but today I feel better, so I can entertain myself a little with you. My companions of the voyage make up their minds and agree with me to resign themselves willingly to suffer seasickness. Ann is always tranquil and quiet, Elizabeth feels cold and tries to keep well-clothed. It is true the weather is cold just like an April morning, but the air is pure and it is a pleasure to breathe it. It is healthy and inspires sublime thoughts, just as a celestial ray would surround us and raise our minds to that God, so good, so dear, and so great. He has made so many beautiful things for us, poor creatures, the work of His omnipotent Hand. The sea continues calm and wonderfully tranquil. It seems to reflect the peace and the features of a soul adorned with sanctifying grace, which communicates to that soul interior peace and joy. From time to time birds come to cheer us. They look like swallows, but I think they are sea-birds. Last night I slept very well, just as though I was in my cell. I dreamt that I received Holy Communion. It is almost impossible to receive Holy Communion here at sea, and today, especially, I miss it very much, because I heard yesterday (to my great displeasure) there would be a religious service held by a Protestant minister. But, thank God, it is now near midday, and no one has mentioned it.

18th August

I have nothing new to tell you, because the sea keeps so calm. It is as smooth as a table, and if we raised our eyes, we could scarcely believe that the ship is going so rapidly. I don't feel ill, but I am not well, and I have no desire to do anything. Nevertheless I am in the happy position of being able to meditate freely. This is a great advantage for me, because I am able to pass the time conversing with the sweet Spouse of my soul. Oh, if everyone had the knowledge of the great and beautiful advantages of meditation and of speaking familiarly with Jesus, if they could experience these heavenly joys, they would certainly envy our happy life (or state). Instead, how many poor creatures are there who do not want to know Him, in order to follow their own passions more freely, blinded by the smoke of the false pleasures of the world! In these circumstances, and at the sight of so many miserable and unfortunate creatures, how much better we are able to understand the great grace that God has given us by calling us to His Divine Service, or, to express it more accurately, to His love. Let us love Jesus, then, my daughters, let us love Him very much. Jesus has ready for us many other graces, but He is waiting to be loved by us more and more, in order to grant these graces to us. On one occasion He said to one of His faithful servants, that if he could find souls who would love Him, as Saint Francis of Assisi did, He would give as many graces as He bestowed upon that Saint, and even greater ones. Indeed, it is true. Let us confess it. If graces do not descend upon us, it is because of our little love of God, which keeps them back from us. And we shall never get a true love for God unless we try to overcome our self-love and the attachment to ourselves and our own judgment. This morning I petted a dog to please a lady, in order that, after gaining her friendship, I might speak to her of our Holy Religion. She is a Protestant; I have already had a few words with her, but I find she is very much attached to her false religion.

19th August

The sea continues to be extraordinarily tranquil. All say they have never seen it so calm. If there were a little movement, there would be something new to tell you. The compliment I paid to the dog yesterday has had a good effect. The lady has been pleased to come to me and to discuss at length our Holy Religion. Naturally, she tries to maintain her own opinions, but now she doubts whether we can make satisfaction for our sins in this world. I would like to be a little more instructed in order to explain the truths of our Holy Religion more clearly, and so be to her a real missionary, but what I cannot do myself will be done by our good Sisters at Rome, where this lady is going to pass the winter, and she will go to see them. For this purpose she has asked me for their address. I would like to convert all Protestants. This is a mission I have very much at heart, and you, my dear daughters, by the duties of your holy vocation, find yourselves engaged in this sublime mission of converting souls. Do attend to it with great zeal and fervor, and try to multiply the grapes of the mystic vine of Christ. You should use every possible means and skill in order to succeed in converting souls, and be certain you will never be wanting in means and knowledge if you love your Celestial Spouse, because the love of Jesus suggests a thousand ways we may use for the interests of His glory. Oh! how beautiful is the hymn of that fortunate spouse who can say, "Jesus loves me, and I love Him! He is the only object of my thoughts. I have printed Him on my hands and in the deepest recess of my heart." Be wise, then, daughters. Let us please Jesus by doing more good for His mystic members, the souls redeemed by His great sufferings and death.

August 20th

The sight of the sea is really enchanting, one can scarcely believe one's senses. The passengers say that this is due to the merits of the Sisters; and it may be so because there are seven ladies of the Sacred Heart on board who are very good indeed. They are going to their Mother House in Paris to prepare for their Profession. Thus you may imagine with what holy sentiments they are animated and what beautiful souls they are. It is rather cool now, and we are surrounded by a temperate atmosphere which speaks to us of the great goodness and munificence of our good and great Almighty God. From the stern of the ship we can see a rainbow which is continually reflecting on the waves, now large, now small. I often go up there to breathe the pure air. This morning I saw marvelous fishes of many colors joyfully basking in the sea, just as our souls should bask in the grace of God. The Protestant lady never leaves us. She likes to stay with us. Today I made her a present of a small cross, on which may be seen the picture of Our Lady. She thanked me so much for this cross, and said to me, "It may be that one day I shall be a Catholic!" Oh, daughters, pray that this may be so. How happy I should be if she entered the true fold of Holy Church. She is a lady who has much influence, and therefore how she would extend our Religion to many other souls. Let us pray. By prayer we can obtain everything.

21st August

The weather continues to be calm. Last night I saw something new and marvelous–the phosphorescence of the sea. It looked like so many lanterns of a thousand colors on the waves around the ship. Fireworks are insignificant in comparison. These made by God are much superior. We were admiring this wonderful spectacle with great pleasure until eleven p.m., and this morning at six o'clock I was at the stern of the ship making my meditation surrounded by the pure fresh air, which strengthens and helps me much to make a beautiful meditation on the happy and fortunate life of those souls to whom God has given the grace of a Religious Vocation, as He has bestowed on me, notwithstanding my many infidelities and unworthiness. The same grace has also been granted to you, calling you to the mystic garden of the Mission of His Divine Heart. What good has He seen in us, oh, daughters! The amiable Jesus has granted us such a precious grace in preference to so many other beautiful souls, who we know would have corresponded much better to this grace than we have. Oh, let us animate ourselves and inflame our hearts with holy ardor and fervor in the faithful and laborious service of our beloved Jesus. Let us love Him very much. Let us strive to enkindle His holy love in all hearts that surround us. Let us offer ourselves as victims for the conversion of infidels and sinners who do not know or love our dearest Lord. Oh, Love is not loved, my daughters! Love is not loved! And how can we remain cold, indifferent and almost without heart at this thought? How can we forget ourselves in folly and nonsense? How can we put a limit to our affection and to our energy when we consider the interests of Jesus? We are Missionaries, my daughters, we are Missionaries of the Divine Heart. If, then, we do not burn with love, we do not deserve to bear the beautiful title which ennobles us, elevates us, makes us great, and even a spectacle to the angels in Heaven.

August 21st

At last we can perceive a little motion of the sea, but very little, only enough to break the monotony of the past days. Every day we have sailed from 387 to 403 miles, and so tomorrow night we are sure to arrive at Havre. How glad we are that on Sunday next we shall be able to satisfy the holy precept of hearing Holy Mass and receiving Holy Communion in thanksgiving for a safe voyage, and to obtain always greater graces which will help us to serve our dearest Lord more fervently and to procure for Him greater glory. Now I begin to realize that I am far from you. Until now I could not persuade myself of the fact. I can see now the great distance that separates us. I am sorry I shall not be able to address you any more, not for one day, nor for twenty, and, in case of necessity, to comfort, console and even correct you, for I know that you even love my scolding, as you are inflamed with the great desire of advancing in perfection, so as to be more dear to that sweet Jesus, Who loves us so much, and in return for all He has done and suffered for us. Yes! in the Adorable Heart of Jesus I can always find you, with the same lively sentiments as though you were present. Go often, my dearest daughters, place yourselves at the feet of Jesus in the Blessed Sacrament. Behold that Divine Heart! He is our comfort, our way and our life. Listen to Him with great faith and devotion. He will tell you all that I desire from you. He will tell you how I love to have you pure, immaculate, very humble, charitable, fervent, detached from all the follies of this world, and, above all, from your own judgment and self-love. He will tell you also how I desire you all to be full of zeal and fervor for the conversion of souls. I will also see you often in that Divine Heart. To Him I shall confide all your needs. I will speak to Him of each one of you in particular. I know the wants of each one of you. I will take a great interest in you and keep you close to my heart. You may be certain of this. Now I want you to pray very much for me, in order that I may learn to serve more faithfully my beloved Jesus, Who is so generous in granting His graces and blessings to His unworthy and miserable servant. I recommend to you the Spiritual Exercises. As soon as the Archbishop returns, go and pay him a visit for me, and give him my heartfelt homage, and tell him I was so sorry I could not see him before my departure. I commend myself to his prayers.

August 22nd

Behold the last day of our voyage has arrived. The sea is still very calm. It is a marvelous sight. From time to time there is a little rocking, the effect of a gentle wind, which one might say is playing with the ship. The ladies complain about it; instead, I enjoy it immensely. They go and shut themselves up in the cabin. At five o'clock this morning, or a little before, I was already on deck breathing the refreshing air. In making my meditation this morning, I transported myself in spirit among you to assist at the Holy Sacrifice and receive Holy Communion. You are fortunate, for you have these treasures in reality, but I only spiritually. I partook of your joy and happiness. Oh, if we could only know how to appreciate the great advantage of Holy Communion, how much greater would be our fervor to receive It well. How much more merit also we should gain, because in Holy Communion the same Jesus, the Beloved Spouse of our souls, works in us for our sanctification. He give thanks for us, He does all for us and for His glory. Have faith, my daughters, have great faith, and perform all your spiritual duties with that lively faith with which the Saints learned to please Jesus and draw down upon themselves and those around them very many and very great graces.

August 23rd

I am at Havre, on the train for Paris, and so I give you my greetings and leave you. Thank God for the perfectly good voyage. I shall not remain in Paris for more than two days. Pray much for me, may the good Jesus bless you all, and each one in particular.

In the train at Havre, 23rd August, 1890

Your Affectionate Mother in the Most Sacred Heart of Jesus,

Francesca Saverio Cabrini

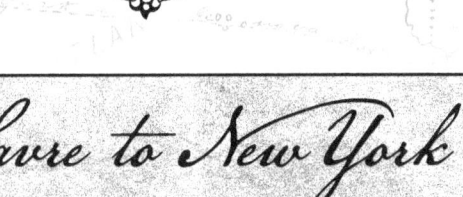

3. Havre to New York
September, 1891

Paris, September 4th, 1891

My dearest Daughters,

May the grace of Jesus be with us all and enclose us in His Divine Heart.

I never felt the bitterness of the separation so much as at this time, my beloved daughters, when saying *"Au revoir* in Heaven," in the name of those of your Sisters who perhaps you may never see again. It seemed to me I had said it also for myself, though I don't feel that I shall die yet. What human weakness! What kind of missionary spirit is this, you will say to me. It is true , you are right; no matter how great the distance that separates us, we are always near to each other, because we are ever found in the little space of this world, which to our small and narrow minds sometimes seems so big. Oh! *How* I would have liked you to have been with us when we went to visit Montmartre! That grand temple which was erected despite the opposition of the incredulous and of the Freemasons, and where stands conspicuously on a large altar the statue of the Sacred Heart, with His arms outstretched. On that day of His great goodness, He seemed to address us in these words, "I protect and guide you with My hands from one sea to the other." Yes, my daughters, a small ray of faith clearly shows us the littleness of the world when compared with God. Why should we give such importance to the transitory things of this life, and allow ourselves to be governed by that which we should despise? Oh, if we at least begin to despise ourselves, what a great thing it would be for us! We esteem and think too much of ourselves, and that is the reason why we never resolve to overcome our many miseries and raise ourselves to that pure sphere where the soul can easily receive the impressions of the Holy Spirit, and see and judge all things as they are in the light of faith! But, my daughters, if we were always animated by the spirit of faith! I asked this grace of Jesus while on our pilgrimage to Montmartre, I asked it for myself and for you. I hope this will please you!

Our Divine Lord has blessed our voyage in an extraordinary way. When we arrived at Modane we met kind persons who had received orders by wire from the Gondrand Firm to help us. They took charge of everything, and took great care of our luggage; none of our trunks were opened, but simply marked. They reserved for us a special compartment in the train, and we arrived very comfortably at Paris in the evening. We enjoyed the sight of the scenery of Savoia, and recalled to our minds the principal events of the life of our Patron, Saint Francis de Sales. We felt so moved, and became so inflamed with fervor, that some thought they saw a relic in every spot, and even in the very waters that the Saint once crossed. Sister Teresa, in her great simplicity, was never tired of praising God for the beautiful inheritance left to His children. I would wish that all my good Sisters had the simplicity of this daughter, because it is not that of the foolish, which is cursed by the Holy Ghost, but rather the simplicity that proceeds from a pure and faithful soul, and which penetrates the very goodness of God and rejoices in It. Oh, my daughters, what an excellent thing is a pure soul detached from everything and from self! She can bury herself in God, Who is the source of all courage. Let us then become pure, simple, unpretentious, raised above all created things. When we have achieved this, we shall begin to realize that true happiness which has awaited us this long time and is in store for us if we wish it.

Havre, September 5th, Saturday

We are on board at last. The sea is beautifully calm and promises a good voyage. Even here arrangements had been made for our arrival. Though it was almost midnight, we had persons to meet us, while vehicles, small and large, for ourselves and luggage, awaited us all in good order. We are traveling under the patronage of Saint Aloysius, who is certainly favoring us. In about half-an-hour everything was in order. We found ourselves comfortably placed in our cabins just as though we were assembled in the Convent. We slept during the few hours that remained of the night, but at half-past five we rose to go to Mass. Not knowing the streets, we were accompanied by a servant to the Church of Saint Francis, and there at the Altar of the Sacred Heart we had Mass, Communion and Benediction. From there we were accompanied back to the steamer, where breakfast was prepared for us, though we did not expect it. About nine o'clock, the Superintendent of the Company who resides at Havre visited us and introduced us to the Captain of the ship, asking him to allow us to go on the first-class deck. This favor was granted to us. In an hour's time we were to start, and all the Sisters wanted to write to our Sisters in Italy, but they were so enchanted with the beauty of the sea, that I was the only one who found it possible to write a few lines. This I did to those to whom I owe gratitude and who favored me with pecuniary and other help: that is, to our Monsignor and Father, that he might give you news of ourselves, and also to the Bishop of Lodi and Archbishop of Milan. But they were only a few lines written very quickly, and I do not know if they understood them, but they manifested my goodwill and the gratitude I feel towards those who look kindly on our Institute, and who assist it for the glory of Jesus and His Divine Heart. The steamer setting sail, we were all on deck viewing this beautiful port and watching the waving of handkerchiefs and hats. Presently we were in the Channel, the Sisters all happy and feeling well, and hoping that the whole of the voyage would pass off as smoothly as this.

Sunday, September 6th

This morning all the Sisters woke up very ill. Some of them thought they were going to die. Sister Cherubina lost her speech. Sister Egidea was almost in convulsions. All the others were seasick. It was a scene of perfect desolation. I alone was able to go around and comfort some and encourage others. Those who trusted in my words arose and tried to eat, and presently were looking quite well. The others, who thought that death was at hand, stayed in bed awaiting it without opening their mouths the whole day. As for Sister Egidea, not being able to find any remedy and not even the doctor, I had to have recourse to one of my usual tactics, viz., a good scolding, and immediately the convulsions disappeared. The effect was such that I became ill myself, and had to be very careful. At the start, seeing how nicely accommodated we were, we thought we might be able to go through our spiritual exercises, but the poor Sisters were not able to meditate. Sister Cherubina thought she really was dying, and was not even able to say "My Jesus, Mercy." They have become like little children. And if I had to depend on them, in their present condition, I should lose all courage myself, but I expect they will be much better tomorrow, and trust they will be able to be on deck where they can enjoy looking at the beautiful fish and other wonders of nature, which elevate the soul, and enable it to meditate on the infinite power, wisdom and goodness of God, Who created those things for our delight and comfort. On deck, today, I have only the company of Sister Agape, who is stronger than all, and Sister Mary Josephine, who, being obedient, eats, and so spends the time nicely and happily. They are followed by Sister Deomira and Sister Mary Gesuina. Sister Salesia with great virtue goes about from one cabin to the other continually, in order to spare me, but even she is not feeling very well. Sister Stephen, after a great effort, thought she would like to dress, but put her habit on the wrong way and came on deck. We felt so sorry for her that we took her back to her cabin.

Monday, September 7th

Today all are feeling well, and can at least get up and take some refreshment. The sea is beautifully calm, and if it continues thus we shall be truly fortunate. The head steward is very attentive to us, and sees that the stewards do all they can for us and that we need nothing.

Tuesday, September 8th

A strong wind that throws the vessel up and down, tells us that this day is going to be a great day, the birth of Her who was to be the Mediator between God and man, our loving Mother. It is a pity that of the five priests on board, not one of them is able to celebrate the Holy Sacrifice. We procured some altar breads when at Havre, but uselessly, so we must satisfy at least spiritually the spark of divine love that is in us, and absorb ourselves in contemplation of the great good that today comes to us through Mary. Mary is most holy, the meek dove of God in this universal deluge of corruption which frightens and depresses us. Mary with the flowery branch of the olive appears in our midst and seeks to give us hope. Adorned with that ineffable beauty of original innocence, she infuses in us great confidence, and makes us feel sweetly that she will present herself before God and obtain for us mercy and salvation.

What an admirable model we have in Mary. She is not yet three years old, and yet she abandons father, mother, country and friends, everything, indeed, and flies to God with the swift wings of a dove. She takes refuge in the Temple, a figure of our convents. She, this privileged Virgin, accomplishes, in the Temple of God, all that from her birth she had vowed to God. Mary sees herself rich in grace, fears nothing, and still she flees from the world and retires. Her profound humility is like a thick veil which she uses to hide herself and her gifts. She seeks solitude and silence, the solitary dove, because she desires to unite herself intimately with Him Who is Her only love. Mary will certainly have exclaimed, "How beautiful are Thy tabernacles!" My God, may all souls burn and languish for Thee! My spirit and fresh are in Thee, O, my God, and my life! O, my God, Thou art my inheritance, Thou art my glory, my joy, my crown! How promptly Mary answered the Divine call, and we? How have we corresponded with the call of God? How do we correspond with the grace of God now? What is our virtue, our conduct? What are our efforts, our generosity? Mary knew her mission, and accomplished it. And what do we do? We also understand what our mission is, obedience shows the way, but do we follow it faithfully? Perhaps we allow ourselves to be carried away by self-love, our corrupted nature, human respect, pride, tepidity. O, daughters, do not lose time. Let us follow faithfully the footsteps of Mary, our sweet Mother. Let us conquer ourselves, cost what it may, and we shall have joy in our hearts and peace in our souls! Let us strive, O daughters, to conquer ourselves, and Mary will cover us with her mantle of virtues; then we shall not feel any trouble in making our journey. Let humility, daughters, humility and great charity, detachment from everything, from ourselves, accompany us everywhere.

Wednesday, September 9th

Yesterday, at eleven a.m., there arose a great wind that caused the steamer to roll like Saint Peter's boat. Some of the Sisters, frightened, asked me if it were a storm. I told them that the sea was comparatively calm, and that something greater was wanting to create a storm. At this assurance they became quiet. The weather continued so the whole day and before the evening the Sisters were quite tired of the swaying, so we withdrew to a small place on deck near our cabins, and there, rather than sit down, we threw ourselves on the floor. We were alone, however, and it was pardonable, though even if we had not wished to throw ourselves down, we should have fallen. The place we occupied was quite near the kitchen, where the Bursar and the Head Steward could see and hear us and they were pleased to hear us praying, regarding this as an augury of fine weather. Being the Feast of Our Lady, we could not allow it to pass without some spiritual exercise. I had been ill also, but, in comparison with the others, my indisposition was nothing. I was, however, able to stay on deck in the fresh air, and as no one spoke on account of the movement of the boat, I was able to join you in spirit and celebrate the Feast of Mary Bambina, the infant Mary. Prayer is a great comfort and works truly. It is the life of the soul, though its effects are not always visible. Of the many graces that proceed from prayer, some are known to us and others not; but this does not prevent its enriching our souls. All the glory of the King's daughter is within. Of her preciously embroidered dress, of her immense riches, we see but the fringe. In Heaven, prayer will be explained in all its pomp and majesty. Pray, then, daughters, pray with unlimited faith in every need, in every difficulty, and do not become weary if in our short lives we do not see the effects of our prayers. Have faith, lively faith, resting always assured that not one of our supplications will be rejected. Oh, faith! how beautiful, great, powerful! Faith produces hope, and prayer is at once the supplicating hope. "*In te Domine speravi, non confundar in æternum.*" Oh, hope of Heaven, thou obtainest so much when we think our prayers obtain nothing, and when our hope seems a delusion. No, our prayers are never in vain, but everything is disposed of by the wisdom of the Omniscient God. Confide in God above all, hope, and you will not be confounded. Repeat often, "*In te,*" etc., and, saying it from your heart, open wide the wings of trustful hope, rejoice in the Spirit, and live in holy joy. You, the elect spouses of Jesus, the true friends of the Divine Heart! Be assured that not one of your prayers will be in vain, for if the Divine Heart cannot grant them, who can? May your joyful countenances make those around you happy!

This morning the weather is not good, but all want to move about, which is a sign of good weather. In fact, at nine a.m. a calm prevailed which rejoiced all. The Sisters gathered around me, asking me if it would continue, and I told them if they humbled themselves profoundly for our involuntary sloth, God would give us good weather and a calm sea. They obeyed, and now it is almost evening, and the weather continues beautiful, and the steamer is sailing at such a rate that we shall arrive in port by Saturday. Oh, obedience, how dear to the Heart of Jesus! Obedient souls delight His Heart Divine. They are His Kingdom, His heaven, His glory. To them He communicates His lights, His gifts, His graces, and often He admits them to His secrets. On them He sheds the rays of His countenance, and renders them perfectly happy in their state. Through obedience, Jesus accomplishes His greatest designs and works on this earth. To our dear Lord, these acts of His Spouses are more gratifying than a thousand sacrifices made from caprice and one's own will. Jesus loves to stay with obedient Religious. He guides them with His wisdom, fills them with His treasures and comforts them with His abundant graces. Oh, happy obedience! Do love this virtue, dear daughters, let it be your favorite. If you are obedient, you will be true Missionaries, you will be blessed abundantly by Jesus and you will save a great number of souls who await your work. None of you should work from self-will. You should have no thought contrary to obedience, but submit as so many little lambs. This is the secret of obtaining peace, and of obtaining great graces and blessings for the Institute. Love virtue, but obedience and humility above all, because with obedience you have given what is yours to God. Be obedient and your sacrifice will be entire, you will be true Spouses of Christ, you will enjoy Heaven in anticipation. Do not have any will of your own, and then you will not make your Superiors suffer. Why should you suffer for the devil? Why should you make a purgatory for yourselves and make others suffer? Why lose peace and make everything desolate on account of your own fancies and caprices? Submit yourself to the sweet yoke of obedience and you will become a haven of Christ, a haven of peace for all your Sisters.

Thursday, September 10th

Last night the weather threatened to break and the Sisters asked me if we were going to have good weather, because if it were bad they had made up their minds where to go and how to spend their time. I told them that if we humbled ourselves profoundly for our faults, holding ourselves to blame for all the acts of frailty that seasickness caused us to commit, God would be propitious to us. At first some refused to acknowledge that they were in fault, saying it was the sea that caused so much discomfort, but remembering the promise they had made of suffering willingly for the holy cause of the Mission, they felt themselves obliged to humble themselves profoundly, and our dear Jesus in the truly paternal goodness of His Heart granted us good weather, and so we are all assembled on the first class deck. You see, humility works wonders. All expected bad weather, and, instead, we have fine weather. Let us learn, dear daughters, to become humble, because God loves the humble, whilst He resists the proud. If we elevate ourselves through pride, God will withdraw from us, with the result that we fall into dense darkness. If we are humble, He will approach us, console us and hear our prayer, and He will send us away justified. No, daughters, God does not make the humble wait long. He runs, flies to satisfy their holy and most excellent desires. It often happens that, drawn by a humble soul, He gives what He has not been asked for. Be humble, daughters dear, the Sacred Heart has prepared many graces in the abundance of His treasures for the Institute. Be humble, His graces are hanging on a thread only. If we are truly humble and simple, these graces will be showered upon us. If we are proud, full of ourselves, He will withdraw His graces. In vain shall we then ask–for He withdraws Himself from the proud and haughty.

But now we must return to the sea. How beautiful and majestic it is in its immensity! It is as serene as a soul in peace with God and its neighbor. The soul thus possessed is a model of peace, though it is working hard all day, and appears to be burning with an ardent fire, which spurs her on to holy action. The mild waves of the sea reflect the rays of the sun in a wonderful manner, sometimes like silver, sometimes like precious stones in many beautiful colors. I should love the Sisters to suggest some appropriate phrases depicting the beauty by which we are surrounded, but all have lost the compass, and the knowledge they once seemed to have has vanished.

Sister Mary Gesuina is very jolly and keeping quite happy. She has recourse to *"Santa Reparata,"* and she does really make amends, for Sister cut her finger very deeply the other day while cutting bread for a poor German Sister, of another Institute, who is traveling third-class in great poverty. As ailments at sea are easily cured, so also the cuts of Sister were readily cured, and she was very happy. Sister Mary Josephine cannot bear the big waves, so when they rise she lies down and eats a piece of an apple, thus quietly forgetting the sea. She would have described everything beautifully, but finding it was more advantageous to remain quiet, she says, "All who want to know about the sea, let them come and see for themselves." Sister Agape is the captain of the sea: she is here, there and everywhere, helping everyone. Sister Teresa has remained two days in bed, so as not to see the Sisters suffering. She thought she had lost her head and touched it to see if it were still on her shoulders.

There is a professor of the University of Washington, a Missionary Apostolic, who inquires regularly about us, but the only complaint we have to make is that out of the five priests on board, not one of them can give us Holy Communion. Every time we come on deck we look for a place to be alone, but after a few minutes we are surrounded by the ladies of the first-class deck, who follow us with their chairs. They appear to be nice people, and to like the Catholic Religion. The Captain and other passengers are most anxious to make us comfortable. All delight in seeing us happy and free from sickness. After all, happiness follows us everywhere.

We are off the shores of Newfoundland, and the Sisters told Sister Teresa that here she could gather some cabbages, so she quickly dressed and came with her apron to get them to make some Italian soup, as we are tired of the French bouillon. Some of our Sisters who never usually think of food, do nothing else but speak about it, not finding anything appetizing. Sister Agape and I eat well-in fact, we are quite unmortified. We praise God for all, whilst some suffer, some keep themselves up, and thus we help keep up the ones who suffer.

Today it was lovely and fine. Some of the Sisters wanted to write, but, though the sea is calm and the movement is hardly perceptible, still they dislike these slight rockings or swayings. The first sea voyage is always a little difficult. When in three weeks time we again embark for Central

America, it will be easier. If you could see the sea at this moment! It is an immense surface of smoothness, and of an enchanting blue, so calm now. A fact incredible after the stormy days we have experienced. One hardly sees a lake so calm and placid. Today everyone of us joined in meditation on the gifts of a humble and pacified soul, the beloved daughter of God. The sea is a lively image of her. How immense and yet tranquil and quiet! A sea which can be so turbulent, yet how submissive when subject to the command of God omnipotent. Our dear Sisters continue to humble themselves, seeing how it pleases our dear Lord. With humility we can obtain immense graces, for humility moves the heart of God, and this unexpected and extraordinary tranquility of the sea is a great grace, Oh, would that God were really appeased; let us no longer offend Him. Do not arouse His wrath by infidelity to grace. Let us trust in the help of our good God, for of ourselves we can do nothing, not even can we pronounce with merit His adorable name. Let us endeavor to be faithful to His holy help, through the merits of Jesus Christ and with the help of His sweet powerful Mother. May she cover us with her holy and spiritual mantle, and make us worthy to serve our loving Spouse faithfully, and obtain for us the graces we most need. God promised to help us, and He does help us. We promised to serve Him, but we do not serve Him with the perfection and energy demanded of us. At times we are indolent, again we do not always have pure intentions, without which we serve ourselves our self-love, vanity and creatures, but not God. Do begin at last to serve faithfully our loving and faithful Jesus.

September 11th, Friday

The weather is still fine, the sea is as smooth as a table, the air light and invigorating. All the Sisters are feeling well, and in this sweet calm all unanimously decided to make their meditation, uniting themselves spiritually with the Sisters in Italy, for at this very hour all the Sisters should be at meditation, or, rather, at the adoration of the Blessed Sacrament. One of us, who desired very much to be near the Tabernacle, saw in a dream a great procession of Saints who were coming with the Holy Eucharist to gratify her great desire. But, only a few days longer, and we shall be able to receive our dear Lord in our little chapel in 43rd Street, New York. He is the Beloved of our souls, the Elect amongst thousands, Who consoles, comforts, strengthens, vivifies and sanctifies us, freeing us from our miseries through His infinite graces and unlimited goodness.

Last evening a Protestant minister gathered together as many persons as he could of the first-class and held a meeting—what the English call a conference—to collect money for the poor sailors' children. It is really sad that so many follow the devil and not Christ. We are so cowardly, that, whether it be from human respect or some other motive, we fear to speak of Christ in public. We see virtue derided, and we remain silent. Why are we so cowardly? We should strengthen our faith in an endeavor to imbue others with the spirit of Christ and to become animated ourselves with the true charity of the Divine Heart, and thus proclaim the truth. Do not be afraid of offending those who approach us, or of being importunate when speaking the truths of our faith. No, if we are filled with the sweet kind charity of Christ, coupled with strength and energy, no one will take offense but rather be conquered. Yes, if there is true charity, the most Sacred Heart will be honored. Sometimes a person will not speak deliberately of our Holy Religion, but praises vice rather than virtue, because such an one has lost his bearings, but if it were possible to find one individual who, with the generous charity and the sweetness of the Sacred Heart of Jesus, could introduce the subject of our Faith gently, correct certain wrong ideas, little by little such a good person would conquer that soul and reunite it with that secure trunk of truth from which unconsciously it has become detached. If such a spirit is necessary everywhere, what must be the necessity of it for those nations who once were profoundly religious, and now, through pride, ambition and a false sense of freedom, have allowed themselves to be carried away and to do what they do not want to do. People on board are already saying, "Why are these Missionaries going to America, while in Europe there are worse despisers of religion and faith ?" These words went to my very heart. If I were not wounded by such expressions, I should not be a true daughter of the Church nor would I have any love for my country. Such expressions dishonor nations, which in olden times flourished amidst true and profoundly religious sentiments.

Do begin, daughters, to humble yourselves, invest yourselves with true, solid virtue, become fervent and true lovers of the Sacred Heart, repairing ingratitude and making supplication for ourselves and for our brethren who live in disastrous times, because deprived of the Faith. Learn to humble and sacrifice yourselves, but with a real sacrifice, accompanied by a true denial of yourselves. Let us sacrifice and immolate ourselves for our dear brethren, purchased by the blood of Jesus Christ; those who through ignorance are losing the inheritance of the children of God and making themselves unhappy for all eternity. Seek to get them out of this precipice by sacrifice.

Saturday, September 12th

At last, with the aid of your fervent prayers, we have arrived at the last day of our voyage. If you could see the sea today, you would not believe it was the same treacherous element which frightens so many. It does not seem like the sea at all; it is so smooth, that the sun is reflected in it, it is so placid, that one might conceive that the sea never moved. I do not remember such good weather even last year, when I was almost tired of the tranquillity of the sea because it was so calm.

Such fine weather is supposed to be the forerunner of a storm, but before this arises we shall have already arrived in port, and so our Sisters who are destined for Nicaragua will not be discouraged to undertake a new voyage. Seeing that prayers are so efficacious in obtaining a prosperous voyage, I shall inform you of our leaving for Nicaragua, so that you may obtain, by your prayers and sacrifices, blessings for that voyage also.

We are going towards the region of heat which I cannot bear at sea, but, with your prayers, why should I fear anything? And for a Missionary, however difficult the voyage, it is always on that small plank that she must seek to extend the kingdom of love of Jesus. Therefore another four thousand miles is very little after all. You pray, and that will suffice. I will do the rest, giving myself up to the Heart of Jesus, He Who is our Good, our All, Our Preserver, our Master, Friend and Spouse. Pray, pray, O daughters, and make generous sacrifices, and then you will see how many graces the good Heart of Jesus will give you. All the sisters are well, happy and contented. They are beginning to like the sea, but perhaps this is because they are about to leave it soon. However, a Missionary must not attach herself to anything, but must sacrifice herself and all her inclinations. Sister Veronica sees now and then some very big fish. She thinks they are whales and sharks. Sister Alacoque talks much of her mission every night, particularly of the school and children. Sister Gesuina makes everyone happy. Sister Cherubina recovered her speech two days ago. The sea made such an impression on her at first, that she lost her speech and thought she would never be strong again. She dislikes leaving the sea now. Sister Pia and Sister Chiara having rested quietly in their cabins are now quite bright and happy. Sister Diomira suffered much, but has always been able to keep going. Sisters Pierina and Angelica and some others are sunburnt, having spent a great deal of time on deck. Sister Salesia has acted as infirmarian, assisted by Sister Agape. Yesterday Sister Josephine began her description of the voyage to send to her brother, but I am sending it first to you, so that you may enjoy it, as I have not time myself to send you an account of my own. All the Sisters ask me to thank you for your prayers. They are far away in body, but not in spirit. As true daughters of the Mother House, they are still very attached to it. All think of you, and are exciting themselves to great virtue. On the second day of the sea voyage the Sisters were feeling so bad that they acted more like children than religious, which fact disheartened me so greatly that I almost repented of having chosen such subjects for so difficult a mission, but I am happy now that I did not disclose my feelings, for the Sisters at length are feeling well and are really good, virtuous and sensible women quite willing to undertake any arduous work, for which they will be rewarded. They will be able to show themselves true daughters of the Church by their true attachment and holy efforts to procure the glory of God. I'm not sure of writing to you again before we reach port, but I will write again from New York and from Manresa, and hope to have much consoling news for you, more so as we are celebrating the centenary of St. Aloysius, under whose protection we are undertaking our work. This dear Saint has always been powerful especially during this year of his centenary, as we have experienced so fully.

The Sisters salute you affectionately and unite with you in prayer, sacrifice and work in the Heart of Jesus and beneath the mantle of Mary.

May the Grace of God be with you all. Your affectionate Mother in the Most Sacred Heart of Jesus,

Frances Saviria Cabrini

On the ocean, 13th September, 1891

4. New York to Nicaragua
October, 1891

On the ocean, Thursday, October 15th, 1892

My very dear Daughters,

As you are well aware, from the account of my last voyage from Europe to America, we reached New York on September 13th, where our Sisters, with many good benevolent and affectionate persons, awaited us with indescribable anxiety. The day following my arrival was the anniversary of my religious profession, a dear and memorable day for me, and for all my good daughters, who look upon whatever concerns me as theirs. We made a great feast of it. We had two Masses, and a sermon by Father Bandini, appropriate to the work of our Mission, treating of the solemnity of the exaltation of the Holy Cross. In the evening Benediction of the Blessed Sacrament was to have been given by His Grace the Archbishop, as he so kindly promised, but, owing to his manifold duties, he was obliged to delegate the Rector of the parish in which our House of 43rd Street is situated, Monsignor Brann, who was assisted by several priests who came to celebrate our arrival. His Grace came to see us the next day, and, with paternal kindness, consoled us greatly.

The following days I visited the various Houses of the Mission. I went first to Manresa with the twenty-nine Sisters who came here with me from Europe. All the Sisters were charmed with the beauty of the villa, which is situated on one of the best sites of the Hudson River. The order and the tranquility of the House pleased them still more. The chapel annexed to it inspires one with great devotion and recollection, and invites us to that kind of contemplation which makes us feel vividly the Divine Goodness of our Celestial Spouse, and makes us understand deeply His will, infusing into us the courage necessary to fulfill it faithfully. Every time I find myself at Manresa I think that, perhaps, when I have worked sufficiently for the Institute, this will be the place of my retreat to prepare myself for my journey to eternity. But this is an elusive dream, a childish feeling. Let us leave to Providence all thought of our future. Let us work, day by day, in the Lord's vineyard, seeking the greater glory of God, in perfect detachment from everything, which is of very great importance to ourselves, for often without our knowing it, we are the enemies of our own souls, troubling ourselves about many things, whilst *"Porro unum est necessarium."* Most of the Sisters remained for some days at Manresa in order to have a rest.

The 21st of September came as a dear and moving feast. Seven of our American postulants, who for a year had given excellent proof of their good spirit, were preparing to put off the white veil of the Postulant in order to take the Habit of the Institute. His Grace came to see us again and, vested in his ceremonial robes, to give them the Veil (or the Holy Habit). He performed the ceremony according to our ritual with impressive decorum and devotion. He gave an impressive allocution, and his sweet paternal words sank deeply into the heart of each Religious. To you, who, like me, have often assisted at these beautiful and ever-new ceremonies, it is needless to speak of the lively sentiments they arouse in all, or to tell you that we spent a happy and heavenly day in community. Even His Grace, in congratulating us afterward, said that the ceremony was always as impressive as if it were being performed for the first time. In spite of all I had to do before my departure, the time flew without my realizing it, and without a day's rest.

The 10th of October arrived in haste, and everything was ready for the continuation of the voyage. The state rooms were visited and the places destined for the Sisters prepared for them. On the eve of our departure, the Archbishop, who is most kind and shows so much affection for our Institute, came again to console us with his presence, and to comfort and encourage us on the new journey that awaits us. He gave us one of those heartfelt sermons which sink deeply into the soul, and then gave Benediction of the Blessed Sacrament, which was preceded by the "*Ave Maris Stella*" and "*Tantum Ergo,*" and sung with great fervor by the Sisters who were leaving. This was followed by a prayer to Our Lady. His Grace afterward entertained us very kindly, and his holy words were a source of great comfort, whilst he assured us that he would pray for us every day during the voyage so that Our Lady and the Angels might accompany us. His secretary, Monsignor McDonnell, assured us also of his most fervent prayers and wishes for a prosperous voyage, and hoped it would be perfectly happy. During the same day, till late in the evening, many good and pious persons came to say goodbye and to wish us a successful voyage. Even the next day some came on board the steamer to pay their compliments and express kind wishes for our journey.

But while we were talking with great animation, the hour of departure arrived. At ten a.m. we were on board the steamer which is called the *New York*, of the Pacific Mail Line. The agent was very good and assigned a stateroom for every two Sisters and a separate one for me. The berths are not so small as those of the Transatlantic steamers, but rather large and comfortable. The staterooms open into the parlor salons, so that the

Sisters can go from their berths to the lounge room without danger of falling, even when it is rough and stormy, for we do not expect this voyage to be as smooth and as beautiful as the last, seeing that we are dealing with a new Mission which needs great graces and therefore new sacrifices to render us more worthy of it. The Sisters were accompanied by many kind persons. A distinguished and excellent Irishman presented us, and warmly recommended us, to the Captain.

At one p.m. the anchor was raised and we glided slowly out of the port, while the Sisters and friends waved their handkerchiefs. We also did the same for about a quarter of an hour, until the distance made Sisters and things imperceptible, and, as the steamer steered further down the bay, we lost sight of everyone and found ourselves abandoned to the relentless waves. Till evening we coasted along the shore, which we should have done all night, I believe, had not a terrific storm arisen which threatened to dash the boat and all it contained to pieces. At one moment the boat rolled from side to side with such force as to threaten to capsize. The Sisters could hardly keep in their berths. I arose and dressed in haste to save them all, hoping at least to die together. Our luggage rolled about in all directions, like so many animated objects. There was nothing to stop it. No one could keep still, not even if seated on the floor. The sea swelled in an extraordinary way. The waves formed mountains as if by magic–one could see, as it were, deep valleys between them. The steamer seemed lost amidst these mountainous precipices of water. The wind worked havoc on deck, and threatened to split the cabins, but limited its caprice to the doctor's only. The following day the poor doctor had to wear somebody else's clothes, his own having been drenched and ruined. The Captain had all the sailors and staff at work as a last resource to save all on the boat, and he only succeeded by steering the vessel towards mid-ocean and sailing across it for more than a day. In the meantime the sea became calm, and then we were able to resume the ship's proper route, from which we had only sailed forty miles. But, God be praised! For during the terrible storm, as the Captain told us, no one was lost or hurt. During this tempest not one of the Sisters was frightened, all remained quietly in bed, ready to perish quietly, but under the bedclothes. I stayed up all night in the stateroom, from which I could see the Sisters resting, and thus we mutually encouraged one another. I was attentive, however, to every movement, for, if there had been any danger, they would have been obliged to dress and try to save themselves when called upon. In the meantime I was praying to Our Lady of the Holy Rosary, in whose month we were voyaging. Then I lighted the candle of Our Lady of Loretto, so efficacious against sea storms, and our Most Holy Mother did really come to our aid, delivering us from the extreme danger which surrounded us!

Oh, how good is Mary! How sweet and amiable. The earth is full of her goodness. All the centuries have witnessed the wonderful and merciful works of her blessed hands. Do we not frequently experience how she evidently loves and protects us? Like a mother full of compassion for each one of us, she pitied us who, in our danger, invoked her with faith. Oh, what joy to be children of such a Mother! We shall always recall the wonders of her love! We then prayed to Saint Aloysius to send Angels from Heaven to save us from the dangers we thought to be imminent, and he, having compassion on us, who undertake all our works in honor of his centenary, sent us immediate aid, and now we enjoy a very quiet, calm and smooth sea. Yesterday the sea looked like a soul, agitated by remorse and pride, who never finds peace with God.

Today is the 15th of October, the Feast of Saint Theresa, and this Saint, who had sufferings of all kinds and had long and painful experiences, has obtained for us a most beautiful day: a clear sky, a vast horizon and a pure gentle breeze. One could imagine that we were at Heaven's gates, from whence emanates a sweet comfort to enable us, as it were, to partake of the grand and beautiful feast which Jesus gives His Beloved Spouse. There is no priest on board, so no Mass, but we have been able to communicate spiritually with great faith. That fortunate prisoner had reason to rejoice at the thought that she once held Jesus in her heart, and entering, as it were, into the Mystical Tabernacle of her Soul, rejoiced as if she really held her Beloved. We, happier still, have received Him many times, and it is only five days ago that our hearts beat together with His, and that He worked with us and was given to us as Holy Viaticum. Today, then, it was not difficult to draw ourselves around Jesus in order that He might charm our hearts, as He once pierced the heart of the Seraph of Carmel.

Today we shall meet a steamer which will take our letters, so I shall write a few lines to New York and Italy, and so contradict as soon as possible those rumors which have led you to believe we all perished in the storm. The danger was indeed real, but we were all calm, tranquil and safe, trusting in our Jesus and the Mission to which He Himself was conducting us in the company of the Most Blessed Virgin and Saint Aloysius, patron of the new foundation. It is evident that we are advancing with great strides toward the torrid zone, though we have not yet reached it. Though we were obliged to put on lighter clothes, we still feel the heat greatly. The breeze, however, is refreshing and comforting.

Yesterday, October 15th, we expected to meet a steamer which would take on our letters, but the whole day passed without one coming in sight. This morning at seven o'clock we sighted a little island, called "Fortune Island," whence came a tug-boat called *Columbus* to take the mail.

After some days on the high seas and, moreover, after experiencing so many dangers, it was a great joy to see land, and we saluted the island with great pleasure. The Captain, always so good and kind to us, gave us a good position in order that we might have a fine view. I strained my eyes to discover all over that island some steeple, so as to salute with double fervor Jesus in the Blessed Sacrament, for it was Friday, and at this hour all our Sisters were making their Hour of Adoration. O, you dear daughters, so fortunate to be so near the Living Center of life.

Blessed are you who feel His Heart beat, who hear His ardent words which fill you with great strength and instill into you a powerful realization of the necessity to correspond with the Love of our Beloved Giver, Therefore, give love for love by the practice of your holy resolutions, which you have made to be generous in sacrifice for the glory of God, by controlling yourselves, always humbling yourselves with all your might, and loving, with true affection, humiliations; by being obedient till death, seeking the perfection of obedience, even to the extent of being so careful as to avoid the slightest transgressions of the orders of your Superior, who speaks to you in the name of God; by being charitable, self-sacrificing, willingly abandoning all your own inclinations in order to make others feel easy, especially your Sisters; seeking to give consolation to your Superiors by perfect renunciation of your will, which you left at the door of the Convent, while, with the cross, you entered saying, "I bring peace, I come to offer sacrifice to the Lord." Oh, yes, my daughters, create peace, sacrificing yourselves always, and never be the cause of sorrow to your Superiors, thrusting thorns into their hearts by your conduct, by your own ideas, which, however lovely they may appear to you, are but branches of a poisonous self-love. The more you are attached to them, the more poisonous they are to you.

Renounce yourselves entirely if you wish to enjoy peace, and let those who are around you partake of your joy, and thus also have the desire, when occasion arises, of cooperating for the salvation of souls. Since I started writing, we have sailed a very great distance and have reached another island called Castel, and we, just as fortunate as you, were able to salute Jesus in the Most Blessed Sacrament of the Altar, attracting Him to us with the most fervent Spiritual Communion. This morning, October 17th, at five a.m., we entered the Caribbean Sea, after having passed the island of Saint Dominic, which we were not able to see owing to the darkness. We were told that this sea is always very rough and stormy, but the Good God deigned to show us that He is the Master of Land and Sea and that all the elements are subject to His Omnipotent Hand, and so He gave us the storm where all expected the calm, and gave us the calm when we expected the storm.

Today is the Feast of one of our most powerful patrons, Blessed Margaret Mary Alacoque, and she, surely, in her ineffable enjoyment of the Divine Heart, has obtained for us a drop of that celestial and sublime dew, and calmed the sea through which we are now passing. She has changed the sky to another hue, clear and blue, smooth and beautiful, in which fly gracefully a number of very white birds, which look like Angels descending to tell us, in their mute but eloquent language, of the feast being celebrated in honor of that stainless Marguerite, purpled by the flaming rays of Charity which burn in the Heart of Jesus. What a marvel of grace God has wrought in the heart of His beloved! Let us also be faithful to the operations of the Holy Spirit in our souls! Let our minds be pure, disinterested, humble, pliant, and then we shall see what beautiful and wonderful things the Holy Ghost will work in our souls. Even the Angelic Spirits would fall into an ecstasy of wonder at the marvelous workings of the Holy Spirit. It is a work worthy of the Infinite Wisdom and Goodness of God. This Spirit works within us, inspires us, instructs us, encourages us, and comforts us with His abundant and perennial lights, with His promptings and impulses in every holy work. Finally, He surrounds us with loving solicitude in keeping us within the enclosure of His eternal and infinite love.

Let us seek the right and sure path of perfection, encouraging ourselves in true Charity towards God and towards our neighbor. The one should never be separated from the other. We should endeavor to attract to the Sacred Heart all those who approach us; that is the object of the life of the Missionary, the Spouse of Jesus Christ. Blessed Margaret Mary Alacoque saw beautifully engraved in the most Sacred Heart of Jesus the names of those who sought to make it known, and the Divine Heart made known to her that these should never be blotted out. The fire of His love is great and wants to spread, and those souls who endeavor to extend It are loved in a very special manner and filled with celestial graces. Which one of us would not like to be that soul? Otherwise we should be like the foolish Virgins, who, for want of reflection, became unworthy of seeing their Spouse and entering with Him into the marriage feast. Let us always have our lamps burning, never weary, and, as soon as we see our oil is diminishing, let us go to the Fountain of Life with profound humility to renew ourselves and to gain new courage. Little time remains, so let us hurry and work, for the reward is already prepared, and will be in the measure that we have prepared it. Jesus is with us. We can do all things with Him. By ourselves we fall, but with God all things are possible.

All the Sisters are feeling well, and are on deck, and whilst they admire the work of the Omnipotent and the immensity of God, they implore graces and blessings on the land that they see. Last evening we passed Cuba.

I have not told you of our pretty invention to keep the sea good, and even to make it more attractive and quiet. At night I beg the Sisters to make big acts of humility, acknowledging our misery. This is very easy, when we live up to the truth and do not delude ourselves, and with this kind of humble supplication we obtain the grace of seeing the sea spread out like a beautiful blue cloth, slightly creased, but brilliant with beautiful colors, creating a charm with which diamonds, gems and precious stones are not to be compared.

Oh, humility, how powerful and beautiful thou art! Do, my daughters, be humble of intellect and thought, as true Religious placed in the school of perfection should be. Have an abject opinion of yourselves. Let each one consider herself the least of all the Sisters and she the only one unworthy to live with the Spouses of Christ, the Beloved of His Most Sacred Heart. Be grateful of God's mercies, for gratitude is the noble sentiment of humble souls. Be humble, therefore, and always truly so, loving to be held of no account, unnoticed, forgotten, ill-treated, despised and calumniated, even in such cases one should remain calm, resigned and contented, as in a garden of flowers. Prefer to obey rather than to command. When you are corrected, do not justify yourselves, never say, "I speak because I have reason to do so." Keep silent and practice virtue whether you are right or wrong, otherwise we may dream of perfection, but we shall never reach it.

With humility, you will increase in grace and virtue, the serenity of the Angels will shine upon your faces, you will not be discouraged in adversity nor elated in prosperity. Your only thought will be to please Jesus in everything, and then you will be like those pure white doves, beautiful and lovely in the sight of God. Your voice will be sweet to the Sacred Heart of Jesus, your prayer will be as perfume in the sight of the Most High, your life will be as a burning lamp in the Community; in fine, your death will be that of the Just, with an immense trust in Him Whom you have imitated, and Who is your All and the Center of your aspirations.

Now, I must tell you how the Feast of Blessed Margaret Mary Alacoque, our greatest Patroness, ended. At four p.m. a bell rang long and loud, and the staff appeared in great hurry. The sailors were running here and there. It was a fire alarm. In less time than it takes to tell, everyone was ready with a life preserver to jump into the sea in case of danger, but carefully, for, as the Captain says, this sea is full of sharks which are seen very frequently. Men were employed in lowering the lifeboats. It was a fine sight to behold, for a dear old lady, who always bestows on us so much attention, told us it was only a fire drill carried out occasionally to keep the staff efficient in the event of a fire really happening. May God spare us such a catastrophe!

At six p.m. we went as usual to dinner, when several people, accompanied by a Colonel from Guatemala, addressed us, saying they were going to give a concert in honor of the Captain, and hoped that we would take part in it also. We hesitated to give our consent, not being accustomed to this sort of thing, but, remembering that we were in very refined company, and that, after Our Lady of the Holy Rosary, we owed the safety of our lives to the brave and valiant Captain, we yielded, begging the Colonel to put our names at the beginning of the program, so that as soon as we did our part we could retire. This was graciously accepted, and half-an-hour after we found ourselves in the first-class salon, where we read an address which was graciously applauded, and then we returned on deck, leaving the other passengers to finish their entertainment, which was really very nice and sensibly arranged. But, after all, they were not satisfied. The Colonel came on deck accompanied by the Doctor and other persons and begged us to sing some of the little hymns they heard us sing a few days before. So we sang, in chorus, *"Gesù mio ver conforto"* ("Jesus, my true comfort") and then *"Maria, che dolci affetti"* ("Mary, what sweet affection"), and our voices, blending with the sound of the waves, were raised to Heaven, while the listeners' faces brightened up with a new pleasure. which, perhaps, some never enjoyed before, It was Jesus and Mary who were passing their celestial rays over these souls, for whom we were secretly praying that they might be given the precious gift of faith. The Captain, not knowing how to show his gratitude, invited us to go on his bridge. He showed us his tri-colored lantern—white, green and red—which is used to avoid collisions, his compass and other nautical instruments, and the plumb-line for measuring. The Captain told us the Caribbean sea is a mile deep, and that the sea near Nicaragua has no known depth, for no one has been able to fathom it. I hope I shall return to you, however, without having to measure such a profound depth. We also saw the Captain's bed, which is a sort of hammock with a small mattress, suspended from the ceiling of his cabin. But very little rest can the poor man have if the weather is not fine, as he is responsible for all lives on deck, for which he is, indeed, most anxious and careful.

Yesterday, 19th, at seven a.m. we arrived at Colon, a port which has the reputation of being very unhealthy and a place of yellow fever. For us, however, it turned out very pleasant, the air, which for the last few days had become cool, contrary to every law of nature, became still cooler as we arrived in the harbor. So whilst we enjoyed a cool sea breeze, we contemplated for the first time a forest of palms which surrounded the bay and made it a charming sight. The railway was quite near the steamer, but the Captain would not allow us to leave the ship until everything was ready for our departure, which was at one-thirty p.m. so we had no difficulty in seeking shelter and food. When the signal was given, he had our luggage put on rail free of charge, thanks to the kindly thought of the Bursar, who also favored us greatly. When we were all in the train, the Captain, accompanied by all the officers, came to bid us goodbye, and told us to keep well and assured us we would have a pleasant voyage up the Pacific.

Even the staff came to say goodbye. One would think we were leaving our own families, but while one was pleased at such an exhibition of kindness, nevertheless, it made one feel sad to leave such genial people, among whom it seemed we could do so much good. God, however, wants us elsewhere, and so, after the signal was given for the departure, we find ourselves flying across the Isthmus of Panama, traversing a forest of palms, and then through a country where nature is immense in vegetation. There are immense stretches of coconuts, royal palms, bananas, bread-trees, tamarinds noted for their beautiful tiny leaves, and another tree called in Spanish *"Asquiera,"* from the roots of which a peculiar kind of flour can be extracted. There are thousands of other trees displaying fruits and leaves which are a source of great wonder. I must say I really saw this time something new which interested me greatly, for up to now I only knew of these wonders through the annals of the propagation of the Faith. We thought we were in India or in China, especially as the train passed through villages of wooden or thatched huts, inhabited principally by Chinese emigrants and negroes. The further we go, the happier I feel in being out here: these are real missionary spots. It is true we have been sent to an uncivilized country, but I hope it will be the stepping stone for a large foundation, from which we may go forth from time to time to bring the knowledge of Christ and His Most Holy Laws in those lands where the Missionary has not yet reached. In fact, we see no churches, and if we see anything of the kind, they are only pagodas or Protestant churches. The sight of this spiritual misery filled our hearts with zeal, though for the moment we can do nothing but pray for these, our unfortunate brethren, dwelling in the darkness. As we can do nothing else, we say our Rosary and recommend these souls to the Great Mother, who, by the mouth of the Church, says to herself, "*Quasi palma exaltata sum in Cades et quasi plantatio rosæ in Jerico.*" Let the Blessed Virgin be honored in these countries of palms and flowers, which are an image of her, and may there be a perfect and complete conversion of all these souls. To obtain this, we trust to your prayers, dear daughters. Pray, pray much without ceasing, and make your prayers efficacious by sacrifice, which you can practice hourly by a perfect observance of the Rule which imposes certain acts of self-denial, and to which I invite all, for Jesus wishes this of you.

But we have been two hours and a half crossing the Isthmus, and we have not arrived at the City of Panama, situated on the Pacific, which ocean extends in front of us with a calmness worthy of its name. Here the boat awaits us, and we are the first to board it, whilst the person to whom we were recommended by the Captain, carried our luggage. It was very soon filled with passengers who were going our way, and we were then transferred to the steamer, *St. Blas,* which awaited us in the bay, and which could not come close to the shore owing to the large number of shoals to be found there. We went on board two hours before dark, expecting to continue our voyage at once, but, when we got there, we had to make a day's stay, which eventually turned out to be one of two very long days. But even then Our Divine Lord remembered His own, because in Panama there is danger of yellow fever, and He thus placed us on the sea to enjoy the sea breeze for two days. We would love to run at once to our Mission, but Our Lord wants us to have two days' delay. We must take this rest in peace.

After ten days fast from Holy Communion, we had an ardent desire to approach the Center of Life. Our desire was about to be realized, for now we see a little rowing boat coming towards us which we hired and in which we rowed to the shore. It was my first experience in a rowing boat, and I assure you I felt frightened indeed to find myself so close to the waters of the largest ocean, especially as the little craft seemed about to capsize every time a passenger stepped into it; but the object of our trip enlivened my faith, and I encouraged the others to follow. In a few minutes we were rapidly making our trip of two miles to the City of Panama, singing hymns in preparation for Holy Communion. At the sound of our voices a flight of birds approached, and accompanied us to the shore. In the Cathedral we were able to satisfy our desire—Jesus came to live in us, to cooperate with us, to unite Himself with us. We went to the Bishop's house, but the Bishop was absent and we were received by his secretary. It was about ten o'clock when we got back to our boat, and, as at this time the sea was at low-tide, we had to walk half-a-mile over the long beach in order to get to our boat. We could therefore admire the beautiful stones, many of very fine marble, which the salty sea usually covers. We amused ourselves by gathering shells of all colors and sizes.

Then once more we rowed amidst the waves, singing hymns of thanksgiving. Here again the birds hover over us, drawn there either by the hoarseness or sweetness of our voices, to adore and praise their Creator Whom we carried in our hearts as in living Tabernacles. Some of the Sisters wanted to know what this procession meant, and I replied that they represented the Religious of those countries who might enter our Institute some day, but one of the Sisters was not convinced of my interpretation, and answered, "They rather (as the birds were about a thousand in number) represent the souls that shall be saved by us." I still argued, when another flight of other aquatic birds appeared, a thousand or more, and eventually we decided that they represented the souls which were to be saved by us in the course of time. Nevertheless, it was a sight I had never beheld before in the five voyages I had already made.

We arrived on board amid the joyful exclamations of all the passengers, who feel for us as if we were of their own. Some of them for fun had tried to frighten us, saying we should never reach the shore, especially as we were hidden from view by a shower which fell near the steamer while we were crossing. The shower only threatened us, for we intoned the *Ave Maris Stella,* during which the spirits of the air vanished, and we only experienced the rocking of the boat, encouraged at the same time by the realization that Our Lord was Master of that piece of wood which separated us from the ocean's abyss. Sitting at the stern of the boat, I put my hands into the sea and bathed them, but I withdrew them quickly when I felt one of them being drawn down vigorously. It could not have been one of those sharks two meters long, but certainly something of the crab species which, when once it grasped, kept a tight hold.

We spent the day in pious readings, interrupted now and then by the arrival of new passengers or fishing boats carrying a quantity of corals for those who cared to buy them. We amused ourselves by watching the little islands, which, owing to the ebb and flow of the tide, appeared correspondingly very small or very large. These islands are joined by narrow stretches of land. At low tide we perceived the remnants of a shipwreck. Who knows how many years ago? The old vessel is so wedged in the sand that no tide can set it afloat. How many poor creatures may have been victims in the disaster! What feelings of compassion does the thought not awaken in us and move us to pray for the repose of their souls!

Yesterday, the 21st, we desired to pay a return visit to Panama, but the passage cost too much so we satisfied our desire for Holy Communion by the thought of having received Our Lord the day before and by drawing Him into the Mystic Tabernacle of our hearts through Spiritual Communion. During the course of the morning the Sisters were anxious to visit the islands nearby. This could be done easily, as the tide was low. They could be reached by boat and then on foot, thus passing from one isle to the other. The trip took only ten minutes and cost very little, so I was able to satisfy their desire. I did not go myself, however, for, if I admit my weakness, I am afraid of the sea, and if there were no very holy motive in view, I have no courage to go where I fear danger, unless I were sent by obedience, and when, of course, one's actions are blessed by God.

Oh, blessed voice of obedience! When that speaks, the Missionary crosses the ocean and gives no thought to the roaring waters, the rising and lowering of the billows, but the ocean becomes to her a sublime and magnificent sight that fills her with admiration, and induces her to praise the Creator for the beauty and wonder of His works.

The Sisters enjoyed themselves immensely under the shady trees. They found other shells, but none so pretty as those on the beach at Panama.

The two days of rest are over, and at seven p.m. the steamer sets sail amidst the salutations of the passengers on the other steamers in the harbor, the boatmen and the waving of hundreds of flags. It is more of a pleasure trip, for we are coasting all the time. The steamer does not seem to move, no sound of the engines is heard, and still the boat is going rapidly. The waters of the Pacific Ocean are really quiet–it does not appear to be what it is in reality.

Yesterday, at five p.m., the Vigil of St. Raphael, we reached Punta Arenas, Gulf of Costa Rica. Here the steamer stopped for the mail of the first Republic of Central America. Owing to the low tide, the steamer was obliged to remain two hundred yards from the shore. Some rowing boats conveyed passengers to and from the steamer. Amongst these was a gentleman who approached us, and hearing that we wanted to send a telegram to Dona Elena Arellano, offered to do it for us. He further told us that as the Bishop had come to Punta Arenas for the Feast of St. Raphael, he would inform him of our arrival, and was sure that the Bishop would be glad to see us.

In about ten minutes he returned to the port, and in half-an-hour's time we perceived a boat coming towards us with two persons in it, and presently we recognized the prelate's dress. In no time the Bishop was ascending the gangway, and he met us as a father awaiting the arrival of his children. We all approached the most excellent prelate, who, sitting in our midst, listened with interest to the account of our voyage and the work we were about to undertake. Now and then he whispered to his secretary, "We must get them here, too," and his secretary said, "Why don't you at once?" He encouraged us greatly, but told us, however, we should have great difficulties to encounter, but we would overcome them and do great good if we maintained the true spirit. Finally he told us that if we had much to suffer, to write to him and he would give us shelter in his diocese. He blessed us and then went, leaving behind him an excellent impression of his zeal and holiness. He is German, possessing an intelligent mind and good spirit, a strong physique and energetic character. He is just the type of person for these countries.

Today, which is the Feast of Saint Raphael, is the last day of our voyage. Just as this angel conducted Tobias to the land of fortune, so he conducts us to these countries where we can accumulate treasures for Heaven by working hard for these abandoned souls. Even here on board ladies and gentlemen approach us and tell us how necessary it is to have Missionaries in these parts who will work with true zeal for the good of the people. Oh! my God, bless our intentions, and give us zeal for the salvation of our neighbors' souls, and communicate to us that energy which knows no measure and overcomes all difficulties confiding in the Sacred Heart of Jesus.

Yesterday afternoon we saw what seemed like a small canal, with waters of different colors, flowing like so many streams in the midst of the salty sea. We asked the Captain the cause of this phenomenon, and he told us it was due to a phosphorous element, and that at night we should be able to see the phosphorescence, which is quite common in the Pacific Ocean.

Here we are, at the Equinox—twelve hours full night. It is interesting to see the succession of both day and night. At six p.m. we are in full daylight, and at six-thirty the sun not only disappears, but we have perfect night. It is the same in the morning. At five-thirty a.m. we are still in darkness, and at six a.m. the sun is high in the heavens. There is a difference of six hours between the time in Italy and Granada, so whilst we hear Mass, you are making the Particular Examination of Conscience, and when we are going to bed, you are about to get up, and thus we are always praising God, which I ever greatly desire.

Whilst I am writing, we have arrived at the end of our voyage. This morning, the 25th, the steamer entered one of the most beautiful gulfs I have ever seen, the Gulf of Nicaragua, off the coast of Corinto. It anchored at seven a.m., about eighty meters from the shore, and soon, amidst the strains of a very fine band, we saw two boats adorned with flags and steered by soldiers rowing towards the steamer. Everyone was asking what it meant, and we were amongst the enquirers. When the boat reached the steamer, a priest and an old gentleman came on board, then other priests and gentlemen followed who had accompanied them. They are the representatives of the President and of the Bishop, sent to meet us. Everyone made way for them to approach us, as we were standing at a distance and little thought such distinguished personages were approaching us. They presented us with salutations from the great men of the Republic and prayed us to go with them, saying our luggage would be seen to. Having saluted the Captain and passengers, some of whom were crying because we were leaving them, we boarded the boats which conveyed us on shore. At Corinto we partook of a good breakfast which had been prepared for us; it being already ten o'clock, our appetites had been somewhat sharpened by the pure air. In the meantime a dispatch arrived welcoming us on the part of the President, and giving us and our luggage a free passage. Thus, after receiving several visitors, we boarded the train at three p.m., accompanied by the same personages who met us on board the vessel.

At six p.m. we arrived at Leon, where a crowd was awaiting us, to see what we were like, I believe, but the place was so full that we could not get off the train, so we were compelled to go further back and take another exit. All precautions seemed useless, for the people were determined to see us. While all this was going on, the Vicar General, sent by the Bishop, came on board the train and read an address to us in the Bishop's name, which was certainly an honor not merited by us.

We were at last able to get off the train, surrounded by soldiers so as not to be crushed to death, Then we got into carriages which took us to an hotel, where, by orders of the Bishop, apartments had been prepared for the night. The owner of the hotel is a Florentine, who had great pleasure in serving us, and treated us as well as he could.

In the evening some ladies and gentlemen from Leon came to visit us and ask us to send seven Sisters to Leon to open an Academy there. It was very hard to convince them that such things were quite impossible for the moment, but in the end they resigned themselves to it by my promising to let them have some Sisters some years hence.

In the morning the Bishop sent carriages to convey us to his palace, as he wished to see us, and though seriously ill through an apoplectic attack which paralyzed his tongue, he got up to see us, making efforts to speak and assuring us that as soon as he was better he would come to Granada to see us.

At eight-thirty a.m. we were on board the train, and at ten a.m. we reached Momotambo, where we took another trip up the lake, and where another breakfast was prepared by the Bishop's orders, the day before. At eleven a.m. we crossed this beautiful lake. Opposite us were several volcanoes, only one of which was not extinct, but from which only smoke came forth. At four p.m. we arrived at Managua, where a train for Granada was awaiting us. One of the Senators and a Deputy of the Government, with other persons desirous to see the Sisters, came to salute us.

At six p.m. we arrived at Granada, where the whole population awaited us. I really think no one could have remained at home, everybody seemed to be at the station. The crowd prevented the carriages from coming up to us, as they wanted us to pass them so that they could see us, but the number of people was so great that order could not be maintained, and we feared we should be suffocated. I was particularly anxious, as some of the Sisters were not feeling too well. I feared they would make martyrs of us through their great devotion towards us. I therefore prayed the soldiers to make room for us, and as soon as I called them they drew near and put the people in order, forming a great procession to the Parish Church, where the parish priest, accompanied by other priests, awaited us to sing the *Te Deum*, after which we were taken to the house which was destined for us, and where with great pleasure we are preparing to open an Academy.

All the children of the town want to attend our school, and boarders from the neighboring districts are asking admittance, but for the present we can only take fifty boarders, for although the house is big, it is not big enough for this tropical climate where the heat is intense. Now and then we have, as it were, a providential breeze which, pure and fresh, restores us a little. We have large enclosures with a variety of orange trees and other smaller plants, and flowers of all colors and kinds. It just looks like the beginning of Spring, and so it will be on Christmas Day.

The good Lady Elena Arellano had all the dormitories in order for the Sisters, and a very nice airy chapel, so that the Director of the Seminary, who by the order of the Bishop had accompanied us, could celebrate Mass and give us Holy Communion. In the afternoon he gave a beautiful sermon inviting people to thank the Sacred Heart for having bestowed on them the grace of having the Religious amongst them. At present Donna Elena is preparing the desks and arranging the program or prospectus, which will be examined by the heads of the families, and so far this has been approved by them, for they say we have brought them true progress. We hope this will result in good to their souls; for this alone have we undertaken such a long voyage. May the Sacred Heart and Saint Aloysius, who is Patron of this house, help to obtain these graces.

All the Sisters are well and working hard to open the Academy very soon. Perhaps they will begin about the middle of December. Those Sisters who feared earthquakes fear nothing now, though we experience some shaking. We have a volcano quite near. Some people want us to visit the country, which offer I intend to accept later on before I leave, so I shall have something to tell you, and not be like those who go to Rome without going to see the Pope.

I beg of you to become true Missionaries, capable of those sacrifices which your Sisters with the aid of the Sacred Heart have made. Seek to perfect your spirit and the observance of the Holy Rules, for you must be holy to be able to go to the Missions, and perfect by observing your rules and customs.

Our great Patron, Saint Francis Xavier, said, "He who goes holy to the Missions will find many occasions to sanctify himself more, but he who goes poorly provided with holiness, runs the risk of losing what he has and of falling away." I become more convinced of this truth every day, and as experience is a great master, let us take advantage of the lessons it teaches and never let a day pass without examining our conscience and making serious resolutions to acquire the virtues we need.

May the Sacred Heart bless and enclose you in His sweet Heart, imprinting His love on yours, and giving you perfect detachment of yourselves,

Your affectionate Mother in the Sacred Heart of Jesus,

Frances Saverio Cabrini

Granada, November 3rd, 1891

5. Genoa to New York
September, 1894

My dear Daughters,

The peace of God be with you and accompany you everywhere with the Most Adorable Charity of Jesus Christ.

Two years have passed since I left the Missions of Central America and the United States and returned to you, and now having to leave you again is very hard, for I have become as one, who, being accustomed to the pleasure of gathering every day variegated and odoriferous bouquets of the most beautiful flowers of your virtues, now goes forth wandering in an endless desert, where nothing but weeds can be found. But I consoled myself with the reflection that, if when I was near you I could gather bunches of flowers which edified me, now that I am far away the memory of your steady and virtuous practices, which make you exemplary Religious, true Spouses of Christ, will give me comfort, and I shall seem to hear a voice saying, "Go, Mother, and do as the Vicar of Christ has told you. Do not worry about your daughters far away. They will relieve your mind by the beautiful and consoling news they will send you. They will do their duty faithfully and keep their promises."

Am I to put faith in that voice within? Certainly you are very good-hearted, and you would never wound the heart of a Mother with bad news, you are sensible and you never break your word. You will try to grow in virtue, try to make sacrifices yourselves, real true sacrifices, in order to obtain that the time and labors I spend be not in vain, and that I may find good ground, good seed, a good harvest. *"Euntes ibant et flebant mittentes semina sua: venientes autem venient cum exultatione portantes manipulos suos."* It was thus that the most eminent Cardinal Parocchi wrote in the commendation he sent. But the first verse is no longer applicable to me, since my daughters follow me with their virtues, sacrifices and their beautiful and admirable fidelity. Shall I fear weather, privations, bad treatment and injustice? No, for the Missionary should fear nothing, outside sin, an offense, however small, against God. Then, what can disturb me? One thing only, that my daughters had lost the spirit of the Institute, had become weak, unfaithful: this would be a sea of bitterness which would trouble me. Let the bond of Charity bind us together as a true family in the Heart of Jesus.

But you wish me to chase away all sad thoughts, and I ask you to assume the usual gayness of the Missionary and to join the company of the good Sisters who surround me. We are fifteen in number, and so represent the fifteen Mysteries of the Holy Rosary. Our Lady of the Holy Rosary is our guide, our star and our comfort. We each drew a mystery, and the one I love most fell to me—"The Descent of the Holy Ghost"—so I shall remain in the upper room during the whole voyage, and from this dear solitude I send a thought, a word to you, providing you say the *"Veni Creator"* for me every day.

At Genoa we received every mark of attention. With the Sisters came several persons, amongst whom was the distinguished family, De Maria, who came to say goodbye to their daughter and sister, Sister Xavier, who showed the true Missionary Spirit. It was admirable how both the parents and the Sisters restrained their feelings, though their emotion was great. Half-an-hour before the departure, Mr. Lamp, the distinguished representative of the German Lloyd Line, introduced me to the Captain, warmly recommending us to his care. He promised to do all he could for us. All luggage was on board, and the *Fulda* had raised anchor, when we perceived a small boat carrying Colonel de Maria and his family and four Sisters of the House at Genoa, who continued to follow and wave salutation till the steamer left the harbor. The *Fulda* is now out of the port and our adieux are ended. We, however, are all united, and whilst we sail beneath Our Lady's Mantle, enclosed in the Adorable Heart of Jesus, you must pray and offer sacrifices to God for us, and Our Divine Lord will smile upon us and bless us. Pray, pray much, for we depend on your prayers, we trust in them, assured that you will obtain for us a very happy voyage and abundant graces.

the Fulda

The 14th September

Today we commemorate the Exaltation of the Holy Cross, and the Sisters not being able to honor the day in any other way, have thought fit to feel somewhat unwell. The sea is calm and beautiful, the air is mild and soothing, the treatment on board is very much like what we have been used to, but, whatever happened, one after another began to feel seasick and retired to their "boxes," as they call the small berths in the stateroom. At dinner I desired all should come to table, but they had to leave at once, not wishing to disturb the others. It is three p.m., and all, feeling well again, have come on deck to see the Balearic Islands, near which the *Fulda* is coasting.

We saw the Majorca Islands, also, the home of Saint Alphonse Rodriquez, and, moved by ardent desires, we begged for some of those sublime and great virtues possessed by this Saint, and which I would love to see imprinted in the hearts of my daughters.

This morning (as we had arranged to do last evening) all wanted to make a regular meditation, but they changed their minds very quickly as they were feeling too ill. Some of the Sisters tried to resist, but had to give in at last. At present all are in contemplation, admiring the landscape, sea and sky, which present to our view a scene of enchantment. Of course it is not like the scenery of Liguria when coasting along the Riviera. There we see a real amphitheater from the sloping top of the Apennines to the sea, the mountains, hills, beach, the sharp peaks, the lofty pines, the soft green, the undulating slopes, the peaceful olive and thousands of fruits and flowers, while the palms and woods and fruit gardens which reach to the sea are beautiful to behold from the deck of the steamer.

From Genoa to Nice, the cities seem to vie with one another in presenting a continual change of view. To tell the truth, until I became acquainted with the beauties of La Riviera Levante, and still more with those of La Riviera de Ponente, I never realized the beauty of Italy. I am happy, now, however, to be able to describe our Peninsula to the people of other countries through which I may pass.

The Sisters having remembered it was the anniversary of my profession, regretted my not being able to receive Holy Communion, for which kind thought I was most grateful. It is only one day since I received Jesus in my heart, and I imagine He is still there. One remembers Jacob's mystical dream when he saw a mystic ladder and angels descending and ascending, who revealed many mysteries and secrets to Jacob and assured him and his descendants of God's protection. Though we are far from the Holy Tabernacle, still even here on the sea there is a mystic ladder which touches Heaven, and the angels ascend and descend upon it for us also. From its summit God looks down upon us and makes generous promises. We can, therefore, repeat with Jacob, "Really, God is here in this place and we did not know it." We are in the bosom of the Catholic Church. We always lay our heads on the dear and mystic stone of Jesus; we agree with Him in everything, and abandon ourselves to Him, tranquil and secure, and by thus doing we merit in Jesus and by Jesus to partake of the good and the graces He brings us. And so I am quite happy to celebrate on the sea the most beautiful day of my life, the anniversary of my profession. Jesus is looking at me from the summit of the ladder, I invite Him to come to me spiritually, and He descends at once into my heart. He deigns to come down to this steamer, the *Fulda*, to bless those who are traveling with us. What a gift, and we knew it not!

Today is the 15th, we have been more fortunate, we do not feel as if we were at sea, but rather wrapped up in a cloud like that of the Transfiguration. There is a charming blue sky above, and below us one can hardly distinguish the sea from the sky. Some of the passengers say we are in the third heavens, others, the seventh; the glorious splendor renders everything so bright and brilliant that the passengers exclaim, "How lovely, how beautiful." We seem to see the portals of Heaven which do not close at the end of the day, because there daytime never ends, for the day up there is eternal and the light which emanates from the Divine Face never fails. There, in that abode, exists no night, no ignorance, no blindness, for everything is seen in God, there, no sorrows exist, no tears, no adversity, no sighs. No, daughters, in Heaven there are no clouds to obscure the Divine Sun, the Eternal Sun of Justice. There is no fear of losing God; no wiles of the enemy, for he has been routed, the world is far away, and the body spiritualized lives in harmony with the soul. No, there is no night in Heaven and the door is always open. Friends reach there at every moment, every instant, they do not disturb, but, rather, render the repose serene and sweet. Oh, sublime City, send down your beams of Light to these regions of darkness, this shadow of death where we still miserably live. Come, oh Supernatural Light, to reveal to us the beauties of that Blessed Country, and detach us from the miseries of this earth; make our eyes so pure that, through the shining crystal of Faith, they may behold the eternal good which awaits us after a short time of sacrifice and self-conquering. He who fights will be victorious, and to the victor the prize is Heaven.

Between one thing and another, yesterday we reached Gibraltar. The steamer steered into the harbor, remaining, however, half-a-kilometer distant from the shore. The small tenders came for passengers who were bound for Spain and for those who wanted to visit Gibraltar. Two of us went ashore to make a visit to the Blessed Sacrament, but the churches were closed, and the cabman told us that they would not re-open at that hour, as the priests had gone to dinner. We then went to buy some Spanish books for our new Mission, but we were handed Spanish novels. None of the booksellers had what we wanted. The cabman tried to console us by telling us there was very little devotion in Gibraltar. He took us then to the Borgo S. Rocco to show us what was interesting. In the Public Gardens we found all sorts of plants. The cabman, acting as our guide, picked bunches of pretty berries for us, and we brought them back to the Sisters as souvenir of this Spanish land.

Gibraltar is grand with its rocks and mountains, which render it one of the strongest fortresses which England has acquired in the Mediterranean. There is stationed here a garrison of six thousand soldiers, with an enormous amount of artillery and cannons of incredible size. The city is small, and contains three Catholic Churches and three Protestant Churches. Though I was told there was very little religion in Gibraltar, all the Spaniards I met appeared to be good, they told me they were apostolic Catholics, an expression which greatly consoled me. Moreover, they wanted to introduce us to the Sisters they love so much, but time was pressing, the Captain having allowed us but two hours, so we hurried on board, where we were received with great joy, just as if we were members of one family. We are very fortunate, indeed. Our company is composed of very kind ladies and gentlemen, who are most thoughtful and respectful towards us. Among the passengers is a Father of the Conventual Order, whom I met four years ago at Hoboken. We were rather importunate in begging him to say Holy Mass, at least on Sundays, but he could not comply with our request, for he had no vestments or other requisites with him. So, here again on this voyage we are deprived of Holy Mass and Holy Communion. But, after all, God wishes it thus, so let us cherish the memory of the last reception of Him, as Holy Viaticum, in Genoa. As I have said before, He helps, consoles and comforts us. We are representing the fifteen mysteries, and God, in His immense goodness, leaves us to enjoy Him. He is our Paradise–the Heaven of our desires.

We left Gibraltar yesterday, and, steering through the Straits, passed Spain. or had a glimpse of it; but we turned with sighs and groans towards Morocco, that poor land to which we would willingly fly to give succor to those poor souls which the Word of God has not as yet reached. It is true, vast crusades of Christ's Missionaries are already on this soil, but the land is vast, the ignorance extreme, and the help is insufficient. May Missionary Priests and Sisters multiply in numbers! The harvest is great, the laborers are few! To you, Christian maidens, do I speak especially, love God, and make yourselves active with the zeal that burns in you, help your poor abandoned brethren, who are the price of the blood of Christ, join our band and try to give a large number of souls to the Heart of Jesus.

Your love must be active as that of Jesus on Golgotha. "*Sitio*," "I thirst," cried Jesus, "for souls." If you love God, come forth, have courage, the devil laughs at the weak, at the timid, whereas he fears and files from energetic souls. Are you fearful? She who trusts in God and mistrusts herself, need fear nothing, because stripped of herself and strong with the strength of God, and with faith and humility, she can defy everything. Mind, dangers only exist for those who put themselves in the way of them, who mix up the things of the world with the things of God. On the other hand, those who are untrammeled with the things of the world, seek God alone and His service, and His glory, run no risk.

Worldlings look with esteem on Religious who despise the pleasures of the world, they revere them and will have recourse to them in their needs. What an honor Christian maidens, if God calls you to extend His Kingdom! Let us be up and doing! Do not refuse and incur the rebuke given to the Foolish Virgins, by neglecting to take advantage of the opportunity which the Institute affords us of cooperating in saving souls, and thus gaining merits, which in Heaven will fructify in an immeasurable reward of glory.

Virgins are chosen Spouses of the King and therefore Queens. If they are Queens, they must have a people over whom to exercise their power—their celestial Mission of Peace. Just as the Virgin, working as a Missionary, gains souls to Christ, so she extends her dominions, and her scepter becomes more powerful and more glorious. Come, prudent Virgins, and enlarge the Missionary Army, come, and make all nations give one another the kiss of peace. Come, for the Kingdom of God has no limits; its limits are those of the globe itself. Come, and let your glory be the glory of your celestial Spouse, the working out of that celestial talent—the sublime vocation of cooperating with Christ for the salvation of souls. Come, for in the Vineyard of the Great Father of the family we are to gather rich and copious sheaves. There are some who may think they are too poor, ignorant and weak to undertake such work. Do not fear, mistrust yourselves and confide in God, for, as I have already said, *"Omnia possum in Eo qui me confortat."* "With God I can do all things." He who calls us is that same Jesus who said, "Be perfect even as your Heavenly Father is perfect." But how are we to attain such perfection? By the grace of Him Who deigns to impose such an injunction upon us. When the Virgin of Christ mistrusts herself and confides completely in Jesus Christ, she can do all things. She becomes powerful, and can at every instant repeat, "With God I shall do great things."

But now I must continue my letter. You will certainly forgive the digression, which was inspired by my great desire to see your numbers increase. I long to help those nations who excite my pity. Today I am alone on deck. All the Sisters have remained in their berths. As we passed through the Straits of Gibraltar and entered on the great Atlantic, we at once felt the roughness of the ocean, and that, coupled with the swaying of the steamer and the roar of thunder, unnerved the Sisters, and they began to fear a storm. Sister Alphonsus tried to be brave, and came on deck to keep me company, but she was hardly seated when she was forced to descend. Then Sister Xavier did her best to be brave, overcoming herself by resting and coming on deck in and out. If she persists in her efforts, she will eventually become a good sailor, Sister Alacoque is quite a success, she rests on a table or a chair from time to time, and at intervals acts as infirmarian to all the other Sisters. Sister Giovannina made several attempts also, but was eventually forced to retire to her berth. Sister Constance is always up and comes to her meals regularly, for she thinks that by eating she will be able to resist the seasickness longer. I believe she is quite right, but today even she is laid up and can eat only what is brought to her. Sister Benedict sighs and believes she is ill, but one can see she is looking brighter than ever. All the Sisters seem very happy and are making the best of their little discomforts.

Today the Captain and the Head Steward begged me to tell them what the Sisters needed, as they felt it very keenly to see the Sisters suffering so much. The kindness we receive is incredible. I experienced great attention as a passenger on the Transatlantic Company's steamers, but the North German Line merits just as much praise. Captain Thalenhorst is a typical sea captain, and his good-heartedness and sagacity stamp him as the right man in the right place.

Today I made up my mind to stay in my berth and rest awhile after the incessant fatigue of the preceding days. I had hoped the Sisters would remain there also, as they had done during these past days, but to my surprise they were on deck, bright and happy and as serene as the lovely sea which we are enjoying today. The sea is of a charming deep blue, and reminds one of the heaven of a soul in the possession of God, a very peaceful heart, a heavenly look. Such a soul is always made more beautiful by Jesus. It listens to His conversations, and loves them because they are purer and more precious than gold or silver, it listens to the precepts of its Beloved and feels they give it life and salvation, for such are fragrant with the sweet balm of grace and wisdom. Such a soul should exclaim, "Enlighten my mind, give light to my intellect, help me with Thy grace that I may happily run the paths of Thy sweet commandments. Do not permit me to stumble on the way, but make me strong with Thy virtue, that I may faithfully do Thy holy will. Work in my weak and unstable heart, that I may fervently desire all what Thou willest, my Jesus, and reject that which Thou willest not. Guard Thou Thyself this Tabernacle consecrated to Thee." To this beautiful soul consecrated to God, every sign from Jesus is invaluable. Such a Religious not only performs what is hourly prescribed for her, but joyfully anticipates His every desire. She no longer lives for herself but for her Beloved, she has, as it were, wings to fly wherever the Divine will calls her, and to do and suffer something for Jesus. Again, this soul imitates the life of Jesus. He was obedient unto death, and the obedient Religious imitates Him in her perfect obedience to her Superiors, to her, every command is easy, for in obedience her path is safe, her work sure, her spirit strong. She is joyful happy, and smiling; she feasts on heavenly fruits; she acquires eternal merit at every moment, and follows in the footsteps of the Saints. It is obedience which distinguishes true piety from false piety. The obedient Religious is victorious over her enemies, for as she subjects herself to her Superior, so she acquires a perfect mastery over the devil, who was cast out from Heaven for disobedience. She has promised to give up her life, rather than be unfaithful to her loving Lord. In the exercise of obedience she has the merit of martyrdom. In martyrdom we sacrifice the body, in obedience we sacrifice the will, our liberty, the supreme power of the soul. Obedience is a penance of the mind, a sacrifice immensely more pleasing to God than any other sacrifice you could voluntarily make of your own choice. One act of obedience is more pleasing to God than a thousand other acts of your own will. The Saints teach us that it is better to eat by virtue of obedience than to fast to gratify one's own will. Saint Mary Magdalen de Pazzi, used to say that the simplest act of obedience is greater than the highest act of contemplation. In fact, we read in her life that when she was in ecstasy the voice of obedience was sufficient to recall her to herself. Learn to love this virtue, which forms the character of a true

Religious. The readiness of your obedience indicates the readiness of your heart, for the hand moves and the feet run when the spirit is fervent. In serving Jesus Christ, you see Him in your Superior. You must consider the orders of your Superior not only as being rightly given, but as being the best for you. If thoughts against obedience come to you, chase them away as you would drive away thoughts against our Holy Faith. See in your Superior not only the authority of God but the will of God. Remember that holy obedience is ordered by God in the Holy Scriptures; therefore it is orthodox, and in faith there can be neither deceit nor illusion.

Conform your will and judgment with that of your Superior, and you will attain to a great height of perfection. Do not regard the natural gifts and good qualities of your Superior, for by so doing you will change Divine Obedience into human Obedience. See in her Jesus Christ, and all will be well, Make all your actions, however small, precious by obedience not by doing your own will. Beg often of Jesus to give you the spirit of Obedience, and, as far as it lies in your power, do all you can to merit such a grace, and blessed will you be in obtaining such a signal favor. Let us trust in the Heart of Jesus, for Its very pulsation is obedience.

It is almost evening now, and we have sailed 389 miles in twenty-four hours. The Sisters seem fairly well, sewing and praying, and meditating either with the aid of a book or by gazing upon their sublime surroundings, which excite sublimer thoughts. Sister Alexandrine, fearing to forget the days of the week, keeps a record of them, and scrupulously reminds the Sisters every morning of the same. Our fellow-passengers take more care of us than they do of themselves; they give us everything they can rather than see us suffer. They treat us with much respect and reverence, and hold the religious habit in great veneration. Some of the merchants ask our advice on their business affairs, and we try to comfort them with the inspirations we receive from the Sacred Heart. Yesterday a waiter told me how sorry he was that he could not speak Italian, so that he might render the Sisters better service. He wants me to act as interpreter, but my knowledge of English is limited, barely enough to prevent me from losing my way or from dying of hunger. When we are on deck there is a very nice gentleman who always acts as interpreter, The Sacred Heart seems to bless us in a very special manner on this voyage.

Well, my dear daughters, help us to praise and bless Him Who with so much care and ineffable love guides and comforts us.

Tomorrow, at ten a.m., we shall see the Azores, and we shall be able to tell you something about them, though we may not be able to visit them as we did Gibraltar.

At five a. m. we heard a whistle which notified us that the Azores were in sight. We, however, did not understand the cause of the movement on deck, but it was not long before our friends came knocking at our doors to inquire why we were not on deck.

It really was a lovely sight! Some call the Azores the Azures, and they really look like a bit of heaven dropped into the Atlantic. What beautiful mountains and hills! The grand slopes are covered with a smiling green that at every twenty meters changes shade. The grassy plains, the heavy-laden vineyards, the leafy woods and enchanting villas make one long to visit these charming islands. More than one passenger was desirous of asking the Captain to stop the steamer, at least for one hour, to see these most fertile Portuguese possessions, cut up into fields, cities and summer resorts, with everything so pretty. Surely wealth and comfort reign there, The good Captain steered the vessel in such a way that the cities of these islands could be seen quite easily. The city of

Punta Delgada could be seen sloping, as it were, into the sea. Its towers, steeples and monuments reflected in the waters. Just as we were passing, a most beautifully colored rainbow appeared in the sky which seemed to unite the inhabitants of the city with the passengers of the steamer. The rainbow seemed to announce the Peace of the Divine Heart which draws the hearts of all people together in ardent charity. Behind this arc there was a still larger and more extended rainbow with lighter tints, it was a sight which made us hold our breath. It looked like a heavenly light spread out to purify the mind and render it capable of raising itself to praise the Maker of Creation, so immense and enchanting and inimitable by man. And, while the arched rays of this beautiful rainbow increased in splendor, and this unparalleled view fascinated us, big bright drops of rain advancing at lightning rate sprinkled us all over, and we were obliged to take shelter. The Azores are beautiful and healthful; it is a resort for invalids, especially for those who suffer from chest trouble. How good God is!

This morning the rainbow reminded me of our celestial Mother, the real Ark, who guides our little company across the sea. Mary is heavenly, and in her loveliness and serenity reflects the rays of the Divinity. She is a shining dart burning and inflamed with charity for us, because the splendors which are in her descend from God, Who is not only an ineffable light but a burning fire of charity. How many wonders we meet with in the love of Mary, how many graces, how many gifts, how many good things come from her benevolent hands, and all are sealed with great love. One look from her, one thought from her fills us with her burning charity. Mary, our sweet Mother, is an ocean of goodness, a fire of charity that burns, in flames and transforms. She is a sun of perennial light, grace and beneficence. No one is excluded from her beneficial heat, for her charity is universal and continual. To all she opens the bosom of her ineffable goodness; she is ready to help all, and even anticipates their desires.

Mary is like the beautiful olive tree in a field where all can see her and have access to her. From her fields flow perennial streams of water wherein the thirsty may quench their thirst. Do not wonder if you see yourselves overloaded with graces and tenderness from Mary, for she dispenses gifts and graces which flow like a stream from that immeasurable ocean of love she bears us.

Yesterday, the 14th, we had the last glimpse of the Azores. The great Saint George did not seem half so beautiful as Saint Michael, though it also had smiling green mountains and valleys and enchanting slopes. In one of the great cities we saw a very beautiful and artistically built Cathedral, but no one could tell me the name of the city. There were several boats full of people, but none of them could approach us owing to the formidable waves created by the movement of the *Fulda*. They waved their hands and handkerchiefs to us. How I longed to tell some of them to go and visit Jesus in the Most Holy Sacrament of the Altar. They certainly would do so, I'm sure. All on board seem quite disposed to believe what we say about God. They are very reserved in manner and speech. We united with the Portuguese and Flemings in sending our greetings to the Churches. We could also see volcanoes; some were extinct, whilst the sharply-pointed cones of others seemed about to burst at any moment and send out fire, smoke and lava.

The scenery of the Azores has disappeared, and rainbows succeed one another, two at a time. The passengers are surprised, but we discern the eye of Mary looking down upon us, as though to console us. Then another thing happened which astonished those Sisters who are strangers to sea voyages. A huge number of water-birds appeared. The sea, disturbed by a north wind, tossed the vessel, and the passengers began to whisper to one another and then to exclaim aloud, "A storm, a storm!" Like the Apostles, they gathered around me, and begged me to tell the sea to be calm. I had to tell them they had little faith and little courage, also that it needed bad weather to bring a storm. If one did happen we need not fear, for we are traveling in the Name of Jesus and under the mantle of Mary. Neither sea, winds nor billows will frighten us. Our faith obliges us to trust in God, and that trust will make us strong even unto death. The sea still continues to be rough, but today the barometer marks "Fair Weather," so we hope to recover the calm that marked our passage from the Mediterranean to the Azores. Sister Constance asked me if I would allow her to complain aloud, but I told her to repeat the words, "How wonderful!" This she does, though she can hardly bear it at all. Sister Pia cannot get up, so she remains in her berth. She is able to eat whatever is brought to her. Sister Xavier is not feeling well, but she keeps me company on deck, as she does not like her berth. Sister Alacoque is quite like a seaman, healthy and active. She is still infirmarian, and knows how to make the Sisters eat. This is the best thing she can do, for it is very bad not to be able to eat whilst traveling, for fasting increases the nauseous feeling and one suffers more. Sister Frances suffers silently and serenely, and forces herself to eat for the sake of obedience. Sister Claver suffers more than anyone else. Our Sisters have made a Heaven of their cabins. One Sister dreams she is at Holy Mass but cannot receive Holy Communion, and then another sees a Saint who comes to console them. They are always praying. The goodness of God is so great that He consoles us in a thousand ways. To raise us up, to provide for us, to console us and to enrich us, He has thousands of ways. Have faith, my dear daughters, whatever you ask you shall receive, for by prayer born of faith you can obtain everything. If, sometimes, we do not get what we want, let us examine ourselves and see whether the cause does not lie in the want of proper dispositions, perhaps a lack of proper spirit, of fervor, of supernatural motives, perhaps our prayers are said with the lips only, with weariness, in a hurry or without recollection and perseverance. My good daughters, how prayer enlivens faith and does everything! Prayer and Faith united are powerful beyond thought. If the Saints have worked wonders and prodigies, they did it through prayer with faith. Have faith! He who prays with faith has fervor, and fervor is the fire of prayer. This mysterious Fire has the power of consuming all our faults and imperfections, and of giving to our actions, vitality, beauty and merit. The fervor produced by a lively faith is like a shower of limpid crystal waters that revive and animate. It lightens all our sufferings and troubles, and purifies all that is faulty and earthly, and gives everything its proper virtue, value and splendor. But, note, I am not speaking of sensible devotion, but of that substantial fervor which is the product of a lively faith. I refer to that fervor and ardor of spirit which consist in the union of the soul with God in perfect conformity of our will with the Will of God. This fervor you will obtain by keeping a mastery over the powers of the soul, and by watchfulness over your senses, rejecting, as far as it lies in your power, all useless, vain and inopportune thoughts. A soul recollected in God receives in its prayers the fervor of God, therefore it can obtain from Him all it desires.

Accustom yourselves to unite your prayers with those of Jesus Christ, so that yours coming in contact with His shall be purified and sanctified. Be assured that after Jesus Himself has purified them, He will present them to His Eternal Father. Pray always with Jesus, always remembering that a soul united with Jesus can do everything. Bear in mind this maxim, "*Omnia possum in Eo qui me confortat.*" Have faith; pray with faith, and good measure and overflowing measure shall be given unto you. Oh, Faith, beautiful daughter of Heaven, come, to our souls and let us honor thee, thou who hast enveloped us with the beautiful mantle of baptism, and hast always enriched us by means of the other Sacraments!

Another gorgeous day! The sea is so calm and serene that one hardly perceives the movement of the vessel! Everyone is up and well. Tired of the rolling and the pitching of the steamer, we said our prayers last evening. We began by humbling ourselves, knowing that humility is the secret that penetrates the walls of the Holy City and the rock of the Omnipotent. Humility is the foundation of every meritorious and virtuous work and of prayer. It is impossible to please God without humility, it is a golden scale that measures the strength of our prayers, and it is, therefore, the measure of their weight in God's own scales. The humblest obtain the most graces, the least humble obtain the least grace, for it is written: God resists the proud and gives grace to the humble, "*Deus superbis resistit; humilibus autem dat gratiam.*" Chase away all sentiments of pride and self-love if you want God to be with you. God will be our strength, and if we are humble our prayers will ascend, like a sweet perfume, to the throne of Heaven, where they will be fully granted. The humble Religious is like a bunch of Spikenard, which, though the smallest and humblest of flowers, is one of the most fragrant. Spread about you the perfume of humility, study profoundly this celestial virtue until you possess it completely and perfectly, and then you will be able to repeat some day, when this life is over, with the Spouse of the Canticles, "*Nardus mea dedit odorem suavitatis,*" while the loving Savior, delighting in your sweet virtue, will give you the eternal kiss of Peace.

The Franciscan Father enquires daily how we are faring, and tells us the Feast of the day, and thus helps Sister Alexandrine, who, having been ill these past two days, has given up keeping her diary, and so we run the risk of losing our bearings. I have met kind friends on my journeys, but never anyone who exceeded the kindness of our good Captain. He is just like a father, always anxious about everyone being well provided for. He especially watches over the Sisters and sees we have the best of attention. The Sisters are having recourse to the Holy Souls before the weather changes. These Blessed Souls cannot help themselves, but they can do so much for us. Let us have pity on them; let them have the principal part of our prayers, for the mitigation of their sufferings depends upon our charity and our prayers. One might almost say the keys of their prison have been consigned to us. The Holy Souls love their Divine Spouse, they desire Him, they sigh for Him, but they need the cooling hand of benefactors to cancel their debts. These doves would love to fly to the bosom of their God, but, woe to them if no pitying hand severs their chains of fire. Come, beloved daughters, draw down upon them a celestial dew which will cool and allay their inconceivable heat. Your prayers will be the dew that will quench the flames of Divine Justice. Comply with the just desires of these souls. You will be doing much to your own advantage if you relieve them by offering for them your Holy Communions, Indulgences, Masses and all satisfactory works. This, you see, will be a work of perfect charity, of immense glory to God, of great joy to the Church Militant, Suffering and Triumphant, because with your prayers you will send many saintly souls to the Kingdom of the Blessed. Have no fear that you will lose your prayers, indulgences and satisfactory works by giving them to the Holy Souls, but, rather, rest assured that by so doing you will become rich in grace and merits in this life and in sublime glory in Paradise. Rest satisfied also that the intrinsic merit of this work of suffrage remains always with you, being of its nature inalienable; only the portion that gives atonement goes to the Holy Souls. Giving up, then, this portion of our works to the Holy Souls, which some do by means of the Heroic Act, we do nothing less than convert every act of satisfaction into merit, and be assured that in the scales of God one degree of grace and merit is of more value than all the works of atonement we may apply to the Holy Souls. Be generous to the Holy Souls, for he who gives shall receive, and he who is merciful shall obtain mercy. The souls whom we set free will become so many advocates, so many protectors who will pray for us, intercede for us, and, what is more, they will interest themselves in our Eternal Salvation.

The 21st The sea is now as smooth as a table. Our sailing is delightful. The passengers are very happy and come to thank us, for they say they owe everything to our prayers. The Captain says that each of us must bring a lovely day, and, as we are fifteen in number, if we have fifteen fine days there will be a surplus of four days' fine weather, for the *Fulda* takes only eleven days from Genoa to New York. At present all the Sisters are feeling well. I always feel better at sea than on land, so the passengers call me a sea-lion. But, by way of a change, I am seasick today. All the passengers were quite surprised that I should have to pay the toll at the very end of the voyage. This impost is generally exacted at the beginning. But Jesus, the Master, does as He wills. We have but to praise and thank Him, for everything is good that He permits.

We have entered the Gulf Stream where everyone says the sea is very rough, but up to now we have enjoyed wonderfully fine weather. Everyone is astonished. So we have reason to praise and thank God for His goodness in commanding the elements to adapt themselves to our comfort and convenience. Love the good God, for the sky, earth and sea tell us to love Him! The immense ocean, set with wonderful gems, reveals clearly the ineffable solicitude (with graces and blessings) with which our loving Creator surrounds us. We look at the sea, the earth with its inexhaustible fecundity, the firmament with its stars, and the whole Universe resects God's attributes, His power, His wisdom and goodness, and we cannot but exclaim with admiration, "How wonderful is God in His works!" The sisters are quite bright again today, so on deck we found a nice cozy corner where we enjoyed our lecture on humility. We then read a chapter on Charity, that sublime virtue which gives a foretaste of Heaven. Those souls united in Charity peacefully repose in God, and await with security great graces from God's goodness. Magnanimous and generous souls are those united in Charity; they are blessed by God, they soar on high; they ascend to Heaven, where they repose at God's feet, and He, rejoicing in them, crowns them with glory. Be charitable, my dear daughters, love one another in holy love in the Adorable Heart of Jesus. Sacrifice yourselves willingly for your Sisters, be meek towards one another, never be sharp or resentful with one another. Try and be the one who always soothes with the balm of peace. Learn how to use that precious magnet of the Charity of the Adorable Heart to Jesus to alleviate pain, to dress wounds and to console in tribulation. Admire what is good in your Sisters, pity their faults and do not envy anyone. What a wonderful sight to see so many souls of different nations and different languages united in one religious family, joined by the ties of the sweet Charity of the Adorable Heart of Jesus.

Though the distance is widening more and more each day, still I'm nearer to you in spirit than ever. Not a moment passes without my thinking of you and working with you. You must do the same and accompany me in the spirit of Holy Charity. Help me with your prayers and sacrifices. When you wish to console me, withdraw into the mystic sanctuary of your soul to see if you have acquired the sweet virtue of Charity. I could desire nothing more. Love all in the Adorable Heart of Jesus, as the Saints love one another in Heaven; love, and God will take care of the rest. Study Charity, love Charity, let Charity rule your souls, and then you can repeat triumphantly, *"Dotavit me Deus dote bona,"* as the Holy Ghost says. Yesterday the staff were making great preparations to protect us from the icebergs of Newfoundland, as we shall be very close to them tonight, but the precautions were not needed, for the Blessed Virgin covered us with her mantle, the Holy Souls interceded for us, and the result was that we had rain during the whole night, which proved very advantageous, for the sea became quite calm. Fresh water and salty water mixed together form a calm sea, and this lesson teaches us how to behave with those who are against us. Raise your hearts on high and accept God's will without murmuring against or criticizing those people who afflict us. Pity them and excuse them as did David with regard to his enemy, for, on hearing himself reviled, he did not defend himself, but said, "Let them talk, because it is God who permits their speaking against me, it is little, indeed, they are saying, I merit more." Thus behaves a soul according to the Heart of God. If we become possessors of such virtues, we would become Saints very easily. Never murmur, never criticize; if you are inclined to use your tongue, use it against yourself. Or, better still, as Saint Francis de Sales inculcates, say neither good nor bad of yourself. Today on deck (I spoke of this yesterday) we were able to enjoy the sun and to say our prayers and make our meditations together. As we were rapt in contemplation, the sun, covered with graceful clouds, formed, as it were, with its rays of gold, the border of Our Lady's Mantle. It seemed to us that Mary, the perfect image of Jesus, was gazing down upon us. As a cloud brightened by the rays of the sun becomes beautifully bright, so does Mary, the perfect image of Jesus, appear brilliant in her Divine Beauty. The fact is, that we imagined we saw Jesus and Mary, beautiful and refulgent, looking down upon us and offering us their patronage so that we might become converted.

But how shall we obtain Mary's patronage and protection? By imitating her. Impress on your minds the life of Mary, her sentiments, her habits, her Immaculate Purity, her words, her actions. Beg Our Divine Lord to imprint, with the fire of His Divine Heart, Mary's image on you, and to make you loving models of His Immaculate Mother.

Mary is the Mysterious Book of Predestination to glory; she is lovable, love her. She is sublime and glorious, praise her. She is benign and merciful, appeal to her. Mary is your Mother, Mistress and Foundress, obey and fulfill her desires. Mary speaks to you plainly; listen to her, trust her with all your affections, she will alienate them from creatures, and you, as angelic spirits, will take refuge in the Heart of Jesus. Offer yourselves often to Mary, pray, work, suffer, recreate yourselves, rest and walk with Mary and beneath the gaze of Mary, and never sadden her in the least.

Yesterday, to our great surprise, the Captain invited us to go over the steamer. I should like to know how to describe the complicated machinery of this great vessel, which transports thousands of persons from the Old World to the New World. The steam power used by the propeller when driving forward this ship is that of fifteen thousand horses. The noise made by the propeller when out of the water is great. I commend you to Sister Frances whose knowledge of ships and their appurtenances is more extensive than mine. She will give you more satisfactory details than I am able. She will explain either out of the store of her own knowledge, or by reference to ancient and modern works on the subject. I can see quite a library of such books spread out in her berth. I was advised to ask Sister Xavier for information as she knows something of these things, but she replied, "Those who want to know the sea, let them come and see." Sister Ignatius set out to give you a very full and learned account of everything, but so far she has written not more than four lines.

The Captain asked Father Mazzetti to celebrate Mass, but the Father had not the necessary vestments, and we had no Hosts. Taking advantage, however, of the Captain's exquisite kindness, we all assembled, both passengers and Sisters, in the largest space we could find and recited the Rosary, priests and passengers alternately, just as we do in the Convent for our Benefactors. This was followed by a sung Litany. We formed quite a fine choir, and our voices, which filled the air, seemed to arouse in the souls of those who stood around (no less than a thousand in number) a host of pious sentiments. A beautiful sermon was given on the day's Gospel by the Father, who spoke with great zeal and emotion, touching the hearts of all and bringing tears to the eyes of many. Then followed hymns to the Sacred Heart and Our Lady, and other prayers. Owing partly to the religious habit of the Father, which made him seem like Saint Anthony returned to life, and partly to the solemnity of the devotions, our poor countrymen almost thought they were in church, though there was not even a Cross to be seen. After the Father's simple blessing, they accosted us and asked us why we did not sing the "*Tantum Ergo.*"

Now that the voyage is at an end, we feel it parting from these poor people who trusted us so much and for whom we have been able to do some good. Oh! if only we could again impress upon them the happiness that awaits them if they are faithful to prayer and to the Sacraments. If we could make them understand that Heaven is the great prize or reward granted to good Christians, to those who are faithful to the laws of Jesus Christ! Oh, Heaven! Who can conceive or express the inconceivable delights that God has prepared for those who serve Him with that internal and external worship He requires of us? The Holy Prophet spoke well when he said, "Rejoice and be glad ye who love the Lord." "Drink large draughts of that river of peace." "Fill yourselves with joy, glory and happiness, because the Lord has said: I shall pour upon Jerusalem celestial torrents of glory that will inundate it with the purest consolations and delights." On that most blessed Eternal Day we shall be rapt in ecstasies of love and gratitude, and there will be an immense jubilee contemplating God face to face. We shall be rapt in His infinite beauty, illuminated by His light, inebriated by His peace, fortified by His Divine Consolations, because to see God and to contemplate His Divine Beauty means to love Him with the most pure and most perfect love, and that love will augment in us joy and contentment and the enjoyment of our souls. Speak often of Heaven to those who approach you, make them love it as well as the virtues which are required before we can be admitted to our blessed country. For if you know how to draw souls there by your zeal, your good example and your exemplary religious conduct, you may be assured the Gates will be opened for you also.

I wanted to go to Heaven, but what with one thing and another we have entered the New York Bay. The Superintendent of the Customs House Officers and Doctor are all on board. We are requested to give our names to a New York representative whilst the *Fulda* is being towed down the bay by three tugs. We disembarked at Hoboken Docks, where we were met by our dear American Sisters, who received us with great joy. A Customs Officer came up, marked our baggage and asked us to say a prayer for him.

I found everything in perfect order here, with much to console me. I cannot, for the present, give you further details, for I have a great number of friends to greet. I will, however, send you further news as soon as I embark on my next voyage.

In the meantime I commend myself to your good prayers, as well as my intentions and new enterprises for the good of souls and the glory of God. I'll work hard and you'll pray, I'm sure, adding some extra sacrifices, especially that of self-abasement. Offer everything as a perfect holocaust to the Adorable Heart of Jesus, Who loves us so much and has done so much to merit for us our beautiful and sublime vocation.

May Jesus bless you and enclose you in His Sacred Heart.

Your affectionate Mother in Corde Jesu,

Frances Saverio Cabrini

24th May, 1895

My dear Daughters,

Peace be to you, so that you may always remain in the Sacred Heart of Jesus.

I must keep my promise to devote all the time of my voyage in describing the little adventures, with their impressions, which have occurred, and, though the vessel is still sailing down the Mississippi, I must fly across to you in the guise of a consoling angel to console you with my visit. You, the chosen portions of Christ's flock, are destined to console His Divine Heart; you, who by your work, prayers and obedience, can procure the glory of that Heart, have become by your precious vocation the chosen portion of my heart.

I travel, work, suffer, meet with a thousand difficulties, but all these are nothing as long as you are faithful, observant and generous, and prove yourselves true members of the Institute. At four-thirty am. the alarm clock warned us it was time to arise and finish packing. The Chaplain began Mass at five-thirty a.m., when we received the dearest token that we could carry away with us–the Maker of the immense ocean we are about to cross. After the reception of Our Divine Lord, calm and joyous, Mother Gabriella and I started on our journey accompanied by our dear Sisters and the distinguished lawyer, Mr, Marinoni, who at all costs insisted upon accompanying us in his own carriage to the steamer. We started off though the rain was falling in torrents and the city so badly flooded that the horses could hardly make their way along. It required great courage, which Mr. Marinoni fortunately possessed, to overcome the difficulties that lay before us, for he knew that in ordinary circumstances the steamer waits for no one, and the time of departure was fixed for eight a.m. However, Mr. Fallon, the distinguished representative of the Company by whose line we are traveling, fearing we should not get to the steamer in time, and not wishing us to lose our connection, postponed the hour of departure by himself arriving an hour and a half late, for he knew the steamer could not set out until he had arrived on board. Of course, we never expected so much consideration, but we arrived on the steamer at seven-thirty a.m. Mr. Fallon is an excellent man. I shall never forget him or be sufficiently grateful to him for his generosity towards us. As soon as he heard of my arrival in New Orleans, he offered me a free passage to Port Limon, a distance of only sixteen miles from Colon, Panama, where our House is stationed, thus saving me the expense of a hundred dollars. He recommended us to the Captain and Head Steward, and we have the best of everything, with a very kind staff which seems willing to do anything for us.

May 25th 1895

"Man proposes, but God disposes." This time I was too sure of myself as well as the good Sisters, who had prepared for me a large number of nice sharp pencils and ruled paper, so that I might write a volume.

This time I am not as good a sailor as usual. Yesterday I did my best not to give in and to do honors to the Captain's table, but I never longed so much to get away, and was forced to contradict my saying that I never suffer from seasickness. Fortunately I managed to stay on until the end of the meal, but shortly after I became the faithful companion of Mother Gabriella and had to resort to the expedient of lying very still. At the moment of writing I am feeling much better, and tomorrow I hope to be able to write more, though I cannot promise for fear of not being able to keep my word. We must abandon ourselves to God's Holy Will, reposing in Him and promising all in Him. How good the Sacred Heart is to us! What does He expect from us for so much love? Nothing but a perfect trust in Him, a continual endeavor to conform our lives with His crucified life, taking Him as a model in all phases of life, walking in the path of His holy love as becomes those consecrated to His Holy Service. Blessed shall we be if we remain faithful to the Beloved of our soul, putting Him in possession of our whole heart, our love, our affections, our inclinations, our feelings. Know, children, the Sacred Heart wants all or nothing. He wants no divided heart, no divisions. Woe to us if we have anxious affections for creatures or for ourselves. All must be placed in the Most Holy Heart of Jesus, all without reserve.

26th May

I slept sweetly and profoundly in the Sacred Heart of Jesus all last night, and I am feeling very well this morning and quite myself again. The sun is shining in all its splendor, but the heat of its rays is tempered by a pure and gentle breeze which renders our cozy corner on deck a most delightful place. The Captain has an awning put up especially for our comfort. The sky is clear and covered with white clouds, which now and then take the form of large shining masses. These clouds seem to remind us of the Novena of the Holy Ghost, and that the Sacred Heart of Jesus is calling us, as He did His Apostles of old to come apart from the multitude, and even here in the middle of the ocean, far away from the noise of the crowd, to implore the coming of the Holy Ghost. Our loving Savior has promised to send the Holy Spirit, but we know also that the Divine promises are fulfilled by means of prayer and in the exercise of sublime charity and union with God.

Though Charity signifies that form of union which necessarily unites all members of Religious Orders, nevertheless there is another union which each one should possess within herself. Our Divine Lord said that prayer is heard when two are united in His name–for example, when the exterior man and interior man are united; the soul and the body; the subjection of the body to the spirit; these two must join together. So, to pray we must unite the body with its feelings to the soul with its imaginations and desires, with its superior powers, memory, understanding and will. Christ then shall be in your midst, united in His name, helping you to pray with efficacy. He cannot pray whose soul is in disorder, whose mind is wandering with a thousand useless, vain and anxious thoughts. The Spirit of God shuns such a soul, and so the poor soul, deprived of help from on high, languishes little by little and gradually loses the spirit of prayer.

Is it necessary for us to make the Novena of the Holy Ghost? Our Lady made it; the Apostles and the disciples made it, by command of Jesus Christ. This shows, therefore, the need we have of making it, especially if we want to possess the fervor of the early Christians, that spirit which makes us true followers of Christ and true Missionaries of the Sacred Heart. Oh! if only devotion to the Holy Ghost inflamed the world, then should we see the face of the earth renewed, and Faith and Charity would triumph over everything. "*Emitte spiritum tuum et creabuntur Et renovabis faciem terræ.*"

If you desire to correct your faults, and you feel that you cannot; if you languish with tepidity and it seems you can do no good, but, still you wish to be fervent, try to be devout to the Holy Ghost, invoking Him often and with your whole hearts. Excite in yourselves strong desires to receive Him, repeat often to Him "*Cor mundum crea in me, Deus, et Spiritum rectum innova in visceribus meis. Redde mihi lætitiam salutaris tui, et spiritu principali confirma me.*" If you invoke Him with a humble and trusting heart, filled with good desires, He will descend with His blessed light and inflaming fire; He will come and penetrate into the very center of your heart, purifying it, changing it, enlightening it, inflaming it, and consuming it with the flames of His holy and divine love.

As soon as we begin to desire Him, He begins to favor us, because pious and holy desires are like the forerunners of God in the soul, and as soon as we, by the grace of God, form a holy desire, the Holy Ghost, as Saint Paul says, will work in us and by us with ineffable sighs. Let us supplicate Him, then, to inspire us with ardent desires which will prepare us to receive Him.

You, dear daughters, know what weight our desires have with the Heart of Jesus, because many and great and special are the graces that the Omnipotent has given you from that first moment that you longed to consecrate yourself totally to His Divine Service. You, yourselves, surrounded and weighed down, I might say, by the sweet weight of so many and innumerable graces received from Him, often exclaim, "Why so much grace and this foretaste of Heaven?" It was our loving Lord, wounded in the depths of His Divine Heart by your ardent desire of being His without reserve, and making Him loved and known to all, even at the cost of life itself, Who put before your eyes, like a victorious army in battle array, this immense number of singular benefits and special graces that He lovingly bestows upon you so that you are captivated by the strong ties of His ardent love for you. And that Lord Who had destined you all for Himself, listening to your sublime desires, how lovingly does He not watch over you continually? What lights, knowledge and holy affections does He not give you? He surrounds you with Holy Fear, He uproots from your heart the love of earthly things, He encloses you in His Holy and Divine Love, He frees you from the snares of the infernal dragon. He strengthens you when falling, He raises you and reestablishes you in your original state of peace. How consoling is the thought of God's goodness! The Holy Prophet David mentions very often in his psalms the kindness of God, awakening in his own heart deep sentiments of gratitude; he, whose heart was made like unto the beautiful heart of God. Yes, every grace which you have received is a special token of God's love for you , the multiplicity and frequency of graces does not diminish, but, rather, increases the value and renders it more valuable.

Blessed will you be, my daughters, if, knowing the gifts of God, you render yourselves more worthy to receive greater gifts.

Know that gratitude for God's benefits is one of the riches of the soul, and that, on the contrary, ingratitude dries up the fountain of Divine graces. Give your tribute of gratitude often to the most loving Jesus. Consider with frequency the graces, both general and particular, that you have received, taking a retrospective view of your lives. If you meditate well, you will perceive the torrents of these salutary waters of Divine grace which have inundated your soul at the various stages and different circumstances of your past lives. With how much care has not the most dear Jesus always watched over you! How admirably He guided you in the way of eternal Salvation! For you God has worked many wonders because He loves you well, but remember that all He has done for you up to the present is but a slight pledge of His great love for you. If you are faithful in His Holy Service, He will work new wonders in you.

Be faithful to what you have undertaken, try to understand the prodigies of love which God has worked in you, learn the language of the Saints, who, on gazing at the heavens, earth and sea, and the starry firmament, repeated within themselves that holy refrain, "Love God and serve Him with fidelity." Oh, how great and wonderful is God in all His works! How we should love Him, my dear daughters! But whilst I am speaking the steamer is sailing rapidly through the waves, almost carried by a very favorable wind.

We have traversed a long stretch of sea in the meantime, and I have passed Cuba without having noticed it, as this steamer is going straight from New Orleans to Port Limon. We are very fortunate this time in not having to visit there, owing to the war which is going on, for we might be suspected as enemies and fired upon, as was done to an American torpedo vessel. We are in mid-ocean, surrounded by the immensity of the sea and a very vast horizon. The waves are mild and placid, they are like an obedient soul responding to the order of the Supreme Maker, who bids them leave us quiet during this voyage,

The first day of our voyage I said the waters of the Mississippi were like those of the ocean, and now I say that those of the ocean are like those of the Mississippi. The steamer is long and narrow, and consequently sails rapidly, but we experience some straight rocking now and then when the wind is very strong. Yesterday the sea was somewhat rough, and the waves gave us a little sprinkling in the face. I paid no attention to this improvised shower, knowing that a sea spray is always beneficial, and that people go to great expense to enjoy sea bathing. However, last night I felt my face all contracted. At first I couldn't imagine what it was, but this morning I found my face all swollen and of a scarlet red. How funny! I never expected such a thing. Did I not feel well, I might imagine that I had erysipelas and so withdraw from the fresh air. But, seeing that I have never had such a disease I regard this as a little trick of the sea, by way of a change, and I remain on deck enjoying the most pure air, this immense gift of God, which refreshes me both spiritually and physically.

27th day

The day is gorgeous; the sea is very quiet, the steamer is sailing rapidly, with no movement, respecting, as it were, our weakness.

Notwithstanding all this, Mother Gabriella will not get up, for only by lying down can she avoid being seasick. As soon as she feels a little better she comes to keep me company. She is, however, always smiling and calm. We have the Captain's servant, who is eager to please us and gives us everything we need. As to myself, I am a perfect fright, face all swollen, eyes closed, and a face as red as scarlet. On board there is no doctor, no infirmarian, no one who understands about illnesses, not even a veterinary such as Saint Francis Xavier once met. I cannot make out what it is; I have no temperature, I do not feel sick, nor am I afraid. So I have decided to remain on deck and watch the beautiful fish that play on the waves, and enjoy the pleasure of writing to you as long as I am able before my swollen eyes are closed altogether.

Why should I be afraid of traveling under the guidance of the Holy Spirit, for we are still within His Novena and in the company of the Apostles under the immediate direction of the Most Holy Virgin, our tender Mother? Then, again, have I not the blessing of the Holy Father that accompanies, strengthens and consoles me? As if His own personal blessing was not enough before my leaving, He again blessed me through the illustrious and most reverend Monsignor Radini Tedeschi, which fact encourages me more than ever in these voyages and Missions, which the Most Sacred Heart extends and enlarges to His greater glory every day.

Frequently I cross the seas, with the rapidity allowed by the progress of science, which every day provides the most rapid steamers, but, believe me, they are very slow indeed when compared with the rapidity with which the Sacred Heart works in His Vineyard. How fruitful is the blessing of the Holy Father! I would wish everyone to understand this, and put confidence in the Pope. Who is the Holy Father? He is the representative of God, of His authority and His majesty amongst men, The Holy Father is the instrument of the Holy Spirit; the depository of the treasures and secrets of God. He is the Key of Knowledge for the Christian People! He has in his keeping the power to loose and bind sin. The voice of the Holy Father is the voice of God; his word is the word of God. He is the living ark of the new alliance in which is found the Divine Law, the Manna of Celestial Doctrine, the precious vase of gold, in which is contained the purity of the Catholic Faith. The Pope is the guide of the people, the ark of salvation for all. He, in the name of Jesus Christ, has the virtue to raise and save Society from its sickness and oppression, if only it will allow itself to be cured and healed by him. This work has already begun in the country of the Angels—England—and is now going on in America, where a great number of Protestants revere, respect and venerate the Holy Father. How often, even in the midst of Catholics, one hesitates to mention the Holy Father for fear of hearing his august person insulted, but it is not so today among Protestants. I have had personal proof of this, for the best news I could give the twelve doctors of our Hospital in New York was that I had the blessing and encouragement of the Holy Father. So also a number of pious objects blessed by the Holy Father were the gifts most appreciated by some Protestant people.

Believe me, my dear daughters, there are many Protestants who have almost the same practices as we, only they do not see their way to submit to the Holy Father, and attach themselves to the true Ark of

Salvation, but the hour seems to be drawing near. Pray, then, pray that these good brethren of ours may understand thoroughly the celestial relations that exist between Jesus Christ and the Holy Father, that they may ally themselves to him, belong to the same family, the same fold, under the one shepherd, the universal pastor through whom we are united by the express will of God. Pray, then, pray with your whole hearts, and, as true Missionaries, offer yourselves as victims to the Sacred Heart to obtain such a grace, so that while the harvest is growing the enemy may not sow cockle.

But if these people wish to enter the true fold, the pastors, who are not real pastors but mercenaries, are not of the same mind. I mean the non-Catholic ministers. I should never finish naming them if I continued. These do not want to become Catholics and to unite themselves under the banner of truth wherein alone there is true salvation. Why? Because they are not validly ordained and cannot unite themselves with the Church like the simple faithful, and because also they are afraid of losing their lucrative positions. You may imagine, then, how they try to keep their followers away from the Catholic Church, so as not to lose them and their own huge salaries. We must, therefore, pray much that the Holy Spirit may enlighten each individual soul, in order that all, in the presence of the brilliant light of the Divine Sun, knowing and confessing the one true Faith, the supreme truth, in union with the Holy Father, may be cured of their false ideas and aspirations, and brought to see the error of their wrong tendencies and desires.

Pray much without tiring, because the salvation of these people does not depend on material force, nor on the vain science that clouds and darkens the intellect; neither does it depend on arms and human industries, nor on sterile and diplomatic congresses, nor on worldly or earthly means. The grace of their salvation can only come from the Heart of that Supreme Pastor Who called together the Apostles, and promised grace and blessings to all their successors who remained faithful to the foundation rock, the Holy Father.

Pray much, dear daughters, for the Sisters who are scattered in the various Missions of the United States, that the good God may assist and enlighten them and render their work fruitful in the conversion of many souls. Yes! pray much during the Hour of Adoration, because if our efforts and our words are not made fruitful by Jesus, we shall never do any good. The conversion of sinners and the sanctification of souls does not depend on sterile cold human eloquence, or the grace of style and flowery rhetoric, but on the fructifying grace of Jesus Christ. Jesus alone can give life to words and arguments. He enlightens the mind, moves the will, sows virtue, and animates us to undertake holy and perfect works.

And it is Jesus Himself Who speaks through the voice that teaches with zeal and faith, Who works prodigies in souls, renews miracles and performs wonders. With what wisdom does the good God work in the heart of man! He respects our liberty, but enlightens with truth and divine light, moves and invites all to the celestial reward. Yes! Dear daughters, it is Jesus our Beloved, Who by His death conquered hell and sin and won from His Heavenly Father, as His inheritance, all peoples. How consoling to think that we and all the people we would like to convert are the Kingdom of Christ, the hereditary portion, the most precious inheritance of Jesus! And how Jesus rejoices in the conversion of one sinful soul! What joy does not the recovery of one sheep give to His Divine Heart? How He clasps it in His loving arms!

And can we not multiply these joys of the Sacred Heart of Jesus, by our prayers, works, and the winning over of hearts and souls who will love Him much? Let us imitate the charity of the Adorable Heart of Jesus in the salvation of souls, and make ourselves all to all to win all to Jesus.

If we act thus, what a harvest of virtues and merits we shall reap, for what we do to these souls, God considers as done to Himself. He marks in the book of life all the trials, troubles and crosses that we suffer for the salvation and sanctification of souls. He enumerates the days, hours and moments that we spend in this holy exercise, and all will be fully rewarded by the sovereign goodness of the Most Holy Heart of Jesus. Even a charitable word spoken will be amply remunerated because everything done for Jesus and with Jesus is great.

28th day

Yesterday, at midday, my eyes were almost closed by the swelling, and I had to stop writing. Today the swelling has greatly diminished, but there are white blisters on my forehead which give me the appearance of a leper. How strange and wonderful! No one here can tell me what it is, but it is consoling to abandon oneself to the most Adorable and most Loving Heart of Jesus, for whilst we are far away from our Sisters, and between the sky and water where no human comfort can reach us, we know that the Heart of Jesus watches over His Spouses just the same. Tomorrow we shall arrive at Port Limon, and, through the kind offices of some good people there to whom we have been recommended by our excellent protector, Mr. L. G. Fallon, I expect I shall find some remedy for this complaint. If we can reach Panama, where our house is situated, then Mother Gabriella's anxiety will cease, for she is quite upset about it, as she does not know what to do for me.

Yesterday, at three p.m., we passed by the Iwan Island, which means the Isle of Big Wings, and some call it a big bird. It belongs to the United States, and is inhabited by fifty men, who spend the greater part of the year fishing. Last night we passed near some very dangerous shoals. The steamer seemed as if it would capsize. The night was very dark, and fear made it appear darker. With all this, we remained very quiet in our cabins, resting as best we could, for the vessel rocked very much. We had no reason to fear, for the Captain had informed us of all that was likely to happen, for he had to stop the steamer to measure the depth of the sea, so as to be sure where he was sailing. Moreover, he told us he was staying up all night, and that the crew would be up and about also. We could afford to remain quiet, for the Captain is a very trustworthy man. He is a Swede, his name Welin, and he is a capable and respectable man. He has traveled right around the world, and almost always in the capacity of Captain of a steamer. The crew is mostly Swedish also, and I regret I'm unable to speak to them of religion, because they have no one to remind them, when we part, to attend to their religious duties. I gave them a small medal which they received with great devotion and regard as a great treasure, even those who are Protestants. I told them the medals were blessed by the Holy Father, which pleased them more, and they put them away very carefully so as to find them during storms. The Swedes have many good qualities. They are sober, simple, courteous, intelligent, and have great respect and veneration for us Religious, and when at eventide they hear us sing the *Veni Creator* for the Novena of the Holy Ghost, the *Ave Maris Stella* and other hymns to the Blessed Virgin Mary, they become reverently attentive, and there seems to be a ray of Heaven falling on their souls. Poor men! What a pity we cannot instruct them.

This morning, at nine a.m., we passed by the Cape of "Deo Gratias," almost touching it, where the coast of Mosquito begins, and a little later we seemed to enter a new sea of bright green colors. It was the current of Rio Grande, a current that plunges with such force into the sea that for several miles it seems to struggle in its efforts to mix with the salty water. At present we are coasting, and will presently pass by Bluefields, then tomorrow by S. Juan del Norte, and at eleven a.m., please God, we shall arrive at Port Limon. I never thought I should have made such a journey, being under the impression that this steamer traveled a direct route, but the Captain told me at lunchtime that a direct line was impossible as he had to encounter many coral banks which are very dangerous. I am pleased we are coasting, and I should have wished to remain a few days at each of these ports, for I like these Indians, having visited them three years ago on my return from Nicaragua. Then I was making a much more uncomfortable voyage than this, for while passing S. Juan del Norte, before entering the sea, I had to change steamers nine times in twelve days, while at night we never traveled for fear of running aground. In Rio it once happened that owing to the vessel not being able to advance, we had to travel by canoes (poor barques), and to make things worse, it was all under a downpour of rain from which we could find no shelter, as there was none to be had. In other small vessels in Rio San Juan there were nests of mice and other vermin, most amusing to watch, but as I could not make friends with such adventurers, I was obliged for several nights to stand and lean against a sofa, the only form of rest I could trust myself to take in such company. In the meantime, Sister Mercedes Cepeda and I were quite happy and making the best of these experiences. We were well repaid, however, for when we arrived at Bluefields we had to wait several hours for a steamer of the Morgan Line which was to take us to the United States. There is no church here, no priest to invite a few times a year to visit these Indians of the Riviera Mosquitia, who are considered little better than beasts by the Government, and whom the Church as yet has not been able to reach. Taking advantage of this stop, we went around to the Indians, and spoke a few kind words to these poor people, who overcoming their shyness and yielding to their respect for the "Black Robes," as they call the Sisters and Priests, they begged us to send them also Sisters and Priests to instruct them and save them. The poor things! How I felt for them! I would have opened a House at once had I the means to do so. Oh, if I could but open the purses of many of the rich to whom the good God has given so liberally of this earth's treasures! If I could only make them understand what a reward theirs would be, if, prompted by their own good heart, they would come to our aid in succoring these poor creatures who still live in darkness. By so doing they would be placing their generous offerings in the Bank of Heaven, where they would fructify a hundredfold, if not in this world, certainly in the next, and their generosity would make them happy with an eternal felicity in Heaven, where God has prepared a profusion of immense treasures for the merciful.

Yesterday, between one interval and another, we saw another part of the east which kept us in admiration of its beauty until evening. Meanwhile, I have stopped the description which I began with such eagerness. Have patience, if I am obliged to cut my narrative short, for the port is within sight, and it seems to move to meet us. There lies in front of it an island called Paseo. This island is so called because it is a pleasure resort where the people of Port Limon spend their holidays. A lighthouse stands in the center. From afar it appears like a gigantic statue, with a large chest, red vest, a black head and a white hat. Here and there we notice some nice houses, well built with verandas, after the Chinese style. These, in the midst of the variegated green of the country around, create a pretty sight, together with a delightful promenade and a rest resort.

Here we are at last in port. Two tenders approach, one with the Doctor and an uncle of the President of Costa Rica, the other with the representative of the Government and other gentlemen. The first ones to examine everyone and everything, the others to satisfy their curiosity.

The Doctor looked me up and down from head to foot. As I had not shut myself up in my cabin, but remained in the fresh air on deck, my leprous appearance has disappeared, and my skin has been completely renewed, just as fine and as soft as silk, giving me a complexion which I never had before. This caused the Doctor to say, "All right," "*tutto bene.*" When the visit was over, the Captain and other persons came to offer us their services whilst we waited for the steamer which was to convey us to Colon for Panama. An uncle of the President, Dr. De Castro, suggested that whilst we waited for the steamer we might as well go to San José, the capital of Costa Rica, for three reasons—namely, because Limon was unhealthy, secondly because he had a Sister, very pious and good, who would be very happy to see us, and lastly because we should thus be spared hotel expenses. It was impossible to refuse such kindness, and so I promised to go after a day's rest. The Captain offered us the hospitality of his vessel, but a large quantity of bananas destined for New Orleans compelled him to leave Limon the next day. The English representative here having had a letter from Mr. Fallon, recommending us to his care obtained for us one of the best places in the hotel, and then went to get a free passage for us to S. Jose. This was a very agreeable favor, as otherwise it would have cost us eight pesos each, which according to the exchange would be eighty *lire*. Mr. De Castro had already given us a letter of recommendation to his sister , and we had already asked the owner of the hotel, who was an excellent Italian, to take care of our luggage and to wake us at four-thirty a.m., as the train would leave at six a.m., when suddenly a representative of the Governor appeared and told us he had received orders from the Government to prevent our entering the interior of the country, the Government having passed a bill which forbade the entrance of Jesuits, and Sisters bearing the title of the Sacred Heart. I laughed heartily at the idea. I asked to see the Governor, whose residence is quite near the hotel. We went, and he received us with the greatest kindness, telling us how to get the order withdrawn. I told him I would make no effort whatsoever, as I had no need of visiting the country, but that I was very sorry, or, rather, regretted that a country that boasted of so much progress had such retrograde laws, which were contrary to the liberty about which they spoke so much, and inhuman, forcing me to remain in an unhealthy place which might prove detrimental to the health of my companion who for the first time was visiting the tropical regions. The Governor was greatly impressed, and that evening, when the leaders of the place came together, they all spoke and discussed the affair whilst we remained quiet and contented, looking forward to receive Holy Communion the following morning, which was Friday and the last day of the month of Mary. Who had caused all this commotion?

A Freemason, who, as soon as he saw two Sisters on board the ship, made inquiries and then telegraphed to the Police to prevent our entering the country. Today everyone is looking down upon him for acting so inhumanly towards two ladies. The more sensible minds are doing all they can to obtain a permit for us to visit any part of the Republic we wish, so as not to let us leave the country with such an unfavorable impression. I told them it would now be useless, as we were leaving for our destination soon.

Here, however, we were able to perform our little devotions, even closing the month of May in a small country church, which is kept very nicely by the parish priest, who is a member of the Mission of Saint Vincent de Paul.

The only church-goers are the converted negroes from Jamaica. The natives go to church but very seldom, and some never, it being a tradition of the last century that church-going is not good for those who claim, as they do, to be *"adelantandose cada dia,"* i.e., making daily progress. What a pity! What a misfortune that they should have departed from the good spirit, the characteristic spirit of the Spanish race! And all this has been brought about by the terrible Masonic influence which moves and dominates everything and everybody more and more in these countries. The devil has placed his throne very comfortably there and extends his net in thick darkness, as seen once by Saint Anthony, and he really catches a great many fish without much trouble, because to these poor things the word "progress" is like a siren, which allures them and offers them the hidden poison which leads them backward instead of forwards.

The closing of the month of May was lovely. In the morning, when High Mass was over, a procession took place during which was sung the Litany, and at three p.m., after some hymns, the parish priest delivered a touching sermon full of devotion and piety. Our Lady was crowned by a child dressed in white and wearing a wreath of flowers, after which the mothers brought their children to the altar to have them blessed by the priest, and then every child presented a flower to Our Lady. It is lovely to see these women in their best dresses of gorgeous colors, with very short waists, and skirts so long that the train measures a yard and a half. Their turbans are of such contrasting colors and their faces resembled ebony. Some were tattooed.

The children were dressed either in variegated colors or in white, which clashed with their black faces and black hands, but their souls were truly white for their innocence and simplicity. Mary seemed to rejoice and extend Her Heavenly Mantle over these people.

But I forgot to tell you about our lodgings. Well, we have a room which has a balcony looking west and another looking east, and both are so well placed as to afford us opportunities for precious contemplation, just as we had on the ocean. On one side we have the immense gulf, with beautiful and green gondolas, not for fishermen, as these people care little for fishing, but for carrying passengers backward and forwards to the land. Some shoals right in front of the balcony cause the water to break into foaming waves which roar like the Falls of Niagara. On the other side stands the park, with groves and fountains, worthy certainly of a greater city, and hardly to be expected in a small country as this, but, as they say, "*se adelantan cada dia,*" so, to show their progress, it is necessary to have parks and fountains that foreigners may admire. Meanwhile we enjoy a pure and refreshing breeze. You may imagine what I mean when I say the thermometer at New Orleans is at 28 degrees, here it marks 25 degrees, but, when the doors and windows are closed, it exceeds 30 degrees (centigrade).

It is said that this is a country of fever, but we have been assured by the doctors, who have become our friends these days, that it is a very healthy country, where people suffering from lung complaints come to be cured. We keep really well, but we regret to be here doing nothing, seeing that we are only a sixteen hours' journey from our Sisters in Panama, where we would love tofly. I hope to be with them soon, and to receive through them and their merits an abundance of the gifts and fruits of the Holy Ghost, for which I hunger and of which I feel in great need; but we must resign ourselves to remain here at Port Limon and to receive the Holy Ghost here. Blessed Will of God, how dear and amiable Thou art when Thou revealest Thyself with so much clearness! When we take a little walk to speak to the negroes, who listen to us with so much pleasure, we always go down to the dock and almost beg the boats to sail off at once to Panama. But none of them take heed, and, leaving one after another for other directions, seem to say, "Have patience! Clip the wings of your ardent desires." In the meantime, the vessel, which is destined to convey us to Panama and which is in port, the Royal Mail cannot approach land owing to its vast size and the shallowness of the water.

June 1st

Today, to the spiritual view of the soul a most beautiful and sublime subject commends itself ... The dear month of June is at hand, in which we all united, both far and wide, and animated by the same faith, will honor the Sacred Heart of Jesus, in order to make reparation for so much ingratitude, about which He complained to His beloved Margaret. This is the month of love, and love ought to transform us all. But what are the necessary means for obtaining this transformation? The first is to approach the Sacred Heart of Jesus in a spirit of humility and confidence, the second is to let grace work in us, following its impulses with fidelity and constancy. The good Jesus, through the goodness of His Divine Heart, makes known to us our ugliness and our misery; but we should not fly away frightened by the knowledge we receive of ourselves, we should rather humble ourselves and beg God to free us from our misery. Be not discouraged at seeing yourselves so far from the perfection of Holy Love, because Jesus desires to grant it to you, to help you in your own efforts. It suffices if we have recourse to Him with a sincere desire to correspond with His graces and to trust entirely to His Love. Let us throw ourselves into the blessed flames of the most Sacred Heart of Jesus, and let that holy fire burn into our spirit, so that it may destroy, purify, renew and sanctify all our thoughts, affections, sentiments, intentions and desires. What have we to fear if the most Sacred Heart protects us? And what may we not hope for, if we confide in the Heart of such a compassionate and powerful Father? Let us fix our gaze on the Wound of the Sacred Heart of Jesus. We shall read in characters of blood the height and depth of the love that He bears us, and we shall always feel, wherever we are, comforted in hoping for everything from His infinite goodness. Very often our prayers are imperfect and deserve to be rejected by God; but the loving Heart of Jesus sanctifies them. He Himself asks for us that which He sees will be for our greater good, and compassionately covers our unworthiness with His merits.

In the secrecy of the Holy Tabernacle the loving Heart of Jesus takes note of our needs in order to help us, and waits for nothing more than to see us at His feet, full of confidence, uniting our prayers with His. Recall often what Jesus said to Saint Gertrude, His Beloved, "Here is My Heart, avail yourself of It to make good what is deficient in your prayers." Another time, Saint Gertrude, full of love, made a fervent prayer (and this is especially good for the Missionary) in which she declared that if it were necessary to travel the whole world barefooted till the Day of Judgment, in order to lead all men to the Heart of Jesus, she would have done so with her whole heart, and would have carried every one of them in her arms so as to satisfy, at least in part, the infinite desires of His sweet Divine Love. Even more, if it were possible, she would divide her heart into as many parts as were necessary to give a portion to all men on earth, and thus infuse into them the good desire to serve God, and thus give perfect joy to His Divine Heart. Then Jesus appeared to her showing her the gift He was about to give her, in the form of a very rich treasure sent by the Holy Trinity, and whilst this gift appeared to rise in the heavens, the Angels seemed to prostrate themselves before Him.

She knew, then, that when prayers and holy desires are offered to God, the whole celestial court receives and raises them to His throne, as gifts most pleasing to God, and that when to one's merits the merits of Jesus Christ are joined, the very Saints themselves respect them. Let us fly, fly, dear children, often to the Tabernacle–as the heart pants after the fountains of clear water. As long as we live in this exile, far from the heavenly country, let us not rest, but labor until we repose in the Heart of Him Whom we love so ardently, as true Spouses and Missionaries of the Sacred Heart. Let us always go to His Divine Heart, think of Him, He to Him, sigh for Him alone and always, because the vehemence of His love for us, is truly wonderful.

By the words of consecration said by the priest in the name of Jesus, the bread is changed or transubstantiated into the body of Jesus, and so the body and blood are present under the appearances of bread and of wine by a miracle of the Omnipotent. After the Consecration, the substance of the bread and wine disappear, the appearances only remaining, like so many veils of love and wisdom to hide from our material eyes our glorious Lord's presence, as also to supply motives for faith, confidence and courage in receiving our Divine Lord into our hearts. As long as the species remains, so long does the Sacramental Presence last, as soon as the species is consumed, the most Sacred Body retires and vanishes. Nothing but wonders are worked on the Altar. The priests, who, during the twenty-four hours, offer the Divine Sacrifice in so many countries, towns and villages all the world over, are innumerable, and thus in a hundred thousand places Jesus is present in the Sacrament of His Love. Could there be an invention more beautiful and more holy than the Institution of this Most Divine Sacrament? Could the Loving Jesus show us a greater tenderness of love? But remember, daughters, that this most Holy Sacrament is like the column of fire that lighted and guided the Israelites to the Promised Land, yet proved dark for the Egyptians. This mystery of the Holy Eucharist is like that of the Cross, a scandal to the impious and the wise of this world, but to humble believers a source of virtue and of the wisdom of God.

Only to the humble and docile of mind and heart are revealed, by the Celestial Father, these ineffable and incomprehensible truths of the Most Holy Sacrament. Such only shall receive these truths into their hearts, because they have received them humbly into their minds first.

Such alone, therefore, enjoy the sweetness and richness of this august Mystery of Wisdom and Love.

These precious pearls are hidden from the wise and prudent of the world. Unfortunate creatures! These pearls have been spread under their eyes, but they do not perceive them; they hear them spoken of, but they do not understand; the reason is that they lack the sense of humble faith and dutiful love, hence their ears are deaf. Oh, if everyone understood what a treasure we have in the Most Holy Sacrament of the Altar, what greatness, richness, sweetness and joy they would possess! But to draw down the mercy of God on the earth, so that all may join the Holy Catholic Church, the Tree of Life, and be saved, what can we do, we Missionaries? We are so poor, capable of nothing, and move in a circle too restricted to permit of being able to help such a large number of souls. We can, however, make frequent and fervent Communions, and by this means we shall obtain everything for these poor sinners, our brethren. We are unworthy, but approaching our dear Jesus and receiving Him, He will give us the kiss of peace, and whilst we give Him our filial affection, He will warm us with His love, purify us with His blood, vivify us with His breath and decorate and enrich us with His graces. "*In me manet et ego in eo.*"

Our Thanksgiving for Holy Communion, dear daughters, should be long, very long; indeed, it should never finish, because it is the continuation of daily Communion. Entertaining myself with God sacramentally, the more I know Him the more clearly I perceive His greatness and perfections. Having this Blessed Presence in myself, it stands to reason that I shall frequently receive the Holy Sacrament. Knowing God, I love Him, and in thanksgiving the spirit of God raises me above the things of this earth; it introduces me into the Blessed Oasis of growing grace and of the Beatitudes. He opens His breast and shows me His Beautiful Heart burning with charity, and He says, "See how I burn with love for Thee! How much I love thee!"

3rd day

Yesterday we had a visit from the most loyal and dearest friend, the Holy Ghost. He loves us tenderly, immensely and continually. We, the portion and inheritance of Jesus Christ, washed and purified in His Blood, have become the living temples of the Holy Ghost, that is, living members and the abode of the Divine Paraclete.

The Holy Ghost, who descended for the first time on the Apostles, always descends upon the Church and upon our souls, because it is our good and most beloved Jesus Who has merited for us the precious gift of the Holy Ghost, by Whom we become rich in grace and in every celestial virtue.

How pleasing it is to the Holy Ghost to see zealous souls that seek to spread the Kingdom of Jesus Christ! We give Divine homage when we convert a sinner, or make known more clearly and more distinctly the knowledge of Jesus Christ. Work, work indefatigably, without tiring, for the salvation of souls. May the Holy Spirit work in you, pray with you and communicate to you His lights, graces and treasures. If you are zealous, He will really enlighten you with His Divine Light. He will assist you in your works and trials. He will support you in danger, defend you from internal and external enemies, and strengthen you by His virtue. Have faith, great faith; faith and confidence, and pray constantly. The Holy Spirit with His immense Charity, will then diffuse Himself into your hearts and in your souls in order to make them stronger with His own fortitude. "*Ignem veni mittere in terram, et quid volo nisi ut accendatur?*"

Yesterday the Holy Spirit wanted to console us even materially, for we received many visits from people whom came to sympathize with us on account of the insult, as they regarded it, which we received on our first visit to this port. They did their utmost to make us forget it, fearing that we might publish it in the papers.

Two representatives of the President called upon us to apologize, saying it was all a misunderstanding, and that we could go to the capital and everywhere, and that we would be very welcome. They begged us to prolong our stay, and by way of inducement offered us a ticket, good for twelve days, so that we might travel at our own leisure. But we were too anxious to leave for Panama at once, and so, after thanking them most courteously for the great favor offered us, we took the steamer for Panama on the 4th. The ticket was made out in my name, and I am keeping it to show you, on my return, the exquisite kindness of the people of Costa Rica.

But here favors still continue. Seeing everyone so very kind, I was able to obtain a free passage, or at least at a very reduced rate, from Port Limon to Colon. I spoke to several, and finally to the Captain of the steamer, *The City of Para*, especially mentioning to him how kind Mr. Fallon had been to give me a free passage from New Orleans to Port Limon. He listened to me attentively, and after some time returned, saying he could not obtain the favor, but that I could take the cheapest ticket and that he would see that I was treated as a 1st class passenger. I did this, and one could see the joy in his face at being able to confer a favor on Religious. He was not content until he sent his own tender to conduct us and our luggage on board. May the Sacred Heart of Jesus bless this good English Captain and his family with graces, spiritual and temporal, for his generosity towards us.

4th day

Here we are on board the Royal Mail steamer, *City of Para*. She is turning around on the way to Colon. What a pleasant sight of the Cordigliera with its high mountains, and the wonderful declivities and points, its aged plants and its carpet of variegated green. We cannot enjoy very much this scenery as the sun is setting, and night falls at once to the almost complete absence of twilight in these regions.

As is customary with all steamers as they steer out of port, the dinner bell rings, and so we must leave this delightful scenery to answer the call. This time we have a most exquisite dinner, as it is done *à la mode Italienne*. But how does this come about, seeing we are traveling in an English steamer? There are four Italian cooks, Milanese and Piedmontese. Having seen we are Italians, and perceiving the favor which the Captain shows us, they also desire to favor us, and in doing so everybody on board benefits, for the Italian cooking is very much appreciated. If the Italians would make themselves respected in matters of religion and morals, as they really could do if they wished, how much better off they would be, Italy would become the great nation it merits to be, instead of being despised as it is now by everyone.

Today, amongst other favors, we received a visit from His Lordship, the Bishop of Costa Rica, the great champion of the Church, Monsignor Thihel, whom I had the pleasure of meeting four years ago when passing on to Nicaragua with the Sisters, through the port of Punta Arenas. He came then to see us and to bless us. Now he came as a friend, having formed a closer relationship with our Institute, consequent upon his several visits to Rome. He came to ask us to open a House in his diocese. He wanted the Sisters who had been exiled from Nicaragua, but it is too late, for, passing through Panama, they were detained, and, with the approbation of the Mother House, they opened a new school there under the highest auspices. I was very pleased with the holy Prelate's visit, and only regretted I had not been able to prevent it, as of course I ought to have visited him first. If I had not been prohibited from entering the capital, San Jose, I should of course have called on His Lordship.

But now, I hear someone asking what was the reason for which our Sisters were exiled from Nicaragua. Do not wonder, for as yet these countries are but little advanced in civilization, and full of disturbances and revolutions. There are some who have studied a little in Paris, London, Germany and the United States, and each one thinks he knows better than the other. They hold themselves in high repute, not wishing to see at the head of the Government one whom they think inferior to themselves. Then, they seek to make friends and induce them to follow the same ideas. Thus they work on collectively until they succeed in removing the ruling President and placing in the Presidential Chair one of their own followers. Very often, one of these satellites, well grounded in these ideas by the first proud usurper, takes the opportunity of overthrowing the one he had previously helped to establish in the Presidency, in the same manner does a third one behave, and so they carry on in this way. Sometimes one of them, still more ignorant, and not possessing the necessary knowledge, wishes to accomplish something even more brilliant, and endeavors to become famous by persecuting religious men and women. This is what ultimately happened to our Sisters. It appears the School was progressing nicely, being filled with children of the best families. Indeed, I was feeling quite happy over the foundation, because, having survived three revolutions, the Sisters there felt encouraged to believe that their position was more secure. Generally speaking, very serious diseases and epidemics break out after revolutions and wars, owing to the unburied bodies of the victims. Fortunately, all our Sisters remained free from infection, and not one of the pupils contracted any illness. It was at this moment of apparent success that they heard that there appeared immediate danger, owing to a new dispute in the Government, which arose through the entrance of some foreigners, who excited the Liberals of Nicaragua, always easily led to rebellion.

It just happened, too, that about this time a young lady, a great votary of the world and its pleasures, touched by the grace of God, was converted, and sought immediate entrance into our Convent. She was not received, however, as the local Superior had first to obtain permission from the Superior General before receiving anyone into the Convent. The young lady had recourse to Dona Elena Arellano, a lady of high repute in Nicaragua, and this lady, owing to the esteem and influence she enjoyed in the country, kept the would-be Nun with her in her house. In the meantime, those who had lost their prey in the person of the young lady, attributed the workings of grace to our having induced the girl to leave the world, and shortly afterward we heard we were to be expelled. To ascertain the truth of this rumor, the Reverend Mother called personally on the President. He received her and her companion with every mark of esteem. He was loud in his praise of our work, and even promised his fatherly protection, which, of course, left them with a sense of assurance of his goodwill. Moreover, the following week he sent a case of prize books for the pupils, which were accompanied by a letter in his own handwriting promising our Sisters every protection.

A month after the President had promised to protect the Sisters, whilst they were quietly attending their classes and finishing off some new uniforms, the new Prefect of the city, Mr. Pedro Pablo Bodan, and the Governor, Mr. Rivos, asked to see the Reverend Mother. On presenting herself, they gave her orders to leave the country at once, and told her that the steamer was lying in port awaiting them. The Superior pleaded that two Sisters were very ill in bed, but they would not revoke the order, and surrounding the house with Military Guards so that outsiders could have no access, and that the Sisters should not have the chance of appealing to the President, they intimated that no outsiders who were within the walls of the Convent would be allowed to leave the house until the Sisters had first left. As soon as the pupils heard of it, they arose in a body against these men, crying and shouting piteously. As soon as the parents of the pupils heard of the matter, they went to the Convent to try and prevent the expulsion, but all was in vain, as the soldiers had received orders to fire on all who resisted. The screams and shouts filled the air. It was a scene of real desolation. The Prefect alone remained unmoved. In the midst of all this disorder, it was lovely to see how calm and serene the Sisters remained whilst they prepared the few articles of clothing they needed for the voyage, trying in the meantime to quiet the children and their parents, and showing how to accept this trial from the hands of God, Who knows how to draw good from evil, and promising to return some day. Two hours later the Prefect called forward the carriages which were to convey the Sisters to the steamer. The Sisters were surrounded by soldiers who accompanied them to the port.

It was just like a funeral cortège, for, the news having spread, a great crowd followed the Sisters, crying and begging them to stay, as their leaving the country was the sign of God's wrath, towards them. They pleaded mercy for their sins. On arrival at the port, the soldiers formed a cordon around the Sisters to prevent the crowd following. The Sisters passed one by one, as they had to be counted before embarking.

A few minutes later two priests arrived on board. They were the Parish Priest and the Chaplain. They, too, were banished, whilst the day before six other priests were exiled to the port of Corinto on the Pacific.

Lady Elena Arellano, who had spent so much money on this foundation, and who loved the Sisters so much, felt she could not let them go without accompanying them, but as this was forbidden under pain of exile, she decided to accept the penalty, and remained with them all the time they stayed at San Juan del Norte, and until they had received orders from the Mother General to found another Mission.

Every vessel that left Granada brought some resident of Nicaragua, who came to console the Sisters whom they loved and venerated, and to whom they brought some help. Even the very Indians of Rama, through the distinguished Don Felice Alfaro, gave the Sisters a substantial sum of money to help them in their distress.

At Granada, Don Constantino Motonco, who had his children at the School, obtained from the parents what was still due to the Sisters, and sent the money on to them, which could not have been much, as this was generally paid in advance. However, it shows how the Sisters had to struggle for their maintenance, especially having several sick Nuns.

And so the good God does not abandon His Beloved servants when in need, tribulations and illness. He knows how to soothe our wounds, and from news which I have recently received, I have reason to praise the Most Sacred Heart, Who so honors our Institute with banishment, though it is so young, poor and the least in our Holy Church.

The expulsion of our Sisters was a celestial dew which fell upon many souls, and changed that delirium of fury and impiety into a solemn act of homage to our most holy Religion. It was a Divine Light dispelling the dense darkness. Let us thank God for having so favored us and made us worthy of suffering for His cause! But you are in great suspense and anxious to know what happened in consequence, and I will satisfy your wishes. The expulsion of the Sisters from Nicaragua not only made an impression on the good, who could not console themselves on account of their loss, but also on the bad. There was one member of the Masonic group, who, touched by Divine Grace at the sight of such cruelty, became sincerely converted. He had been one of the worst enemies of the Church, attacking Her even by his writings and his speeches. Now he became one of Her greatest defenders, after having witnessed our expulsion, and went so far as to refuse a public office which was offered to him, rather than sacrifice his intelligence and good convictions. His answer was, that a true Catholic could have nothing to do with a Government so brutal, impious and cowardly, whose heroism consisted in oppressing the weak, stamping on religion, and outraging Sisters, whose sole crime was to instruct innocent youth by means of self-sacrifice.

This refusal gave room to much criticism and mockery, and made him many enemies, but nothing could make him turn back. He knew well what he would have to put up with. but he said the example of the Sisters helped him. They, being innocent, had suffered so heroically, hence why should he not suffer, who merited so much punishment for his past misdeeds against the Truth? He would rather die than withdraw from the obligations of the true followers of Christ!

He gave up all his Masonic decorations and his whole library, which was very large, he handed to the Bishop. In thanksgiving for so great a grace, which he appreciated according to its worth, he had a solemn High Mass celebrated, inviting all his relations and Catholic friends to assist at it, and receiving Holy Communion with his whole family. He still remains very good, rising at four a.m. to pray, while at six he goes to High Mass, and receives Holy Communion weekly. He has renewed his library, filling it with books of sound doctrine and Christian piety, amongst which are the *Imitation of Christ*, *The Christian Year*, and the *Martyrology* and the like, and intimates that his family should read these at certain hours of the day.

Therefore the expulsion has had one great good result for the inhabitants of Nicaragua, a result which is most consoling. Let us supplicate the Sacred Heart that such may always be the effect of the sufferings of the Missionaries of the Sacred Heart, for then we do not really leave the Mission but, rather, change it into a better one. It is now eight months since the Sisters left, but they continually receive letters from one family and another, and some even bearing the name of the President of the Republic. Please God we shall return someday, but not at present, as the actual government cannot guarantee the privileges and liberty which we require for the success of our work.

Yesterday, at four a. m., we perceived the lighthouse of Colon, and a little later the monument of Christopher Columbus. At seven-thirty the English steamer was already in the hands of the Custom House officers. Friends and relations had come to meet their expected friends, and I strained my eyes to see if there were any Sisters to meet us and to convey us to Panama, but there was no one about, as the Sisters had been told that the steamer would not arrive before midday. They had, therefore, only left by the eleven a.m. train. We knew nothing of this, and as I had determined not to sleep outside the Convent that night, whatever happened, I made my own arrangements. For a moment or so the whole place appeared to me like a desert, seeing that no one had come to meet us, especially as I had sent several letters and, recently, even telegrams announcing our arrival. However, I made up my mind to act, and approaching the Captain, I begged him to allow me to remain on board until the arrival of the train. Then taking a cab, I went to the Prefect to ask him to give us a free passage to Panama. He not only favored me in this instance, but said he would do anything for our School in Panama. When everything had been arranged, we returned on board for dinner, where there were two Sisters awaiting us with tickets for all four. The Captain very kindly allowed the new arrivals to dine with us, and at two p.m. we were on our way to Panama. After three hours and a half amidst the beautiful mountainous scenery of the Isthmus, we arrived at Panama, where at the station we met our Sisters, and within a quarter of an hour we were within the Convent, blessing the Sacred Heart for having given me back those Sisters whom for four years I had not seen. After a short rest, I was anxious to look over the house which a number of distinguished persons obtained from the Government for our School, and which already shelters the children of the highest families of Panama.

The house is lovely. One could imagine easily to be on board a steamer, because on the south and south-west it is surrounded by the sea, whose proud waves beat against the walls of our garden, throwing a spray of water, whiter than milk, with small pebbles which the children take for sweets. The room which the Sisters have prepared for me is surrounded on two sides by large orange trees, the fruit of which touches my window sill. One window looks out on a path which leads to the sea and the lovely isles in it, which seem to be playing in the bay. These isles really serve as a defense or a sort of port for all vessels that come from California, from all the Southern ports, and from Europe through the Straits of Magellan. Such a long voyage, however, is only made by ships and very seldom by the Transatlantic steamers. In our garden we have six kinds of palms, bananas and coffee trees and various kinds of fruit, the names of which I do not know.

Today I wanted to visit His Lordship, the Bishop of this city, but the person who was to obtain the audience for us said the Bishop would send word himself. This message was hardly delivered, when His Lordship arrived so as to greet me first. He is a very distinguished person, and inspires great confidence in one. This is a very favorable augury for our new foundation, which seems to have gained already such a good footing. A great number of persons called on me, saying how happy they were that we had come to stay, a favor that they had long desired but which for many reasons they had failed to obtain, especially owing to the expulsion.

Yellow fever is prevalent here, but, as far as we are concerned, I can attest to the contrary, as the Sisters have had no fever whatever during the nine months, in fact, they are in better health. The heat here is no worse than in Nicaragua. We frequently have very refreshing breezes which strengthen and invigorate us.

Before closing this, I want to give you some news of the work that is done by our Sisters in New York, and how the Sacred Heart blesses our Mission there. But you know the only free time we have is when we areon the ocean, so I will speak of it another time on another voyage, which I may make either on the Atlantic or on the Pacific. Here on the Isthmus we are really at the apex of the world. The position of the house is such that I imagine I can see every part of the earth in that immense space of water which is in front of us. It serves us as an object for meditation, and this is not disturbed by the desire I have of taking the first vessel that sails to the places where the need is the greatest. But where shall I go? The calls are many, and if I cannot go to all places where we are needed, as commanded by Rome, I will do my utmost to comply with obedience as far as it lies in my power. Pray, daughters, pray from your heart, so that we may be able to do all that the Sacred Heart wants of us. Study to become observant, for with perfect observance you will become Saints. Seek to increase your number, so that I may increase the number of Houses for the good of souls. I can assure you that the people are well disposed, though they are uncivilized. They only need someone to speak the Word of God and instruct them.

Tell the young ladies who have received so much from God, tell them not to bury their talents, but, corresponding with the sublime grace of their vocation, to come forward and unite themselves with us and become Holy Religious, to work in these endless fields where the harvest is rich, but the laborers are few. Tell them to come and carry the sheaves into the granary of our holy and august Religion. Tell our friends not to cease helping us with their offerings, as the work extends in proportion to the means at hand. And blessed are those who have placed their charitable offerings in this treasury, because they will be rewarded a hundredfold, and will receive blessings in this world on themselves, their families and undertakings, while heavenly blessings, to their consolation, will follow them at the last day, when they will depend totally on their good works and generosity. I send, then, from my heart, my best wishes to all, imploring special blessings from the Sacred Heart of Jesus on all, assuring them that I shall not forget them in my poor prayers, and will have them remembered in those of the Community. And you, my dear daughters, I leave you in the Heart of Jesus, where we must remain united together, though we are four or six thousand miles apart. The Missionary knows no distance—the world is so small. Space is an imperceptible object to a Missionary, because she is accustomed to dwell on eternity, to which she wishes to conduct all the souls she can—those souls which have been redeemed by the Most Precious Blood of Jesus Christ. Open your hearts, oh, Missionaries of the Sacred Heart, open your hearts and souls, do not be content with little, but become holy by sanctifying all whom you approach under obedience, and console your Mother, who, though far away, loves you and delights herself in the beautiful garden of your virtues.

May Jesus bless and enclose you in His Beautiful Heart, where I find you every hour and every day.

Affectionately yours in Corde Jesu,

Mother Frances Saverio Cabrini

7. Panama down the Pacific and across the Andes to Buenos Aires

October, 1895

12th October, 1895

My dear Daughters,

Peace be to you, and may you repeat often,
"Omnia possum in Eo qui me confortat!"

Della piaget del costato
Quanto é larga l'apertura
Ivi il porto é preparato,
Lungi, o figlie, ogni paura;
Sto alla Vergine afferrata,
Presto al porto saró entrata.

"What a long voyage, what a hard voyage Mother is undertaking at present!" Such is what I hear you say, whilst I detect the sadness and fear depicted on your faces. I believe I am the calmest amongst you all, and I am, really so, as far as my voyage is concerned. Jesus still lives. Mary, the Mother of Grace, is always my most tender Mother, because she is the Mother and Foundress of our Institute. It is Jesus and Mary who have always seen me through thousands of difficulties, and will they abandon me now? No, I shall never do them such an injury as to mistrust their power and protection. During all the sixteen years the Institute has existed, they have done everything for me. They have accomplished everything wonderfully. If, sometimes, things were not so successful, it was because I acted too much on my own initiative; when I left the work to them, I had nothing to regret. I go forward, then, as tranquil as a child reposing in its mother's arms; in that safe ship of the Sacred Heart of Jesus I go to fulfill my mission. Holy obedience and the blessing of the Holy Father accompany me and remove all fears. I fear nothing, repeating continually my motto, "*Omnia possum in Eo qui me confortat!*"

The wind roars, the heavens darken, the treacherous waves arise and beat against the steamer, everything turns topsy-turvy. We are threatened with a terrible tempest. All this matters nothing; I have given my trust, I must keep my word of honor, and with faith and confidence. I hope, with God's grace, to go on repeating, "*Omnia possum in Eo qui me confortat!*" We are Missionaries. oh, daughters, and the Missionary should never shrink from difficulties and dangers, but, rather, confiding in Jesus and resting on Mary, she will overcome all difficulties and escape dangers.

Difficulties! What are they, daughters? They are the mere playthings of children enlarged by our imagination, not yet accustomed to focus itself on the Omnipotent. Dangers! What are dangers? The specters that surprise the soul, which having given itself to God, or thinking it has done so, still retains the spirit of the world, or at least many sparks of it, which fly up from the ashes and flare at every gust of contrary wind.

It is necessary, dear daughters, to invest ourselves with the true spirit, to live a life of true faith, lively faith, and not to deceive ourselves and the grace that is always in us.

In Holy Baptism we solemnly renounced the world, the devil and the flesh; but we must prove that renunciation by our daily actions. When we entered Religion, we said, "I am crucified to the world and the world is crucified to me." But such a promise should not be a mere empty saying; in reality we should live as if we were people of a Holy Nation that belongs no longer to the world. When we took the Crucifix of the Missionary and became more generous in the service of God, we said, with the impulse of the ardent soul, "I shall be happy to shed my blood for Jesus Christ, and will welcome the blessed day in which it shall be given to me to suffer something for the Holy Cause, for the salvation of souls and the glory of God." Sublime words! And who would be false to such an oath made by so courageous a soul? O daughters! Let us meditate profoundly on the sublimity of the state to which God has called us–that of working for the salvation of souls! In the presence of such contemplation, we can never shrink from our promises or lose courage, if only because of the judgment and reasoning of the world!

"But I am weak!" With God's help we can do everything; He never fails a humble and faithful soul. "But I am so fragile!" If you are humble and constant, God will be your strength, and, having been made strong with the strength of God, what shall we fear? The devil is terrible, but he is like a chained dog–he cannot disturb you or hurt you without God's permission. Therefore, a humble and faithful soul need have no fear of the devil. "I have failed in generosity, I have fallen at the first temptation, now I shall not be able to do anything well." Have you fallen? Then, humble yourself, and, with a lively act of contrition from the depths of your heart, ask pardon with great humility and renew your promises to God and those who represent Him; then be up and doing with more courage than ever to repair your defects.

October 12th

Yesterday was a red-letter day.

The thought of leaving, after a stay of four months, our dear Sisters, who so edified me and whose virtues made the Convent of Panama, a sweet habitation, was painful.

To leave those young ladies, our pupils, who endeared themselves to me by their nobleness of heart and cooperation in the cares and sacrifices expended by the Sisters in their regard; who surrounded me daily to hear a few words of advice, which as yet I can hardly express in their own language; the efforts they made to overcome themselves and to render me happier each day by guessing my wishes; all this combined to render my departure more painful. The steamer was lying at a distance of three miles from the shore, and they all came on board to see me off. The noble and generous Signor Don Ernesto Icasa, the father of one of our dear pupils, had placed at their disposal his comfortable launch. The representatives of the heads of families in Panama and the patrons of the new School, also came on board and introduced me to the Captain and the Head Steward. They are very distinguished persons, not only on account of their social position, but for the virtues and generosity that distinguish them.

From the very first moment that I arrived in Panama they did all in their power to further the development of the School and to place its preservation and progress on a sound footing. Many were the sacrifices and acts of self-denials they made in its regard. The evening before my departure, the Committee came together to assure me that during my absence they would do everything in their power for the Sisters, and even attested the same in writing, adding a letter of commendation for me to present to their friends when I reached Ecuador, Peru, Chili and Argentine. Many ladies, our good friends, came to the port to see me off. Amongst others was the Bishop's Secretary, the Parish Priest of the Cathedral, who came with good wishes, which, because they are accompanied by God's blessing, are always valuable. This good priest had been invited by our Chaplain, to give us Benediction of the Blessed Sacrament, so that my voyage might be blessed. So many demonstrations of kindness touched my soul, indeed, and rendered more and more deeply painful my leaving Panama, a town with so many noble and generous people.

On board the steamer, Messrs. Icasa, Espinosa, Della-Ossa and Lewis introduced me to the Captain with many expressions of recommendation. Mr. Casa gave a finishing touch to the leave-taking by paying for the voyage and handing the tickets to the Bursar himself, making sure that I should enjoy all the advantages procured for me. There was also the comical side which served to mitigate the sadness of the last moments, for the Consul, Mr. Della-Ossa, took the Captain by the arm, saying, "You know, Mother has had no supper yet." "Of course," he said, "she shall have it presently," but Mr. Della-Ossa persisted so much, that the Captain thought he wanted him to go to the kitchen himself for my supper. The Captain was very amused, and called the Steward to conduct us to the dining room, but I begged him to wait a few moments, as I wished to see the Sisters and children return, as the tender was leaving at once, it being six p.m. Night comes on with remarkable rapidity in these equatorial regions. The waving of the handkerchiefs could not be distinguished after they had gone about fifty meters, so we went to our cabins, Mother Chiara and I. These were just like a little Convent. The two cabins communicated one with the other and opened, out on the deck, which is four meters wide and one hundred long, where we can walk about freely and enjoy the air. The dining room is very near, and very comfortable, we might have wished for all these conveniences, but we could hardly have expected to find them. After supper, and after having said some prayers, Mother Chiara went to bed, whilst I sat alone facing the lighthouse of Panama. Looking to the left of it, I thought I could see the Sisters at recreation gazing in the direction of the steamer *Mapocho*, and afterward absorbed in prayers in the chapel. I also thought I could see all the five lamps burning, three before the Blessed Sacrament and one each before Our Lady and Saint Joseph, which, by raising and lowering their flickering lights, seemed as though they wished to unite with the Sisters in praying for a good voyage for me. I then united with you in spirit, and prayed in return that you might receive the most precious graces which you need always in order that you may accomplish your mission, i.e., to lead to God all the souls that are brought into contact with you.

Between nine-thirty and ten p.m., and very quietly, the steamer began to move, and, having turned round, it passed in front of Flamengo Hill and made straight for the south. I continued as long as I could to look on the left-hand side of the lighthouse, but little by little the darkness that surrounded us became so dense that everything was rendered imperceptible. Then, having lost all hope of again seeing you any longer, and of hearing your voices raised in singing the hymn of the *Ave Maris Stella* as an invocation and prayer for me to Our Lady, I also retired to rest.

On the morning of the 12th, as soon as I arose and had said my prayers, I turned towards Panama to see if I could get a glimpse if not of the town, at least of the coast, but the water that surrounded me was like a leaden space. The heavens were so clouded that I could not distinguish the points of the compass, which might have helped me to look in the proper direction. I then looked into the Sacred Heart, where I could see you in deep contemplation like so many inflamed seraphim in preparation for Holy Communion. It was a most consoling vision for me, and I hastened to unite myself with you in Spiritual Communion, offering it to the Eternal Father in union with your Sacramental Communion.

The atmosphere seems to have changed its nature, for, proceeding towards the Equator and even while on the Equatorial line itself, instead of feeling the great heat which we were told to expect, we felt rather cold, so much so that we were obliged to put on heavier clothes. One would think the steamer had mistaken its route and had steered towards the North Pole instead of going to the Equator. Two blankets were not sufficient, and we had to wear shawls when on deck, but despite this I feel the cold to my very bones. I should have loved to have used those two cushions you had so carefully provided for me, but no matter how much I stretched my arms, I could not reach Panama to take them. I imagined also how disappointed you were to have forgotten them, but there is no need of your being upset, for everyone is so attentive to us on the steamer, that we need nothing,

Then, while crossing the Equator, it is not becoming to wish for too many conveniences, because we are near and in a straight line with Quito, where Blessed Marianna lived in such austere penance, though this is rather to be admired than imitated. What a pity that M. Gabriella is not here, now that we are passing the Equator, seeing she wished so much to see the line. It is like a shining dark blue band stretched just above a globe, and is really beautiful to behold. The sea seems to end there. To one of the lady passengers who desired to see the line, the merry company placed a thread across a pair of eyeglasses, so that she thought she really saw a great beam dividing the two hemispheres. However, notwithstanding this joke, the combination of sky and water forms such a beautiful spectacle, that one would think it was the actual line of division where the South begins and where a twofold nature appears to exist, for whilst the thermometer registers 27 centigrades, the air is so cold that it caused us to shiver.

You must not think it is always like this; everyone is surprised at this phenomenon. I am not so surprised, accustomed as I am, now, to see so many changes from the hand of God, Who, in the economy of His Most Holy Providence, always has new wonders for those who completely abandon themselves to Him. I, in fact, rejoice to be able to give you a new description of these equatorial regions, of which I have heard hardly anything except that the heat is excessive and unbearable. It might be that the Lily of Quito, the Blessed Marianna, from her sepulcher in the Andes, or, rather, from Heaven where she sits happily at the side of her loving Jesus, sent us this fresh breeze to mitigate the heat of the voyage, which we undertook from Panama in honor of Saint Rose of Lima, the Patroness of America. We shall visit her tomb and receive Holy Communion at her altar.

October 16th

Yesterday we arrived at Guayaquil, where we intended to go ashore to receive Holy Communion, but two hours passed before the custom officers and doctors came on board. Then there arrived a Peruvian priest, who during the revolutions, had left Ecuador and settled in Peru. He had hardly reached Guayaquil, when he was banished anew to Peru, and embarked on our steamer. I made up my mind after this information not to go ashore and have the police following us, as everybody is held in suspicion, Signor Alfaro not having as yet fully settled his Government.

Guayaquil is a beautiful port. Its entrance resembles that of the Mississippi at New Orleans. We have to sail up this river for more than six hours before we reach the port. They say the vegetation is charming, but I cannot describe it as we arrived at night, and after twenty-four hours we again sail at night. The town resembles Genoa for its scenery, only it is not so high and healthy.

Seen from the steamer, the city, with its beautiful houses built with architectural regularity and well-painted and in shape semi-circular, reflected in the water, is very fine and not inferior to a European city. When illuminated at night it is a wonderfully pleasant sight, and, judging from the tall steeples towering over the houses, the churches should be beautiful. But now these temples and houses are deserted and present a desolate spectacle, for the first thing the revolutionary Alfaro with his followers did was to banish Priests and Sisters. The latter took refuge in Panama and then returned to their Mother Houses. Some were not banished, but a troop of rough men entered the convents and treated the inmates so brutally that the Sisters fled in despair from the country. Some of these poor women suffered so much, that they were still ill when I called on them ... But you are not to be frightened. If you are banished from one place, you should, like the Apostles, shake the dust from your shoes and enter another country. Hunted from the second, you can return again to the first, and so you will not abandon a large number of souls who desire to take advantage of the good you can do them. At the present moment, having no business in Ecuador, I simply pray the Blessed Marianna to look down upon her country and obtain that it be again enlightened with the light and faith of former days.

October 17th

Yesterday we left Ecuador and entered the waters of Peru, and at seven a.m. we arrived at the port of Paita. It looks like a city of desolation, and at first sight it saddens one's heart. No trees, no grass, no fountain are visible. Surrounded by low and dry mountains, it is a real desert. Yet it is one of the most healthy ports, and large numbers even from Ecuador come here to enjoy its curative advantages. In fact, the air one breathes here is pure, light and balsamic, and really restores one. The sea is tranquil, and they tell us it never gets rough at this point. It has such a beautiful blue soft color that one would think it a fallen portion of the sky. But to us it appeared even more beautiful and singular, for, as we looked around to see if we could find a steeple to which we could turn our thoughts to Jesus in the Blessed Sacrament of the Altar, a flock of white birds suddenly whirled around us, making a strange noise, at which Mother Chiara broke silence, saying, "What can this mean?" "Oh," I replied, playfully, "they are inviting us to their country as they did three years ago at Panama, and we will go there when we can." While we were talking and amusing ourselves with these peculiar birds, a priest came on board, and approaching me, after a few salutations, asked me what was the object of our voyage. Having told him, he said we should remain here and open a Mission. In the meantime, he said, he would see to our going ashore immediately. I had a difficult time in endeavoring to persuade him that it was impossible for me to stop here, at which he seemed very much disappointed. However, determined not to be outdone, he shortly afterward appeared with the Governor and Mayor, who promised me all sorts of things, salary, etc. At first I thought that, as there was a great deal of business being carried on on-board, that these people wanted to trade with us, but I soon discovered that their intentions were very good, and that they only desired to get a religious education for the youth of their country. Of course, I could not gratify their wishes, and they finally took my address, and I theirs, with the hope of satisfying their wishes at a later date. Meanwhile, two beautiful days have passed away without our being able to receive Our Divine Lord or hear Holy Mass: the Feasts of St. Teresa and of Blessed Margaret Mary. Had we been without the consolation of prayer, this long voyage would have been insupportable. What a gift prayer is! It is the real treasure of our soul, our being able to give to God the worship of perfect adoration. Prayer is the channel through which the most precious waters of grace continually and copiously flow from the Heart of God. Precious waters, daughters, these are, for while they sanctify us, they render happy our Holy Church, of which we should daily try to become more worthy. Prayer is always useful, because it can penetrate everywhere, and where there is misery and poverty, there it enters to enrich, to give life, grace, comfort and salvation; its zeal is like that of God's Angel, its activity is greater than the most ardent fire, its velocity is like the thought of the Cherubim. Oh, the spirit of prayer knows no obstacles, admits of no delay, despises dangers; its end is the glory of God, the prosperity of Christ's interests, the extension of His Kingdom, our own sanctification and that of our neighbor! Oh, what happiness, daughters! I go accompanied by the powerful and wonderful means of prayer. I am, then, most happy in the midst of the foaming waves of the sea. And you, dear daughters, pray, pray always, and incessantly practice the spirit of prayer, which must form your happiness.

October 20th

On the 18th we had two landings—one at Port Eten and the other at Port Pacasmayo—and yesterday morning we had another at Port Salaverri, where we still are, though, judging from the scenery and commerce, it does not appear to be a place of much importance. There is a big trade here in sugar, cocoa, rice and cotton, which form the principal riches of these countries, apart from the mines of gold and other metals which still abound in Peru, though not so much as they did at one time. Now it possesses another source of wealth, the natural and rich guano composed chiefly of the lime of sea-fowls. From the Equator to Chili, all the coast, whether plain or mountainous, is but one desert. There is not a blade of grass, not a tree, nothing that gives the slightest indication of vegetation. Nothing can be cultivated, for there is no rain except at intervals of five to seven years. In the intervening years, millions of birds, destined by Providence, deposit in certain places quantities of fecal matter, from which is extracted the guano which is so much valued all over the world for the cultivation of fields.

In these parts we have seen many practical innovations. The sea is almost always so rough that boats coming to a ship with passengers, cannot always get near the ship-ladder, and then what is done to put the passengers on board? Well, something very curious and very funny takes place. They take a barrel cut open on one side and place the person in it. They then attach it to the chain which they use for hauling merchandise. The person is then pulled up and let down into the ship. The poor creature, who is suspended between the sky and the water seems very much afraid, and this applies not only to the women but to the men also, for even when they reach the deck they appear stupefied and as if not quite sure of having escaped some sort of danger. Yesterday one of the usual stowaways of these ports, taking advantage of the conveyance of merchandise, managed to get on board, but the officers, who are quite practical, as soon as they saw him accosted him and told him to leave the steamer at once. It was a most difficult task for him to climb up the ship, but it was more difficult to descend, so they took him, put him into a sack and then attached the sack to the chain and let him down. He must have been accustomed to this sort of thing, for he remained indifferent and as fresh as a rose.

We were detained in this port of Salaverri, which is as important as it is inconvenient, for two days, owing to the large quantity of cargo we had to take on board. Some years ago a large dock was built here to facilitate the work of embarkation. It was hardly finished, when there arose a tremendous gale which destroyed it completely, not leaving a trace of the work, while the expense of construction was so great that the promoters did not feel disposed to rebuild it. The ocean is very rough here, and the waves break so violently that they actually frighten us. The cargoes are brought across in large and strongly-built boats, and, notwithstanding their size, they often seem to be on the point of foundering as the great waves sweep over them and hide them from sight, while we remain in terrible suspense until we see them rise again above the tremendous waves. Amidst the force of the waves, these unfortunate boats roll from one side to another, though they are in the hands of ten strong rowers with long broad oars. The one at the stern, who acts as steersman, has a bigger oar than the others, and works with all his might and main. Others come with *"balzas,"* a boat of somewhat primitive construction and formed of planks of long big trees. Called *"balzas,"* these planks are as light and spongy as cork, and offer great resistance to the water. By means of these boats they transport bags of charcoal which is used in these parts. It is said to be a safer form of transport than any other kind of boat. However, I should not care to trust myself on one of them except under obedience, in which case fear ceases and is replaced by a trust which brings security.

Obedience! Oh, dear word, Obedience! The revealed word, ray of true light, which descends upon us from the Father of Light, as a manifestation of the Divine Will by means of His representatives on earth. He who does the Will of God feels great peace, tastes Heaven in advance, and what great joy is ours, oh, daughters, who live under obedience, or, rather, in the State of Obedience, really, actually and continually doing the Will of God. *"Ego quae placita sunt ei facio semper."* Those who live under obedience are sure of their way, because in the practice of obedience there are no errors, no deceits, no illusions, nor darkness. Obedience! Obedient souls are the delight of the Heart of Jesus, Who has said His treasures are always open to His Beloved and

Faithful Spouses. It is they whom He makes the dispensers of His possessions, on earth and in Heaven. Do you love Jesus, daughters? Do you want to be His faithful Spouses? If so, love obedience. Obey always, for God's sake. Let every command be easy to you, on account of the faith you have in Holy Obedience. Are you sure of the steps you take, of the solidity of your work, of the strength of your spirit? In the way of obedience not only will you walk, but you will fly like royal eagles and spend a quiet and happy life, being able to repeat to yourselves, "I am sure I am doing God's Will." Remember, no one ever became a Saint without obedience, for it is obedience which is the favorite virtue of all the Saints. Do not do things by halves, but let your obedience be entire and perfect, just like that of Jesus. Firstly, in the performance of it, by following promptly, entirely and happily all that is ordered by the Superior, secondly, as regards the will, by not wishing for anything but what the Superior wishes, thirdly, as regards your judgment, by judging and thinking as the Superior judges and thinks. Which of you, daughters, has not contracted debts with God in the course of your life? Well, a sure way and means of paying your debts to God is that of submitting oneself to a true and perfect obedience, seeing that obedience is of far greater value than any penance whatsoever you can imagine. "*Melior est obedientia quam victimae.*" Most sweet will be the death of obedient souls.

Always late, we arrive at Callao only on the 22nd. I rose at four o'clock, and at five-fifteen I called Mother Chiara to get up in the hope of going ashore at six a.m. and then taking the train for Lima, where I wanted to satisfy my desire of receiving Holy Communion at the Sepulchre of Saint Rose. But very soon our hopes vanished, for at seven-thirty none of the customs officers had arrived, and no boats were allowed to come near the steamer under penalty of a heavy fine. They came at last, but what was our surprise to learn that there was no train to Lima until nine a.m. I didn't know what to do. Mother Chiara had fought long enough with the sea, and it was impossible for her to remain fasting much longer. As for myself, I did not want to lose my promised Communion in honor of Saint Rose, having made many promises to her and having confided to her care the rest of our journey and the interests I am engaged in furthering. I could manage the fast all right, having had no trouble with the sea, only playing with the waves, as it were, delighting in their impotence and their breaking and rising like foam and mist, which resembled at times some part of the Niagara Falls, which I saw near Buffalo, U.S.A., about three years ago. We took the train and arrived in Lima at ten a.m. We hired a cab to the Dominican Church, where we were able to satisfy our devotion. On the Altar where I received Holy Communion there was a statue of the Infant Jesus with His arms extended, bearing a celestial smile on His face of extraordinary beauty. He seemed to gaze on me and to say, "It is here I have waited to favor thee, through the merits of my beloved Rosa, whom you have come to honor." The look of this Infant, so real, penetrated the very depths of my soul, and such was the comfort I felt, that I forgot all about my fast, as well as all other human wants, so much so, that I found I hadn't even taken as much as a sip of coffee, and it was one p.m. If it is thus Jesus rewards a little sacrifice, what will He not do for souls who are really faithful to Him ?

But let us return to the Dominican Basilica, where, after Holy Communion, the Reverend Fathers showed us the different Altars, especially the one where Saint Rose's head is venerated. The Saint's head is enclosed in a silver urn placed above another urn which contains the ashes of Blessed Martin de Porres. The Altars are all adorned with big statues, some of which are truly beautiful. The Saints are so realistically represented in life-size, that one would almost think they could speak, but amongst the statues are some which are dressed, according to the taste of the individual who honored these particular Saints, but which does not tend to enhance devotion. When the statues are adorned with taste, and especially when the colors correspond as far as possible with the natural features of the Saints, then the Faithful show them more love and devotion, otherwise they do not appeal to them. On leaving the church, we saw many women placing their finger on a leaden seal at the mouth of a leaden pipe, which was enclosed in a column where the Holy Water fount is placed. With a finger in that position they prayed with great fervor. I asked them why they did so, and a woman, surprised at our astonishment, answered, "But do you not know that this is an authentic seal from Rome, and that by placing your finger on it and saying an Our Father, you relieve a soul from Purgatory?" Not to surprise them more, I also touched the seal with my finger, and then said a *Pater Noster* for the Holy Souls. To tell the truth, I never heard of such a devotion in Rome. But we were not satisfied with venerating only the head of Saint Rose. So the guide told us to go to St. Rosa de los Padres, where we would find the rest of the relics. We went in the direction shown us, and presently in the place pointed out to us, we found a beautiful new church, very devotional and well kept. The good Sacristan showed us the relics of the Saint, which are distributed amongst the different Altars. In one of the chapels there was a large crucifix and glass case, where we found the remains of the Saint. The crucifix is the one she used herself. At the two sides of the Altar there are two glass cases, each containing an arm of the Saint. On another Altar we saw the cross of wood on which, prostrate on the floor, she used to pray, and to which she used to tie herself in order to imitate her Savior, her Spouse, when she was not undergoing other crucifixions—those of the spirit, which are better—real crucifixions in the strictest sense, which serve so well to purify souls and unite them intimately with their Beloved. From such crucifixions, this beloved of the Crucified, of whom I speak, had much to suffer. On another Altar we saw the discipline and the instruments of her penance, while in a frame is placed a letter written by the Saint herself. On this same Altar was a picture of Our Lady with the Divine Infant of rare beauty in her arms. This picture captivates the soul simply by looking at it. It is believed that the picture represents the Infant who gave the mystical ring of marriage to Saint Rose, and to whom the Saint always had recourse for advice before beginning any new enterprise. The Sacristan then took us to the spot where stood the Saint's house, which is beside the sacred edifice we had visited. It is a large piece of ground, whereon are laid the foundations of a large church bearing the form of a Latin Cross. When the large, beautiful and strong colonnades had almost reached the cornice, a terrible rebellion broke out and threw the whole city of Lima into confusion. The Religious were ill-treated, many being sent into exile and their Convents destroyed. Since that unfortunate episode, there has been no thought of continuing the magnificent work already begun. It is a great pity, for the place would become a celebrated Sanctuary, seeing that it holds the well of the Saint, which corresponds with the center of the church, while there is the grotto in the garden where she used to withdraw for prayer, and which would be one of the aisles of the church, to say nothing of the precious relics above-mentioned and others which are deposited in various Convents of the Sisters. Having satisfied our devotion towards the Saint, we went to visit the Apostolic Nuncio, Monsignor Macchi, who received us very kindly, and gave us a very kind letter of recommendation to the Superintendent of the South American Company, asking that he might let us have tickets at reduced fares, for which reason I had called on him. We spoke of our voyage, and he gave us instructions to visit certain places for the purpose of transacting business matters connected with our Missions. He knows all the coast as far as Valparaiso very well, having traveled on this very steamer to pay a return visit to Monsignor Casanova, Archbishop of Santiago. With the blessing and good wishes of this good Prelate, I visited another part of the city so as to have something to write about to you. Lima is beautiful when compared with the other cities I saw in South America, but I cannot call it really beautiful. It resembles the old portion of New Orleans, U.S.A., where the poor people of that great town reside. We only saw something really beautiful when we entered St. Peter's. You may compare St. Peter's with churches to be found in Genoa. Dressed-up Saints are banished from this church. Everything is well ordered, becoming and richly appointed. It was one p.m. when we entered St. Peter's and Mass was being celebrated, at which we assisted with great consolation, after ten days privation of the Most Holy Sacrament. The architecture is superb, a good style. with rich and various kinds of marble. From the altar hung beautiful tapestries, elegantly and profusely embroidered in very fine gold. The statues were also numerous here. They seemed life-like and in good order. It was the last day of the Octave of Blessed Margaret Mary Alacoque, and on one side of the High Altar there was a temporary altar in her honor, adorned with lilies and roses, with a background of beautiful pink cloth which threw out in high relief the roses and the lilies. How happy I was to see our Patron in the midst of this triumphant altar, truly appropriate for this virgin, whom the good Jesus, in the loving designs of His goodness, pre-ordained from eternity to establish and propagate the devotion of His Divine Heart, manifesting to her Its wonders of piety, clemency, power and love. This dear virgin, worthy daughter of St. Francis de Sales, corresponded with such rare fidelity with the designs of her celestial Spouse and worked with such ardent and generous zeal to fulfill her vocation, that both Heaven and earth were moved to admiration. Words are inadequate to express how much she suffered and worked to diffuse such a rare and salutary devotion, for the demon, who knew the incomparable advantages that she would bring to the peoples of every nation, worked against our dear Virgin Protectress with such satanic violence, that, to human understanding, it seemed impossible to conquer and overcome his attacks. But truly loving and faithful souls are not discouraged, and it was thus with our Blessed Margaret. She knew that the work she was destined to establish came from Heaven. Her courage and confidence did not waver. Entirely abandoning herself, like a strong and true Missionary, to the loving piety of her beloved Jesus, coupled with the industry of an enlightened and generous charity, she knew how to triumph over all obstacles, meriting thus to see before she died this Divine Heart known, loved and glorified by a large number of devout souls. As a recompense for so much generosity of action, Blessed Margaret Mary now contemplates in Heaven the beauty of the Divine Heart. She enjoys peace, happiness and sovereign delights, and can at every instant talk to Him unveiled, implore and obtain great graces, and she will certainly implore them for you if you honor her but especially if you imitate her. She will comfort you with her most powerful intercession. She herself carries your ardent prayers to the throne of God, and, as a reward for your zeal, she will place you all in the loving Heart of Jesus, and obtain for you the grace to live that same life, which is all humility, all meekness, all obedience, all sacrifice, all love.

At St. Peter's we met the Jesuit Fathers, who told me to visit the Ladies of the Sacred Heart, where we could get some refreshments. They have a Government School, a lovely house close to St. Peter's. Many years ago, before the great rebellion destroyed everything, this house belonged to the Jesuits, being a celebrated college and novitiate. Now the Jesuits have a smaller house opposite the Convent of the Sacred Heart, but it will be enlarged in time, as their schools are always frequented by the principal families of the town. The Reverend Mother of the Ladies of the Sacred Heart received us very cordially, and whilst they were getting our lunch ready, she conducted us around the house. It is a very nice place, indeed, and the arrangements are so well carried out, that it is most suitable for the different classes of children who frequent it. The good

Sisters wanted us to stay overnight, but I could not do so, having some business to attend to at Callao concerning our voyage.

I wanted to visit the Cathedral, but they dissuaded me from doing so, as it is ugly within and without, the exterior having been ruined by the cannon fire that was directed against it. This will surprise you, but I can explain the fact at once. One of the first acts of these revolutionaries is always to attack the Cathedral of a town, and the first of the two hostile parties who gains possession of the Cathedral is considered the victor. Perhaps their intentions are good, for those are declared the victors who have the good fortune to secure the Sanctuary for themselves, but we cannot deny that they deface God's temple and destroy the most beautiful monuments. They say *"adelantados mucho,"* which means very enlightened, but, to tell the truth, their customs and manners are those of the aboriginal Indians.

I like the custom of having Holy Mass at one p.m. This is done daily in all the churches, at which many men and women assist with a truly edifying devotion. There is a society in Lima which defrays the expenses of these late Masses.

We returned to Callao towards evening. Our steamer had already reached the docks, so there was no necessity to take a small boat to go on board. Both officers and crew were glad to see us again, inquired how we liked Lima and how our trip went off.

The next day the Captain introduced us to the Superintendent, Mr. Kenny, of Callao, and succeeded so well with the English Company, that he obtained a thirty-three percent reduction for us. We, who could not expect more, were quite satisfied, but not so the good Captain, who said that as soon as we reached Valparaiso, he would go to the General

Agency and get us a fifty percent reduction, as he admired our life of sacrifice, for which he said we deserved every consideration.

Callao is a very important port. It has a very nice large dock, to receive the steamers, which is only opened and accessible when the steamers arrive.

October 29th

We have been "coasting" since the 15th, that is, since we left Guayaquil. The coast is so dry and sandy that one would imagine we were sailing along the great desert of Arabia, instead of being on the waters of the Pacific. There are no trees, no grass, only a variety of rocks. For two days we have been sailing along certain mountains whose peaks are all one height and look like a big extended wall, broken by a few valleys and watered by torrents that descend from the Andes, which, before rushing into the sea, form creeks, but eventually yield to the force of the formidable waves and then mix with the salty waters of the sea. In these valleys are cities and towns that export vegetables and fruit to other places which suffer drought, and where the inhabitants as yet can find no means of growing a tree or any plant whatsoever, the soil being too poor for the cultivation of even a garden. This occurs especially at Chala and Antofagasta, where all the mountains contain great quantities of saltpeter, which, evaporating, rises during the day to fall on the earth at night under the aspect of a thick fog which burns up every kind of vegetation. These great mountainous walls arise like impregnable fortresses defying the heavens. Now and again they take the form of heights, from which the slope extends itself like a mantle and ends in a scarcely perceptible bay. There a town is seen to arise and a port where many steamers enter, especially sailing vessels, which lie in the harbor for weeks awaiting a cargo of saltpeter, which they transport to Europe through the Straits of Magellan; if the vessel is a steamer, it goes round Cape Horn; if it is a sailing vessel, it takes about four months to complete the journey. This saltpeter is used in Europe to fertilize the earth. From this arises the Proverb that we take the best part of the bread and leave them the crust, which means that they have little if any profit. But the Proverb does not apply in the commercial or financial world, much money is made out of various silver, tin and iron mines, as well as out of saltpeter and guano.

During these days of our journey we stopped at sixteen ports: Guayaquil, Tombes, Payta, Pimentel, Eten, Pacasmayo, Salaverri, Callao, Tombe de Mora, Pisco, Chala, Quilca, Mollendo, Ilo, Arica, Pesagua. It is lovely to watch the train as it travels through these mining countries, playing, as it were, on the edges of the precipices, which lie below the zig-zag rails. In some parts there are funiculars owing to the steep slopes, and accidents are frequent. But all this does not retard these lovers of buried treasures from continuing their traffic. These big mountains are called little hills by the people here, and so they are when compared with the great Andes, just as we regard the hills in Piedmont in comparison with the Alps and Apennines. To reach the Andes it is necessary to cross this desert for about nine miles or more. The Cordigliera is really portentous and imposing. It begins in the island of Diego Ranires, southwest of Cape Horn, enters South America through Patagonia, and then runs northward, forming a reef first along the Pacific Ocean, whose waters little by little penetrate the Cordigliera, making deep bays. But even here the Andes are not very high, the lowest parts measuring two or three thousand feet and the highest nine thousand feet. Entering Chili, the chain begins and rises until it reaches to a considerable height in Bolivia. One can admire what is supposed to be the highest peak of the Andes, the Aconcagua, the height of which is from twenty-three to twenty-four thousand feet above the level of the sea. With a height of about eleven or fourteen thousand feet, this formidable range continues all through Bolivia and Peru, now and again thrusting up other heights or peaks covered with perpetual snow. At intervals one sees traces of paths, in communication with different countries, and at this point the lowest height is about sixteen thousand feet above sea level. Even at this height there are fields like those on the plains, for the Cordigliera is about four hundred miles wide. On one of these is to be found the famous lake Titicaca, which is the highest in the world. All along the coast of Peru and reaching the line of the Equator, this range runs until it unites with the volcanoes, the most celebrated of which are the Chimborazo and the Cotopaxi. There we see with wondering eyes peaks which seem to touch the very heavens, and often appear cut by the clouds and reduced to vapor. These peaks then break into three divisions. One takes the north-west direction until it reaches the sea of the Antilles, another passes through the center joining the above and reaches the Antilles while the third turns to the north-east on the east of the Orinoco, enters the State of Venezuela and reaches the sea of the Antilles. It is said that the hottest part of the earth's interior is at the Equator. Those who live in the Isthmus say that the mouth of the interior furnace or of hell is on the Isthmus. Also it is said that thence one can also go straight to Heaven, if not too immersed in earthly things–if so immersed, one falls into hell, and, amongst other miseries, there is the gnashing of teeth. In the whole length of the Andes exist active volcanoes, which, in the neighborhood of the Equator, are so violent that one of them by its eruption—the Cotopaxi—has formed another mountain right beside it. The Andes run along Columbia, presenting to the sight many pretty and imposing views, thence it continues on through Central America and Mexico, where we also find extremely active volcanoes. Entering into the United States, they bear the name of Rocky Mountains along the west coast. Then, taking a course through Alaska to Asia, they reach the Aleutian Islands, forming a connection between the Arctic and Antarctic, having on the west the Pacific Ocean. In the north of Asia there is another chain that runs along the other side, and to the west there is another volcanic chain that seems to merge into and lose itself in the sea, though it reappears in Australia, where it throws up volcanoes, renowned for their peculiarities, which are crowned here and there, as it were with lakes of fire. The Pacific Ocean seems closed, both on the east and the west, by an unbroken chain of volcanic mountains. I have described the Andes for you, because our fellow passengers, who know we are traveling over and will probably cross the Andes at Valparaiso, speak a great deal of the Andes, and their beauty and the facts which make them famous—very often with maps in their hands—and thus every point is described so vividly that I imagine I can touch it with my hand. Having to cross the Aconcagua, I shall have something to tell you about it. In the meanwhile, I think the Cordigliera presents a good lesson to the Missionary, running as it does all over the earth, without fear of seas, atmosphere, unhealthy places, etc, and almost teaching us when it rises towards Heaven with its great heights and when it humbles itself, hiding itself in the waves of the sea; it preaches also when it sends out fire, smoke and lava, adding force to the winds that lash within its gorges. In Boyaca, for instance, especially in the Popayan, to which place we have been invited, it thunders terribly every day, with lightning that seems to reduce one to ashes; so in all this one can very easily find food for pious meditation, on death.

October 31st, Iquique

Within the space of a few days we stopped at four ports Iquique, Tocohilla, Cobija and Antofagasta. We had hoped to reach Iquique early in the morning so as to be able to go to Holy Communion, but the steamer arrived a little late at Pasagua, and the Superintendent of the port would not let us land, so we had to pass the night there on board. In the morning the staff was very busy importing and exporting the merchandise, as well as in receiving and landing passengers. Having arrived at Iquique at night, the vessel loaded very hurriedly, for we were a day behind and the Captain did not wish to lose any more time. We had sufficient leisure, however, to go ashore before sunset and pay our respects to the Bishop, as Monsignor Macchi desired us to do, and so we seized the opportunity of meeting that worthy Prelate who is a real missionary to a population of twenty-five thousand inhabitants. The first thing he did on taking up his episcopal duties was to build a beautiful and very devotional church, and he has since laid the foundation stone of a second, which he hopes to complete in six months, an easy task here, as the churches are made of wood. We visited the Blessed Sacrament rather hurriedly, as the evening was far advanced and we did not relish the prospect of committing ourselves to the waves in the dark, more especially in this open port and for a distance of five miles.

Mother Chiara, who finds this voyage very long, thought we had reached the Red Sea to open a mission in Africa; it is very funny, indeed, the waters are of a bright red color–blood color, in fact. Perhaps it tends to remind us of the heavy wars between Chili and Peru, in 1880, when so many fell victims, especially among the soldiers of Peru. At the summit of the mountains, which run along the coast, and form a kind of wall, the Peruvian soldiers took up their position, but were surrounded by the Chilians, who are noted for their strength both on land and sea. They were driven over the edge and then precipitated, both horses and men, into the sea, and to such a depth (which in these parts always extends to some miles) that not even the remains of the combatants could be recovered by the Peruvians.

Iquique is lovely; its roads are large and straight, it has also pretty houses, though they are not very high, and well-kept shops. especially those of the Italians, who are quite numerous, and who are very comfortably circumstanced and are held in respect. There is, however, not a tree nor a blade of grass to be found anywhere. Neither is there a well nor a stream. Water for drinking and for domestic purposes has to be procured at the distance of a day's journey from the town, and so also with regard to cereals, flour, fruit, vegetables, wine, olives, sugar, coffee, forage, almost everything has to be imported by sea from other countries, so you may imagine what it costs to live in this city. Fortunately, it is inhabited by the rich, who pay the poor well, so that all live comfortably. The air is good, but the people here do not live long, and foreigners, who are not very strong, fall into rapid decline. Notwithstanding, the emissaries of the devil have penetrated here and have done grave harm. How is it that the emissaries of the devil have less fear than the followers of Christ? Let us reflect on this, to humble ourselves, for often we think of health and dangers before we give ourselves up to our Divine Lord, the glory of God and the salvation of souls.

Since we left Panama, we had on board a Protestant minister, one of the worst type, being an Irishman from the north-east of Ireland. This minister came from Chicago and is stopping at Iquique. You should have seen how he tried to capture, now one and then another of the young men. With one he stayed till midnight preaching his errors. Fortunately, the young man, as did the others, made light of him and his statements. When he saw that they made fun of him, he began preaching Liberty of Conscience, but he only made matters worse for himself, and then, with his Bible in his hand, he tried to force his diabolical interpretations on his listeners. He finished off by becoming, both he and his wife, objects of ridicule. So far things were most consoling. He thought he was going to find those who would drink in the doctrine he offered them, but instead, he met with excellent Spanish-Americans, who were well instructed in their religion. But at Iquique, I fear he will play havoc. The only hope lies in the strength of the Bishop, who is studying every means to weaken the efforts of these proselytizers and repair the harm they do.

See how dangerous these times are to our faith, to our august religion and to sound morals, for the emissaries of Satan, violent apostles of unrestrained liberty and freedom of speech, make use of all kinds of opportunities and snares, and go not only into the towns, but even into remote villages to spread their errors and doctrines, which are, as you know, condemned by the Church. It seems as if all the diabolical powers of hell have combined in directing their satanic efforts to combat and persecute the Church, her doctrines and her morals, her laws, her worship, her ministers, and all that she possesses of holiness and reverence, In the meantime, the weak, lukewarm, incautious, drink in the venomous errors, the fatal maxims of which pervert the mind and corrupt the heart, miserably dragging innumerable souls to eternal perdition. One cannot but grieve over this terrible war which the demon never ceases to rage against our holy Religion. One trembles for the frightful future that awaits the world if God does not show an efficacious way out, which must be something out of the ordinary, as the evils that are now affecting the Church are extraordinary.

Continuing our journey, and passing several ports, we arrived at Antofagasta, an important port for the merchants of Sucre and Potose. It was a lovely morning, and we were longing to receive Holy Communion in order to be able to overcome the dangers and vehemence of the foaming waves, which at every stroke seemed about to capsize the boat. Antofagasta is a lovely city, which is being magnified by the construction of beautiful houses, squares and pleasant walks. It has one Catholic Church which is really beautiful, and which helps one's devotion and is an aid to recollection, On our arrival, one Mass was just being finished, but another began immediately, as if providentially arranged for us. So we received Holy Communion and refreshed ourselves spiritually after the long fast we had been forced to make. When we had finished our devotions, we visited the parish priest, who is a very pious and zealous man. He was delighted to see us, hoping we would open a House there, but he was equally disappointed when he heard what our destination was. He learned all he could about our Colleges, hoping that some day we might settle there. We made calls at Tocopilla, Cobija, Taltal, Caldera, Calligol, and also at Coquimbo, where we spent the day, and where we rejoiced at seeing some vegetation, after having sailed for so many days along the dry arid coasts, where at night one could not enjoy the bracing sea air because it is marred by the fog which rises from the land steeped in saltpeter. This fog falls in the shape of very fine rain, and instead of restoring, dries up every plant it meets and shortens the lives of the people who live there. At Coquimbo we found that Spring was advancing, and from the neighboring city—Serena, so famous in Chili—there arrived an abundance of lovely fruit, peaches, pears, figs, melons and cucumbers, and all such things that one would expect, not merely in Spring but also in the Summer and Autumn. The grape, however, ripens only once a year, i.e., in the month of January, when it is full Summer, whilst we in Lombardy freeze like crows.

At last the dear steamer, *Mapocho*, arrived at Valparaiso, our destination, the following morning. After having passed the length of that long desert, one seems to have entered the Vale of Heaven. It is a beautiful harbor, much like that of Genoa, and, like it, also, favored by nature. It is really charming. It seems a large city, and appears larger than it is, for it is built on the slope of a hill, or, to speak more correctly, on the boot of the Cordigliera. It is so steep that from the lower part of the town, which consists of a long row of cottages, you ascend by means of a funicular railway, which resembles a house lift, and, looking out of the windows, you discover you are hanging over a deep precipice. Mother Chiara closed her eyes, for it made her feel faint. As soon as we got into Valparaiso itself, we went to Mr. E. Escobar, who is a very distinguished person and to whom we had been recommended, but there was great sorrow and desolation in his family, for Mrs. E. Escobar was very ill and almost on the point of death. The relatives, who had come to help and console him, were ill also. Mr. Escobar, however, wanted to see us and to show his interest in us. He sent us to the excellent parish priest, Padre Manero, who, in return, recommended us to the Ladies of the Sacred Heart, who have a very nice School here. These good ladies received us as if we were their sisters, and would not let us leave them. We had our luggage to see to, as also our crossing the Cordigliera. We then went to visit Mr. Severin, another friend, to whom we had been recommended. He was very kind and very energetic. He took all our luggage and deposited it in his own business premises, ready for despatch to Buenos Aires at the proper moment. As his family is at Santiago, he asked us to go there and visit them, and also the city itself, which is really beautiful and deserves a visit. Even the Ladies of the Sacred Heart extended a similar invitation. They wrote to their House there in order that a room might be prepared for us. Four days later we boarded the train, and passed along the charming coast, which resembles the western coast of Genoa. Then we passed through superb villages, and entered the mountainous region at the foot of the Cordigliera. After passing through the Great Plains, we reached Santiago. The journey lasted four days. We went to the Convent as if going to one of our own, and were received with great cordiality. The day afterward we visited His Grace, Archbishop Monsicasanova, who is held in great esteem by the whole Republic. He received us very kindly, and thought we had come to open a House, but when he heard I was on my way to Buenos Aires, he assumed an authoritative tone and said I had to rest a few months there after such a long voyage, and in the meantime visit the country and settle on a foundation, to which I should return as soon as possible. Though his words were very pleasant to listen to, they were really like so many thorn pricks to my heart, as I saw that I was losing time in traveling whilst I had so much to do, and the time seems to pass so quickly. But it is useless to worry about it, as the Company of the Cordigliera can afford us no means of passage owing to the mountain roads being closed to traffic by the snow, which is about three metros high, and the road will not be passable until November. We must have patience, for nothing happens by accident. Everything takes place according to the all-wise Time Table of Divine Providence. God has His designs, and wishes me, perhaps, to acquire a good knowledge of the Republic of Chili. In fact, both the Sisters and Mr. Severin are so good. Mrs. Severin takes us out for carriage drives almost every day, so we have an opportunity of getting to know the country well. Santiago is very nice and interesting. It has wonderful churches, beautiful buildings, stupendous squares and magnificent gardens, with enclosures for animals and fountains for fish, displaying every kind of plant representative of every climate and country.

The character of the Chileans is gay, open, strong and energetic. They love progress almost to excess. We showed them several of our prospectuses. Thus they became acquainted with the instruction given in our Schools and tried their best to make us stay, promising to fill our School with children. Amongst other great men of the Republic, one, who has a child four years old, said, "You must come back within two years' time, if not, during the war we have with the Argentines we'll take you prisoner, and then make you open a School for us here, as I want to send my little girl to you."

I spent twenty-five long days here, long, indeed, for me, as I did not want to lose time. Finally, they informed us that the roads were open and that the first caravan was about to start. Both the Sisters and other good friends tried to detain us, saying that the first journey over the Andes is often dangerous, and that if we were overtaken by bad weather, we should be in danger of losing our lives amidst the mountainous passes, But nothing could induce me to stop longer and continue that involuntary rest. I felt I was ready to face any difficulty.

We first visited a Chapel of St. Philomena, the Wonder-worker, so much venerated here. We received Holy Communion at her altar, begging her to unite with St. Rose in protecting us. We made our thanksgiving at the back of the church, near an altar on which is venerated a picture of the martyrdom of the Saint. Whilst I was absorbed in prayer to the Saint, who inspired me with great confidence, telling her all my needs and necessities, a very gentle voice whispered in my ear, "*Esta es una pequeña limosnita,*" "This is only a small offering." I was so absorbed in laying my petition before the Saint, that I thought the words I heard were an illusion of my imagination, and so I made no movement. Again the soft voice repeated the same words. Then I raised my head, and, looking around, I saw someone offering me pieces of gold. I turned and saw it was the holy man, Canon M. Marchian Pereira, Guardian of the Sanctuary, who very humbly kept on saying, "*Es pequeña, es pequeña mas es St. Filomena que la da,*" and then quickly withdrew. The gift was of the value of 100 *lire,* which the good man felt urged to give us without being asked, and I received it all the more gratefully, as obviously the good Saint had begun to help us even before we had finished our petitions to her.

Having finished our thanksgivings, we went to thank the good Canon, who said he was only too happy to help us, as we were Missionaries. He made us presents of books, pictures and the cords of the Saint, which are worn by her devout clients. Then he gave me an image of the Wonder-worker, asking me to keep it in my pocketbook. He himself placed it there, saying, "Keep it there, Mother, and you will never be in need of money for your Institute." I was very much impressed, as he seemed to be inspired. You may imagine that I shall treasure this picture as a precious relic.

On the 23rd of November, supplied with large baskets of pastry, fruit, wine, honey, etc., and accompanied by a number of ladies and Sisters, we took train for Los Andes, a town at the foot of the Cordigliera, where we were to pass the night, in order to be ready on the 24th, after having observed the Feast of the day, for the journey by caravan, which was to pick us up in a place further on.

As Los Andes we were received most kindly by the Sisters called Hospitaliers, to whom we had been recommended by the people of Santiago. They gave us the best room in their poor Convent. The next morning, other Sisters of the same Order, from another House in the neighborhood, came to bid us farewell and accompany us in the train as far as the Chileans have been able to go, up to the present, with their railways up these great mountains, which, the higher we go, the steeper and higher they seem to run.

At eleven a.m., after having heard Holy Mass and received Jesus in the Most Holy Sacrament of the Altar, Who, like a Valiant Giant, was going to conduct us over these great heights; after having had a good breakfast, which, owing to the keen air, seemed to be more appetizing than usual; favored with the blessing of the good parish priest of the town and accompanied by a larger company of the good Sisters Hospitaliers, who came in great numbers, we boarded the train along the river, which has its source in the Aconcagua. We passed through a chain of mountains in a pleasant and picturesque country, which, while presenting awe-inspiring scenes, greatly delighted the passengers. We crossed a small bridge, called the "Soldier's Jump," feared by everyone. It spans a chasm between two rocks of grey stone so narrow and deep that the bottom cannot be seen. One only hears the strange rumbling of the rushing waters in the fearful depths below. Certainly, if anyone had the misfortune to fall into this abyss, they would never again behold the light of day, nor would it be known what manner of death they had had. It did not make much of an impression on me, because I seemed to remember having seen many of such horrifying chasms. I, however, enjoyed the impression made on these good Sisters, and how enthusiastically they spoke of it as they drew near to and passed over it, and how they pitied us with regard to the rest of the journey that awaited us. Shortly after we had passed the "Soldier's Jump," the train stopped and we alighted to take our places in the coaches that were drawn up to convey the passengers. The good Sisters returned by train, after having helped us to make ourselves as comfortable as possible, while we with good mules—six to each coach, following always the course of the same river—penetrated into those vast gorges where only now and then a few pines of harsh color and dark green appeared.

The river was swollen, and in several places its foaming waters with their milky spray made a terrifying noise. Further on it looked as if we were going to be covered by the mountain, as a part of it appeared to fall over the river. At some points the heights were magnificent, whilst behind the mountain the river descended in the form of a precipitous cascade. Then suddenly it slackened its force and took the form of a small torrent, the waters of which seemed to play with the pebbles, and, amidst the enormous rocks, deposited in the bed of the river. Then it widened again to thousands of bends, which we had to follow with great exactitude, as the river was our only guide along the route. Finally, after a journey of five or more hours, we reached Juneal, which consists of a few houses amidst the mountain peaks. This was to be our grand lodging for the night.

Some arrived earlier, other later, than ourselves. We were about forty-five passengers, who, early the next morning, were to undertake, in a caravan with mules, the journey through the most difficult pass of the Cordigliera. As soon as the coaches arrived, the passengers rushed to go to bed for the night. We made our way also, but, as the others were quicker, they arrived first and consequently were served first. Not knowing what to do, we went to the one who was to drive the caravan the next day, and, as he inspired us with very little confidence, we were very cautious in our dealings with him. At first he was somewhat rude, but finally, at our repeated requests, he softened towards us. He told us that on the other side of the mountain, where he pointed with his finger, there were first-class apartments, better than these, where he and his wife were going to put up, and that if we went there after supper we would find everything all right.

Shortly afterward an old man, of pleasant aspect, resembling somewhat St. Joseph, said to me, "I am one of the muleteers appointed to act as guide to one of you tomorrow, and as I am going to sleep on the other side of the mountain, you need have no fear." His kind way and serious character inspired us with confidence, and so we went to table with more courage, and ate of the coarse and badly cooked food and hard black bread as if it were the most dainty food, for the air of the village sharpened our appetites in a most extraordinary manner.

At table all spoke of the morrow's crossing; some of its great dangers, others of their fear of the mists which are fatal to those who are crossing the Pass. Stories were also told of the frost that in some of the passes freezes the limbs, and of the atmosphere which hurts the eyes and causes the skin to bleed.

A delightful description, indeed! Still, with all this discouragement, I felt safe and happy, for I knew if Our Lord had so far helped and blessed us, He would do so to the end. I also took comfort in the hope of meeting with something new which I could tell you, since, to myself, after four long voyages, everything appeared quite familiar. I felt sorry for Mother Chiara, who heard all this, and who, I thought, might have changed her mind after her departure from Valparaiso. But when I asked her which way she preferred to travel, by land or sea, over the Andes or through the Straits of Magellan, she answered, "A thousand times over the Andes rather than by sea again." So I said to myself. "All is well."

When the meal was over, we took a little air in the bright moonlight, which shone very brilliantly. The mountains appeared to touch the sky and seemed covered with a beautiful blue mantle, and raised us to a state of sublime ecstasy. The earth had the color of the sky, while the passes of the mountains wore a blue of a darker shade, and gave one the idea of great clouds saluting their smiling queen. And really, that night the moon in all its splendor seemed to represent to us the beauty of our Queen, our Mother Mary, *"pulchra ut Luna,"* who had come to console us with her maternal look. Those who work in the Lord's Vineyard from morning till night are well rewarded if at the close of the day they receive a loving look from her who, after God, forms the happiness of the Blessed in Heaven.

We wanted to prepare the points for our meditation, but nature had already prepared them for us. Looking at the moon and sky, which seemed turned towards us, I thought I heard the sweet voice of Mary, with that of the most melodious voice of our dear Jesus, transporting us into an ecstasy of love. Methinks I saw the purity and holiness of Mary and the complacency of God in her. What a great sweetness, what a great joy in contemplating Jesus! But the night was advancing, and we had to go to rest, though it did not seem we should need sleep in this fine air. We abandoned ourselves to the care of our Heavenly Mother, and to her messengers who are the Angels particularly destined for pilgrims. Happy and tranquil, we turned towards the shelter on the other side of the mountains.

Reaching a certain point, we lost our breath. A sort of weight oppressed us, and we could not understand what it was. Then we saw the old shepherd who resembled St. Joseph, running towards us to tell us to hasten, as we had reached the "puna," a Spanish word meaning shortness of breath caused by the unstable temperature. We hastened our steps, and soon reached the spot where the air was pure and bracing. It was, indeed, a strange phenomenon, this shortness of breath in these mountains, and, if we had stopped longer, we might have died of suffocation. But the silver moon still shone in its silent language telling us that Mary, the Mother of God, still watched and protected us with incomparable tenderness.

Having reached the inn, we found, what we had never expected to find amidst these rough mountains, a beautiful spring bed with good bedding, which the old man pointed out to us with much satisfaction and pleasure, He told us there was a key, and we could close ourselves in by barring the door. He told us also not to fear, for he would be in the stable next to the mules' stables if we needed anything–an admirable instance of God's Providence, and we reposed quite tranquilly. But the night passed in a moment, and at half-past three the noise of the shepherds preparing the mules and packing the luggage awoke us suddenly. We felt more tired than the night before, as we had had very rough treatment during our five-hour coach drive. We mustered up courage, however, arose at four a.m., and dressed ourselves in long brown cloaks trimmed and lined with a kind of cheap fur, which were given to us by some ladies of Chili. We looked like two monks, but we began to feel the cold, and these cloaks were of great service to us.

We descended to the first inn, where all were breakfasting, and we took our milk and coffee and hard bread as fast as we could, as everything was ready for the journey. We went out into the open and saw two beautiful mules, with new equipment and two comfortable saddles. We thought they were for an opera singer and her companion who formed part of the company–but this time we were mistaken, for the nicest mules were for us, orders having been given that they should be assigned to us by the Superintendent of the Transandine Company. However, thankful we were for the favor, we were not so willing to accept it, because it meant that we were to be the first to mount the mules, and, not being experienced, we preferred to see the others do so first in order to learn the art; but we had to give in. The St. Joseph of the previous evening came forward and stood with crossed hands so that I could mount the mule. As I refused, the whole company stood around to see what was going to happen next. The poor shepherd, so good and patient, went into the house and brought me a chair, which I accepted willingly. I then mounted, placing myself in the saddle and putting my feet in the stirrup, while taking the reins, I drew the mule round whilst the muleteer mounted his mule, and, moving forward, made way for me. Mother Chiara followed my example, accompanied by another muleteer, who, though he might not have resembled my St. Joseph, was very good also. All the others mounted their mules with much less trouble and followed us in procession.

The mountain was steep, but the pass for more than an hour was lovely and smooth. It was almost a pleasure to see the long procession that appeared to be climbing with a certain devotion, as the caravan looked like a devout band of pilgrims so it seemed to me. Taking my beads in my hand, I was about to invite all to recite the Rosary in honor of the Queen of Heaven who had so blessed the day, and all certainly would have willingly replied to my invitation, as they seemed quite pleased to have in their company two Religious who appeared to them, owing to their goodness and faith, to be a guarantee for a prosperous journey across the Cordigliera. My project of the Rosary vanished very soon, for the beaten path had disappeared and we were obliged to make our way through the heavy snow. Two muleteers proceeded in advance, and having found it passable, shouted for us to follow their track. When we had got over one difficulty, another appeared. Afterward, we found ourselves on the brink of precipices many kilometers deep. Then I tried to keep my mule away from the edge, but the poor thing, knowing that it had an unpractical traveler in its saddle, always kept going straight, no matter how much I pulled it from one side to the other, and thus it would not obey me. When it approached too near the edge of a precipice, I shouted and spoke to it in Spanish, but to no purpose. The only thing that seemed to hurt it was when I attempted to alight.

These terrible precipices almost turned Mother Chiara's head, and, no matter how often I told her to sit straight, she lay like a sack of flour on the mule's back, her head resting on the poor animal's neck. Fortunately, the muleteers were more than good, and as in such difficulties one has enough to do to attend to oneself, I felt sure they would not fail Sister.

Gradually we ascended higher and higher, when from afar we heard the shout for all to alight. Something's the matter. A great chasm caused by the melting snow was an obstacle to further progress, unless we proceeded with great precaution. There was a general alarm; the men grumbled about the imprudence of conducting the caravan by this route, and the women cried quite hopelessly. Mother Chiara remained in deep silence. She lost her speech. Certainly she now repented of having chosen the Cordigliera instead of the Magellan for our journey. Her only consolation was that when she raised her head I looked quiet and happy as one enjoying a magnificent spectacle. It was truly grand in all its horror. We were at a height where one perceived an immense abyss on one side, whilst on the other there was a vast expanse of pure white snow, while further ahead there were heights awaiting us. But just in front of us was that large crevice, long and deep, which seemed ready to swallow us up and bury us. The muleteers, though not without fear, tried to make some of the mules jump the crevice, and seeing that it could be done, encouraged the passengers to do the same. I, as you have heard, was at the head of the line, and I was willing to be the first to go forward in order to encourage the others, for, to speak truthfully, I was not a bit afraid, feeling quite calm. My guide had his staff ready, as he thought he would have to carry me across, but I told him I could take longer jumps than the one across the crevice. He very respectfully showed me the danger, and then watched me attentively, knowing I would not fail to tell him or call him if I needed help. I jumped, or at least attempted to, but, probably owing to the cold and the keen air which deprived me of strength, I realized too late that I was like a feather, which, however much it is thrown forward, does not move unless carried by the wind, and so I should have buried myself alive had it not been for the muleteer, who, seeing the danger, dismounted and, stretching his feet across the crevice, held me back on one side of the chasm until he, with the help of his comrade, sprang across to the other side, where he drew me by the arm after him into safety. The shock produced such palpitation of the heart that I thought I should have died. The good muleteer took me aside, and I fell fainting in the snow. I couldn't speak a word, and it was obvious from the frightened looks of the good man that he expected a tragedy. But this was not God's Will. As soon as I was able to speak, I told him to go and help the others; and I hadn't to tell him twice, as the need was urgent. I remained alone, stretched on that white bed of snow, and little by little, helped by the pure air, the palpitation ceased, and I was as lively as ever. I arose to find that all had crossed the dangerous pass and that the muleteer was waiting for me to mount my mule again.

We resumed our journey, and arrived at a higher point where we had to go through snow five meters high, which had been cut through by the Transandine Company for the caravan. It was a grand sight in passing through the fortress of snow, but not quite so pleasant to myself, as I was afraid of not being able to bear the cold. They told me to keep on my eyeglasses, so that the cold and great whiteness of the snow should not injure my sight, but I preferred to see where my mule went, not trusting to my eyeglasses, which I did not find very helpful. Pulling the elastic, I put them sometimes on my forehead, sometimes on my chin, but not in front of my eyes, except when I was obliged to look closely. In God's good time we reached the "Cumbre," which is the topmost height which can be crossed in the neighborhood of Aconcagua, and here we remained some time.

What a majestic sight, what a charming view! We seemed to see the whole world at a glance. There we saw the boundary line between Chili and Argentine. We had said goodbye to that dear country in which we had lodged or sojourned for a month, and which, unknown as we were, had proffered us every care and attention. We wanted to enjoy the sea view, but the fog was descending, and so we were deprived of that enchanting sight. The muleteer made signs to me to mount the mule at once, but I begged him to let me enjoy this sublime and inspired moment of meditation. A little perturbed, he turned and begged me to get into the saddle. The poor man had every reason, for it was past eleven, and within half-an-hour's time the atmosphere of the mountains would have proved fatal to us.

Just about the same time, from the other side of the top of the mountain, one of those good employees of the Transandine Company arrived upon the scene, and, after saluting us courteously, told us that he had orders from Santiago to come and meet us, and, if possible, to make our journey a little easier. He then took my reins and conducted my mule down the steep mountain by the shortest paths. The descent was steep and stony. I thought I should fall every moment. The mule would slip now and again, but this good man encouraged me, and told me we had to keep to this path in order to get as soon as possible to a comfortable hotel. We reached there at midday, whilst the snow fell heavily and the mountain had entirely disappeared in a thick fog.

The landlady of the hotel received us with a motherly heart and placed us at table, where lunch was already prepared and which we enjoyed, as it warmed us after the cold we had experienced. When lunch was over, they called the heads of the different families one after another to write their impressions in a large register kept for that purpose. Our companions on the journey had been very much upset when they had to cross the crevice, so you may imagine what they wrote. I, however, wrote one of my most beautiful impressions of that passage. The hotel-keeper and all were surprised to see what I wrote, and said I was the first person, especially at this dangerous time of the year, who spoke well of this crossing, and more so because the writer was not a man.

The fact is, that I was very pleased and happy to have ascended such a high mountain, and, therefore, incidentally have an inducement to excite or incite myself to ascend the heights of holy perfection, a mountain much higher than that of the Cordigliera.

The Celestial Divine Spouse calls His beloved with the sweet name of Columba, "*Una est Columba mea–dilecta mea.*" He calls her Columba, not only because she should be gentle, meek and mild, but because she has to fly the heights of the Lord, without tiring, rising continually towards Heaven with perfect detachment from earth, raising herself on silvery white wings by the purity of her affections and intentions.

About two p.m. the coaches were ready to convey us to the station, "Punta de Vaca." We set out up the slopes and down the valleys. We traveled along the Mendoza River, by way of a path rough and dangerous, owing to the rocks that seemed to crush us at every instant, and owing also to the breaks of the great river, which looked rather dangerous.

At seven p.m. we arrived at the Punta de Vaca, where we expected to repose quietly, after the shaking we had had on the mule and in the coaches, but, an hour before we arrived, the caravan from the Argentine, which the next day was to cross the Andes, had reached Punta de Vaca and had taken possession of all the accommodation. What were we to do? The bell rang to go to supper, and we took our places at table with our luggage beside us on the floor, not knowing where to place it in safety. When the frugal meal was over, I asked the inn-keeper to give us a place to rest if possible. He very courteously said he had not received any orders regarding us, but that we were not to be alarmed, because he would very soon be able to provide us with beds. In the meantime, night was advancing, and the only room in the inn was full of men drinking. At nine p.m. I again begged the inn-keeper to give us a room, and he said he would do so immediately. Half an hour later he told me all the beds were taken except one in the hall, which of course I did not accept. So I turned and sat down at the table in the corner of the room with Mother Chiara.

It was now ten p.m., and the men went on drinking, the alcohol was producing its effects, and we heard a lot of movement, shouting and singing. I then began to feel uneasy, but, looking around, I saw an American gentleman from San Francisco who had crossed the Andes with us and, like us, had been unable to get a bed. I prayed him to remain near us, as I feared those men. He was the only one amongst that excited crowd who inspired me with any confidence. He felt so sorry for us that he induced the inn-keeper to give us a room in which there were two good ladies and a boy, but the boy retired to make room for us. We called down hearty blessings on that good man, and fell upon our beds exhausted and motionless till the morning. At seven a.m. we were at the station and took train. Still traveling along the Mendoza River, we crossed new mountains and valleys, and in the afternoon reached Mendoza, the first and nicest city on the way from Chili.

We were received by the Good Shepherd Sisters, and it was a great relief for us to find a safe religious home after such a journey and nights of fear and danger. We visited the lovely churches of this city and then went to the Jesuits, who encouraged us greatly in our mission to Buenos Aires by the news they gave us. They told us we should have enough work to do there. We visited the Franciscans, who blessed us as Sisters of the Third Order of St. Francis. Our next visit was to the Slaves of the Sacred Heart of Jesus, a newly-founded Institute in Cordova. The Sisters received us with great kindness, and they would have kept us for a few days had we not already arranged our journey with the Argentine railway company. We were to leave the next night, when we would be crossing the Pampas at great speed for two days, and with very few stops.

The Pampas is beautiful! It is an immense plain, where only now and then one sees a peasant's hut, lost, as it were, in the immensity of the expanse. We saw horses and mules in great numbers, flocks of sheep and goats at pasture in all directions, without a guide, in that never-ending country, the boundaries of which the owner knows nothing about nor cares to know. Now and then we could see skeletons of animals and carcasses not buried, left there, abandoned. But the train flew on without minding anything in the midst of the long thick grass of the virgin prairies, and on December 1st we arrived at the capital of the Argentine. Now I must stop, with the promise to write as soon as I have finished my work on this foundation, when I shall return to you and then go elsewhere, as obedience ordains.

Let us live in the meanwhile abandoned to the Will of God. I shall work in His vineyard, you helping me with your prayers, in which I so much confide. Prayer, confidence and total abandonment in God will always be our sure arms! We are good for nothing, but in God we can do all things. *"Omnia possum in Eo qui me confortat."*

May God bless you and close you in His Adorable Heart, wherein resides the throne of peace, an anticipated Heaven. Love Jesus much, and think of nothing else. Work with great zeal for the glory of God, under the banner of holy Obedience. Do not seek rest on this earth, but be ready to die on the battlefield in company with Jesus, with the assurance that the more you fight the greater will be your crown, a crown that in Eternity no one can usurp.

Such is the wish of

Yours affectionately, in The Sacred Heart of Jesus,

Mother Frances Saveria Cabrini

Buenos Aires,
August 8th, 1896

My dear Daughters,

Jesus be with you, and may His most sweet peace draw you to His Adorable Heart, and retain you there by the superabundance of His Divine Love.

How lovely it is to journey under the mantle of Mary Immaculate, who is attired in blue and white, and who sheds about her rich silver rays!

It was an hour after midday on the 8th of August, when, after eight months spent in founding the Academy of Saint Rose, blessed so much by the Sacred Heart, I began my return journey to you, after two years absence from our dear and beloved Mother House, the center of our most sublime aspirations, where we imbibed the essence of the most beautiful virtues, which should enable us to be an example to the world, and so be able to convert it. "You are the light of the world, the salt of the earth," Jesus said, when from the mountain He spoke to His Apostles. And you, Missionaries of the Sacred Heart, belong in a certain measure to the Apostolic family. Have you not to continue the Apostolate of the great Mission of Christ? To you also is entrusted the Mission of being the salt of the earth and the light of the world. How can we accomplish such a difficult and sublime task? It is very easy when you have the heavenly protection of the Virgin of the Argentine, so revered by the people of Buenos Aires. She is dressed in blue and white, with rose-colored lips, and carries an angelic smile, that diffuses silver rays which convince and inspire confidence and illuminate without injuring the eyes, despite their brilliancy. She is as white as the snow in her immaculate purity; she is heavenly in her grace and demeanor, all celestial in her majesty as Queen of Heaven, in her nobleness of mind and in the magnanimity of her thoughts. She is silver by reason of the rays of light which emanate from the heroic virtues she practiced, which form a halo around her head and render her face shining and majestic. The Areopagite spoke well, when, after the Ascension of Our Lord, he pictured Our Lady as a Missionary encouraging and consoling the devout faithful: "If I had not known there was only one true Lord and God, I should have prostrated and adored Holy Mary as a Divinity. And the help needed to imitate our Holy Mother Mary is to be found in herself, if with great faith we place ourselves under her mantle of protection. If you find Mary, you find all. *"Inventa Maria inveniuntur omnia bona, ipsa enim diligit diligentes se, imo sibi servientibus servit."*

If we venerate so many Saints, and witness so many miraculous wonders in souls, all these graces come from that immense source of blessings which is Jesus Himself, and through that inexhaustible channel of grace which is Mary. Have faith in Mary, endeavor with great earnestness to imitate her virtues, because, at every moment, this Mother of divine love responds with the words the Church puts into her mouth: "I give fruit of a pleasing odor, my flowers are the fruits of glory and sanctity."

Mind! These words are not intended for you by way of a reproach because of the sterility of your works. You, who by celestial grace, have been transplanted in the fertile field of the Church, and in that glorious garden of the religious life, what fruits have you realized? Perhaps leaves only, or some faded flowers, which die on the bushes the very day they opened their petals? No, daughters, henceforth let there be seen in you true devotion to Our Lady, our Mother and Foundress. That devotion consists in the imitation of her great virtues. But let us return to our journey.

I carry in my mind imperishable memories of Buenos Aires. Having arrived on the 10th of December, after having crossed the Pampas from Mendoza to the River de la Plata, I did not know where to go, not knowing anyone except Reverend Father Brogi, with whom I had become acquainted two years previously when he passed through Genoa, having been sent by Reverend Father Rinaldi to say Mass at our Convent, the latter having acted as Chaplain to us at the beginning of our foundation in Genoa. I took a carriage and, with Mother Chiara, went in search of Father Brogi, whom we found after a two hours' journey. He received us with every mark of kindness, and, after having given us an excellent dinner *a l'Italienne,* accompanied us to the Archbishop, Monsignor Ladislao Castellano, who received us like a father, and was pleased to begin his episcopate with a foundation of the Missionaries of the Sacred Heart in his new and extensive diocese. The Vicar General, Monsignor Espinosa, was present, and encouraged me by giving me several visiting cards to present to the principal families of the town. I asked him to write something in the form of an introduction, but he said, good-heartedly, I could write what I liked. Father Brogi then presented me to the Secretary General of the Curia, Monsignor Terrero, a very popular and estimable person in Buenos Aires. He, also, encouraged us, and later acted as our Chaplain. In so doing he came to our aid in a great difficulty, as in these parts there is a scarcity of priests.

There was a great stir in the Episcopal Palace owing to the forth-coming pilgrimage to the grand Sanctuary of Our Lady of Lujan, in honor of the installation of the new Archbishop by the Archbishop of Chili, who had come over purposely, and also in celebration of peace between the two countries, which had been fighting over the boundaries of the two countries, Chili and Argentine.

Amongst the many persons, priests, etc., at the Episcopal Palace, who encouraged and consoled me, the Reverend Father Kierman must be mentioned. He was impressed by the great name of Missionaries of the Sacred Heart which we bear, and was full of compassion at seeing me so forlorn and suffering, as he said. So he decided, on the spot, to do all in his power to help me to make a good foundation. He helped me to make the acquaintance of all at the Palace, and when he perceived I was a little troubled and timid, he encouraged me by saying, "Courage, Mother, we will help you." And he kept his word and helped us in every way and in every difficulty, and never left us until he saw the foundation progressing and on a secure footing. Father Kierman is a beautiful soul, and to great knowledge he adds an admirable simplicity. He seems to have adapted to himself Our Lord's own words, "Be as simple as the dove and as wise as the serpent." How beautiful it is to see souls who, like doves, fly over the earth, shedding over it their benign influence without being caught in the snares of the world. They fly, as it were, with always fresh zest, anxious to do good even when physical strength is wanting. They fly without tiring, or, rather, without being conscious of fatigue, until their works are surrounded by a halo of light, while their beneficent influence is always of great good because they are blessed by God. Having finished business at the Curia, Reverend Father Brogi took me to a very good Italian family, at whose house I passed the night, and the next day we took up residence at the Convent of the Sisters of Mercy, Savonese, which had been established in the Argentine twenty years previously. Father Brogi, in his great charity and nobility of heart, gave me all the necessary help to commence the foundation, and came every day to present me to the principal families, and to assist me in getting to know all the parishes of Buenos Aires. This going about was a great help to me, because it enabled me to find out which were the best localities for a new foundation.

After having gained some knowledge of the city, and after visiting about sixty houses, I decided to take one in the central part of the town, and, as it pleased the Most Sacred Heart of Jesus, I found a very nice house, spacious and well lighted. It was even better than it seemed to be. Strange to say, many of the ladies had tried to dissuade me from taking it, as it was rather dear, saying that for the first two years we should have only six or seven pupils—not more until the people began to have confidence in us—but I felt a secret inspiration which I could not account for, and so I decided to take the house at any price. The courage thus shown in undertaking a difficult enterprise made a good impression on the people, so much so, that the principal families brought us their children, and this went on so well, that, when we left, the Academy was already full and I had to arrange for a second and larger house. When everything had been arranged with the landlord, I thought of going into the house at once, and arranged to open it on a day that would make the opening memorable, viz., Christmas Day. The good Sisters of Mercy did everything they could to prevent my leaving them on such a solemn day, but I was determined to go, and so, at ten a.m., December 25th, Mother Chiara and I went to our new home. Thus the real Founder of the first House of our Institute in the Argentine was the Infant Jesus, in Whom I placed all my confidence and to Whom I fully abandoned myself, hoping that He would overcome all my difficulties, in His tender mercy and immense goodness of Heart. And the Holy Child knew well how to do it, and wonderfully so. On the eve of the opening of the House, I sent two telegrams, one to Codogno and the other to New York, calling several Sisters who were ready and anxious to assist in the work of the new foundation. They set out at once, and within a month the Sisters had arrived from New York, while a little later the other Sisters reached us from Italy. Mother Chiara and I awaited them with the greatest anxiety, for, being only two in number, we could not keep the House going by ourselves, as the requirements of the House increased every day owing to the clients whom the Dear Founder had won for this new foundation.

On March 1st the College was opened, and since then the number of pupils has so exceeded all expectations that I had to send another telegram calling for more Sisters, as enthusiastic as the others, and in a short time they were with us. Early in May our children, so intelligent, were ready to appear before the public. So we decided to have a solemn inauguration of the College. According to the custom of the country, a committee of eight ladies had to be chosen as promoters. They are members of the principal families, and chosen amongst the best. The first one selected becomes the Godmother of the School. On this occasion it was Mrs. Uriburo, the wife of the President of the Republic.

Mr. Buoje, Mayor of Buenos Aires, sent the gardeners of the public gardens to adorn the House with flowers and boughs. The Superintendent of the Catholic Club sent men to adorn the chapel and parlous with curtains, carpets and fringes, etc. At eight a.m. the next day, the chapel and parlors were full of people awaiting the arrival of the Archbishop, Monsignor L. Castellano, who celebrated Holy Mass, the solemnity of the occasion being enhanced by the devotional strains of an orchestra. As soon as the Mass was over, Monsignor Espinosa delivered the opening allocution, in which he spoke of our Institute as if he had always known it. Such is his goodheartedness. After lunch, the

Archbishop returned with many other priests and members of the principal families. The formal opening was made conspicuous by the presence of the Archbishop, Mrs. Uriburo (the President's wife) and representatives of the several school authorities. The children gave an entertainment partly musical and partly recitative, the event ending in a great chorus and a tableau, in which the Sacred Heart was represented blessing the New Foundation, and placing a new diamond in Saint Rose's crown typical of the new School. The whole function was so pleasing to everybody that a photograph had to be taken. It makes an excellent picture, and I shall bring the photograph to the Mother House. In Buenos Aires this photograph carries the imprint, "The Paradise."

Before beginning the ceremony in the morning, the Archbishop blessed the Altar, which is very artistic and made in the form of a temple. It was presented to us by the Rector of Saint Michael's, Father John Deleye, a very pious and generous priest, who does much good, and who himself possesses and loves solid virtue. He is just one of those souls who lives to do good, and who helps to constitute the real happiness of a country. He saw us at the very commencement, when I was alone with Mother Chiara, and when the House was like a great vase without a single ornament. He immediately sent us two candlesticks and a beautiful lamp for the statue of the Sacred Heart, which Maria Brandon, a very good lady, had given us. She helped us a great deal in the beginning, and accompanied us in all our visits to the people of the town. The statue of the Sacred Heart was the first to arrive in the House, and I thought I should have gone into ecstasy the first night I was able to recollect myself before that beautiful image, that seemed to speak and say to me, "My dear daughter, be quiet, live trustingly, put no limit to your faith; I shall see to this House through the intercession of my beloved Rosa." How good, dear, and amiable is the Sacred Heart! One glance alone, one word only, falls deeply into the heart, revives and reassures.

We named the College after Saint Rose, according to the promise I made when I had the pleasure of visiting the relics of the Saint in Lima. The Saint kept her word. She blessed our voyage, our arrival in Buenos Aires, and the foundation, and she still continues to bless the School, for which reason I leave it without any anxiety. Everyone is pleased at the name of Saint Rose being given to the School, as she is Patron of the Republics of South America. I should love very much to be able to perpetuate this lovely title, or the new foundation itself, by building a beautiful sanctuary in her honor. I would do it at once if I were able to find a soul so good and generous as to give me the means with which to do it. Not knowing where such a kind person is to be found, I shall engage the Wonder-worker herself to find a benefactor and bring him or her to me.

Whilst I have been telling you about the new foundation, we have already done a good part of our journey. We have reached Montevideo, where the steamer stopped, and I, with my little angel companion, got into the Captain's tender to go ashore under the guidance of a kind gentleman to whom the Captain had recommended us, and who took care of us and showed us the way to the Cathedral. In a very short time we found God's House, where we were able to receive Holy Communion, which will satisfy us on our voyage at least as far as Las Palmas in the Canary Islands, where we hope again to receive the Living God of the Altar, Jesus Christ, our Love, so that He may fortify and comfort us for the rest of our voyage.

At Montevideo we were also able to hear Mass, and thus comply with the Sunday precept. We assisted also at the Pontifical Mass which was celebrated to implore the glorification of the Venerable Gianelli, Founder of the Sisters "dell 'Orto," and Bishop of Bobbio. We then visited the city for a little while, which is well worth seeing. There are beautiful roads, spacious squares, sumptuous monuments and splendid gardens. All its features gain much from the fact that the city is built on a hill almost surrounded by the sea on either side. It presents an enchanting view, combined with excellent climate.

It is a rather large place, but not too thickly populated. The commerce is not great, as the city is near Buenos Aires, which monopolizes everything on account of the immense progress made there every day.

Montevideo is lovely, and we like it because it is laid out in European style; but Buenos Aires is beautiful and large, and if, today, it is not in accord with our taste, the reason is only because in its vastness it is a mixture of good and bad. For instance, you may walk about ten "*cuadre*," which would be about a kilometer, and you imagine you see before you the beautiful palaces of Paris, when immediately following, for about twenty blocks, or two kilometers, you see nothing but small dwellings of one story high, so small that they seem buried in the earth. After another long journey, one finds beautiful, sumptuous palaces, the Recoleta and, more especially, the Street Alvear, which are really charming. Your wonder increases when you visit the Palermo Walk and public gardens that can rank with the best of their kind in Europe for their extraordinary pitch of cultivation and magnificent conservatories, as well as for the cultivation of the trees and the zoological enclosures. The city of Buenos Aires is only ten years old, but if it advances at the present rate for another ten or twenty years, it will rival New York, provided that civil disturbances do not arise and ruin it. Of this, unfortunately, there is always danger, as the inhabitants are good but of a turbulent disposition. Recently there was danger of war with Chili over the boundary question. Buenos Aires clings to her rights, but Chili desires to appropriate a little more territory, because her boundaries are so narrow. Lately they agreed, the Argentines having ceded a part of their land near Tierra del Fuego. The two Archbishops contributed greatly by their influence and kindly offices in obtaining this concession, viz., His Grace, Monsignor Casanova of Chili, and the new Archbishop of Buenos Aires. On my arrival at Buenos Aires, both Prelates made a pilgrimage to the Sanctuary of the Blessed Virgin of Lujan, in company with General Rocca, President of the Interior, who was acting for President Uriburo, who, owing to illness, was absent. There were present several high officials and an immense population. The eloquent Monsignor Hara, Vicar Apostolic of Valparaiso, gave a magnificent address, in the course of which he was continually applauded by the two representatives of the Republic and all the people present. Finally, after having spoken of the privileges of the Blessed Virgin, and of the great miracles worked at Lujan, and after having said that Chili could give nothing worthy of the Blessed Virgin, as she was already covered with gold from head to foot, he thought the best gift they could leave in the Sanctuary would be the Flag of Chili, which would remain as a sign of peaceful accord with their sister Republic. This was answered by a frenzied cheer from the immense crowd. It made a peculiar impression upon us to see this renowned Sanctuary reduced, as it were, to a theatre. But I quickly countenanced this kind of irreverence, as it seemed to me, in God's Church, when I remembered that these countries had only recently been civilized through our Holy Religion, and that the faith of the people, at least, was good, for it leads the rulers to decide the destinies of the people in God's own Sanctuary and to invoke the blessing of God and Our Lady. Mother Chiara and I also went to the pilgrimage, for as soon as we arrived at the Curia, the priests, who surrounded us with every attention, gave us first class tickets so that we might take part in their great festival. I accepted the tickets with great pleasure, and as the nation prayed for peace, I, too, raised my voice in union with theirs. I considered the country as my own from the first moment of my entry into it. But, in the midst of this country's great exaltation, I collected my thoughts and prayed Our Lady to bless our new foundation, promising if she did so and all went well, that I would return to thank her before leaving Buenos Aires. Everything succeeded beyond all expectation. So, a week before I left, I returned with comfort and consolation to this Sanctuary, for whilst I confided to the Holy Mother of God the care of the House, I felt that this powerful and miraculous Mother had assured me of her continual protection. Of her love and her protection I had another proof, as did also the Sisters who accompanied me to offer their vows and thanksgivings to this Mother of Grace.

We had no sooner left Buenos Aires, than a shaft of most luminous rays, the brightness of which outshone those of the sun, shot forth from the heavens and descended and encompassed us during the rest of the journey until we reached the Sanctuary, where the wonderful Virgin of Lujan dispenses her ineffable treasures of grace and blessings. This was a sign from Our Lady to show us how visibly we enjoy Her special protection.

Oh, how good and amiable is Mary! She is a propitious Morning Star; she is the inspiring guide of all our enterprises, and for this reason the Missionary Sisters of the Sacred Heart should fear nothing. Our great Mother and Foundress is near God, even united with God. Hence, she can do all, wish all, obtain all from God. Oh, the greatness of Mary! She has been constituted the fount of all graces, the sure channel of Divine mercy, the ladder to Heaven, the gate of Paradise. Mary, O children, is that mystical holy mountain, that mountain adorned by the Holy Ghost, that mountain from the summit of which springs; the source of the clearest water, dividing itself into infinite streams which water the whole world. Therefore, our Houses, our works, are absolutely secure in the hands of Mary, as long as we show her faith, invoke her and imitate her virtues, as true Missionaries should do. If you desire to convert the whole world, invoke Mary, for she is that bright cloud, as seen by the prophet Elias, rising from the sea, gradually spreading over the whole heavens, and then breaking into rainfalls on every part of the earth, so that it covers even the remotest inhabitants of the globe. Yes, you can do everything with Mary. She extirpates heresy, eradicates schisms and destroys idols. She causes our Holy Faith to triumph everywhere, and increases and spreads the Fold of Christ which her mystic waters irrigate and fructify. Confide everything to her, then; do everything under her auspices, and do not leave her for one moment. Invoke her always, and she will cleanse your hearts and make them worthy of your high vocation.

In the meantime our journey continues pleasant. It's wonderful; we hardly notice the movement of the boat, the sea being so placid and tranquil. I cannot write much, as the passengers are so good and don't leave us for a moment. Sometimes, with the little angel, the postulant who accompanies me, I am able to withdraw to some quiet corner to pray, but we never have time to finish the Rosary before we have a crowd around us. We cannot find a place in which to hide ourselves. You will have patience with me, then, if you find this epistle is short. I have become a Professor of Modern Languages, for I am giving a lesson a day to the President's sister-in-law, Mrs. Tezanos Pinto de Craseres, who is anxious to speak Italian well by the time she reaches Italy, and especially Rome, where her husband is engaged at the Peru Legation.

At table near the Captain sits a great literary man, a Neapolitan, and the conversation naturally falls on History, Literature and Science, etc. When the Neapolitan goes beyond the line, I keep silent for a moment, and then, with kindness and firmness, I affirm the truth. Slowly, without his noticing it, I induce him to approve what is right according to the standard of truth, justice and the Will of God, and to acknowledge that real happiness is to be found in good alone, according to the dictates of our Holy Religion. One day he asserted that, in order to become converted to better things, he would have to suffocate and extinguish the whole ardor of his soul and the vehemence of his human passions, and so would have to reduce himself to the condition of a mountain of ice, indifferent to all things, even the most beautiful and great. I pointed out to him that the flames of human passions, which always leave a void and a sense of dissolution, become changed into celestial flames through grace, and that the supernatural light of Heaven, once let into the soul, grows so wonderfully that the human passions become a volcano of Divine Love, a real fire that nobody can extinguish as long as goodwill remains in the soul.

Have we not had the brightest examples in this direction? An Augustine, a Magdalen. Did they become mountains of ice after their conversion? Quite the contrary. We should never have had these prodigies of conversion and marvelous holiness, if they had not changed the flames of human passion into volcanoes of immense love of God. But the present generation is too miserable and unfortunate! It studies, studies everything but religion, and, meanwhile, runs with the velocity of a train towards a ruinous precipice. Oh, dear Jesus, what terrible ruin! But in Thy mercy turn not Thy face away from us. Arise, great Giant of Love, arise, O my Beloved! Come into the field of the Missions of Thy beloved Spouses, who desire to bring into Thy Kingdom every human soul. Come! We wait, desire and sigh for Thee. Come, refulgent Sun, with Thy bright and vivid rays, that they may brighten the earth enveloped in dense darkness! O Jesus, the Desired of Ages, Love all on fire for Thy children, hasten and give life to those who are sitting in the darkness of death! Through Thy Most Holy Heart, heal the gaping, bleeding wounds of sick humanity! We, Thy Missionaries, turn our eyes and our hearts always towards Thy Divine Heart, and, if Thou wiliest, all those confided to our care will be saved. Yes, if Thou wish it, it can be done, for Thy very Name indicates salvation, grace, unction and love. The more I invoke Thy sweet name, the more I find it dear, sweet and amiable. Thou art my life, my all, console then her who loves Thee, console Thy poor servant and save, yes, save this sick generation, which you have trusted to us. Look upon those souls whom Thou hast redeemed with Thy Precious Blood. Look upon them with love and mercy. Wound them with the darts of Thy burning charity, warm and transform all, in Thee.

Having passed the equatorial line, we reached Pinedo de San Pedro, which is a rock of considerable size, after a four hour journey. It presents a very pretty spectacle with its slender points. Seen at sunset, it looks like a pretty sailing city, and my companion asked me if there was any likelihood of our going there some day to establish a Mission. I asked her if she wanted to convert the birds, which are the only created things that find an asylum there, but she thought that if ever we went there we should find someone to convert. Well, of course, she wants to convert the whole world, and, in the fervor of her desire, appears to have the faith of Abraham, who merited to see his spiritual children multiply like the sands of the sea.

Between one thing and another, we have reached the Canary Islands, stopping at Las Palmas. There is a beautiful gulf, and the city presents an enchanting sight. We arrived at six a.m. on the 23rd, and, as it was Sunday, we arose at once so as to be able to go ashore for Holy Mass and to have the happiness of receiving Holy Communion. In fact, the medical inspection on this occasion did not detain us long, and Captain Bocacelli, who does everything he can for us, gave us sufficient time to satisfy our desires. At six-thirty we were descending the gangway, and we took the first boat that came. The four priests who were on board, seeing us so early astir, took courage and came along in our boat. In about ten minutes we reached the shore, and took one of the primitive carriages with a small lean horse, so lean that my companion asked if it was a donkey, and expressed the fear that it would not be able to carry all six of us, especially as the weight of one of the Franciscan Fathers was equal to that of three of us. But we very soon found that the horse was strong and fast, for it galloped off at great speed to the Church of Los Padrecitos, the Servants of Mary, which is a very pretty church, where we heard Mass and received Holy Communion. We then got into our carriage again, and very rapidly completed the whole of the trip, passing en route through the market, in order to show off, as it were, our new carriage. We visited the Lazarist Fathers, who opened a House here three years ago. One of the priests with us was a Lazarist. They received us with great kindness, and at breakfast gave us the first grapes of this year, 1896. It was a pleasant surprise to us, because when we left Buenos Aires it was quite winter. We visited the Cathedral, the architecture of which we greatly admired as well as its riches, for the country is comparatively poor. The altar is noteworthy for its table of finest silver and lamp of great value. These inhabitants are very fortunate, indeed, for in their midst religion triumphs. Having paid all our visits, we returned to the boat and were conveyed to the steamer. It had been amusing to note the ingenuity of my companion. As soon as she arose in the morning, she asked me what the mounds of earth were, and wondered how they could remain straight without falling down. She wanted to know the cause of the different colors, why the houses were built on the tops of the mountains, and averred she would never ascend to visit these houses. You may imagine her bewilderment when the horse conveyed us to one of these small houses situated at such a height. As we journeyed along a mountain near the port, she saw a stretch of yellow sand very smooth and flat, like a piece of beautiful material, and could not help wishing to carry some of it away with her as a remembrance of the country.

Going ashore did not do us much good; rather it did harm to everyone, because for a few days we felt as if we had just put out to sea. We saluted Cape Moro and Morocco, and then turned towards Gibraltar to admire that enchanting rock. This could easily be done, as the Captain steered the ship as close as possible in order to give us an opportunity of seeing everything and of photographing the scene. Here the steamer did not stop, but continued sailing quite near land, and we enjoyed for a whole day the most beautiful and charming views. We could see all the towns lying along the coast of Spain, with its gulfs, bays, mountains, chains, etc., and as there were passengers on board who knew Spain, they explained all that was of importance. They enjoyed my being so interested in everything, little realizing, perhaps, that for me everything was important, as my thoughts spread over all Spain, for I desire to open a House in that country, not only to do good, but to obtain religious vocations among the Spanish, which would help the work in Spanish-America. Now and again I turn my thoughts towards the West Coast of Africa and Morocco, for I have aspirations to go there also. I should love to fly and save the souls there, but this cannot be done during my lifetime, as there is too much to be done in the Americas. May God bless us and help us to spread our work, and thus save a great number of these good peoples, our brethren. In the meantime, let us help with our prayers. Prayer is the greatest relief at all times, especially when an amount of work has to be undertaken and when I see that things are impossible owing to our limited means.

Prayer is powerful! It fills the earth with mercy, it makes the Divine clemency pass from generation to generation, right along the course of the centuries wonderful works have been achieved through prayer. We are the dust of the earth, and our days are like the grass. Man is here on a pilgrimage, and shortly will be no more, but the mercy and clemency obtained through the power of prayer will always produce in people generous and salutary effects.

Now we are at Barcelona, and again this time the Captain gave us sufficient time to go ashore to receive Holy Communion. May it please God to bless the piety of this rare and singular Captain! I have been very fortunate in enjoying the kindest of attentions in all my voyages, but the insight and tact of Captain Bocacelli, who discovers in my aspirations that which acts as the hinge on which all other inspirations turn and which gives value to the others, is beyond expression. This time he sent us in his own boat; by seven a.m. we had reached the Cathedral to go to confession and Holy Communion, rendered more fervent by the inspiring devotion of many ladies who were in the sacred edifice. When our devotions had ended, an excellent Genoese gentleman, Di Ovada, knowing how we desired to see Barcelona, asked us if we would allow him to accompany us on a visit to the town. Knowing his marked respectability, I accepted the invitation. He first took us to breakfast, and then conducted us in a comfortable carriage to the public gardens and various churches. The beauty of the principal places of this city does not yield one jot to that of Paris. Barcelona is a trading city which in a few years has grown twice its original size. It is more of a cosmopolitan town than an ordinary Spanish city, for it includes in its population representatives of almost every race on the globe. But the progress achieved has brought one of the worst possible misfortunes on the town, i.e., that of evil living and irreligion. Therefore, we must open a House here in the course of time which will become a beautiful Mission and will do much good.

So, now, up and multiply your numbers and increase in virtue, for the harvest is great and too much for your small number. Make others follow your good example, so that I may be able to summon up courage to do a great deal of good for these souls, who will soon be lost if we do not hasten to their aid.

In the meantime, make use of prayer, work with prayer. Have confidence in our Beloved Jesus, and always abandon yourselves to His Adorable Sacred Heart, and have hope, ever mistrusting yourselves and confiding in Him alone. For however weak and insignificant you are, you can surely do great things. *"Omnia possum in Eo qui me confortat."*

Now I must leave you, hoping to see you all very soon and to rejoice at your progress in virtue.

May Jesus bless you and enclose you in His Beautiful Heart, wherein always I meet you.

Affectionately in Jesus Christ,

Mother Frances Saveria Cabrini

August 27th, 1896

Liverpool, November 5th, 1898

My dear Daughters,

May the beautiful Heart of Jesus, our Hope and only Love, our Life and our All, shower upon us that light of truth, that fire of love, that have come to inflame the hearts of men.

Love us, Jesus, with Your sweet chains,
Of that pure love we fain would claim;
Our wings to Heaven we open wide,
To leave low earth, and there abide.

This is the seventh time that I leave Europe to go to the Missions of America. Yielding to a secret inspiration of the soul, I visited this country—England—that was once the Isle of Saints, and which, through the passions and pride of its king, lost the faith.

I was comforted by the blessing of the Holy Father, who at the end of July gave me an audience and encouraged me, with benignity, to go all over the world and carry the Most Holy Name of Jesus everywhere, thus to draw souls into the bosom of the Church, where alone there is salvation. With fatherly goodness he inquired about my program, and noticing my poor health, he asked how I could undertake so much work. "I, who am so strong, could not do it," he said. "It is true I am old, but I am much stronger than you." The affability with which he deigned to speak to me, encouraged me to remark that, as I was his spiritual daughter, I possessed his moral strength which enabled me to go around the world, and I was sure I should not lose my strength by serving that dear Jesus Who chose me to be a Missionary of His Sacred Heart. Then, putting his two hands on my head, he showered blessings upon me, telling me to pray, for him, as his heart was overwhelmed with sorrow on account of the revolutions prevalent in many countries.

Then the Supreme Pastor, that Father of souls, not wishing to leave his little Missionary unconsoled, gave me a generous offering for my voyage, together with presents for those who helped the Missions most. He said many other nice things, but I must leave these to the Mother Superior of the House in Rome, who was with me on the occasion of that memorable audience. All I can say is, that with the blessing of the Holy Father I can go all over the world and no fear shall overcome me, no matter how difficult the way, and no matter how many the obstacles which may come before me, whether from spiritual or temporal enemies. The Pope has spoken, God has spoken through him. I shall go everywhere without fear. Oh! how powerful is the blessing of the Pope! He is the visible head of the Church on earth, he is God's representative, the oracle of the Most Holy Trinity, the instrument of the Holy Ghost, the trumpet of the Redeemer, the mouthpiece and word of Our Lord Himself. The Pope is the shining lighthouse of Divine Wisdom, and so his words and his blessings are that true column of fire that guides me in every danger and every difficulty. Do pray, daughters, pray for the Holy Father, pray for the Ruler of Church's destiny, pray for him in these difficult times. We must do so, as we are under obligations of filial gratitude to Leo XIII, who loves and favors our beloved Institute as if it were his own beloved family. Speak, children, to everybody concerning the Pope. Make them unite themselves with him, for he who is united closely with the Pope, however far he may have strayed from the right path, returns to God's ways in the end.

The Holy Father wishes our Institute to be prolific of Saints, as he said to the Sisters whom I presented to him after my audience. We are under an obligation to comply with the desires of this holy old man. I imagine I hear, however, someone asking how they can become Saints? Oh, daughters, do not fear difficulties; it will suffice if we follow our holy vocation faithfully. That sweet and most loving Jesus, Who has called us to follow Him, gathering us to His Divine Heart, helps us every day on our journey. It is He Himself, the good Jesus, Who has called us to follow closely in His footsteps, through the observance of the Evangelical Counsels, so that we may be holy and perfect, like unto Him. That dear Redeemer has marked us with the sign of predilection, taking us from the darkness of the world. He has introduced us into the House of His Divine Heart and surrounded us with His admirable light. As long as we remain faithful to our vocation, Jesus will always be in the midst of us, inflaming our hearts with Divine Love. He will try our faith and our love sometimes, by allowing us to be tempted and tried, but, if we are faithful to our vows, and if, trustingly, we invoke Him, not forgetting that the Fount of every good is in our midst, He will soon console us and leave us flooded with His light and celestial joy. He will always be with us in the time of our trials, He will walk by our side and help us out of all difficulties. He Himself has called us to follow Him closely, and has promised to help us; surely, He will keep His word. We may have to suffer a long time on the road to the Mount of Perfection, but we should not be frightened, for, what does she, who ignores Christian suffering, know of what is grand and wonderful? The science of suffering is the science of the Saints. Let us rejoice when an unexpected cross visits us, when a sorrow afflicts us, because these are the precious fruits of the mystical vine, destined to produce inestimable merits unto Eternity. Then, when you have suffered, dear daughters, do not go round sighing, as one who knows not the privilege of the Cross, but raise your eyes and smile sweetly at suffering, which is like a beautiful country white for the harvest. She who knows how to gather copious sheaves will receive a large reward. Learn how to unite your sufferings sweetly with those of Jesus Christ, and, then, your sufferings endured for Jesus and for His Adorable Heart, will be as so many drops immersed in the immense ocean of the Most Holy Passion of Jesus Christ. In like manner, our trials and our sorrows offered up with those of our most loving Jesus, will be not only sanctified but made Divine and worthy of Eternal glory. In suffering for Jesus we partake of His sufferings and riches, so that, during our earthly pilgrimage, grace will never be wanting, either to ourselves particularly or to the works of our mission-the salvation of souls. Be wise, then, dear daughters, and do not squander your sufferings, but submit to them without murmuring and with supernatural motives, remembering that in every sorrow a wonderfully secret work of grace is revolving within the wheels of our predestination.

November 6th

I begin again today my correspondence with you, after having passed a quiet night, so quiet, indeed, that one hardly realized one was at sea. So much was this the case, that dear Sister Frances, who is with me, was astonished, seeing that she was prepared to suffer any amount of seasickness and all the other inconveniences which occur during this season of the year. We have reached Queenstown after sixteen hours navigation. It is Sunday, and we should like to go ashore and hear Mass and receive Holy Communion, but the steamer only makes a stay of half-an-hour to collect the mails. So we have to resign ourselves and send our aspirations to the Solitary of Love, Who is in the Blessed Sacrament, in the devotional churches of this beautiful Irish city, where He receives the homage and reverence and the warm love of the Irish people, still animated with that lively faith which was implanted in them by that great Missionary, the fervent Apostle of Ireland, Saint Patrick.

But it is necessary to return to the account of my voyage, because you wish to know all that takes place en route. I left Rome after having finished some very grave business relating to the affairs of the Institute which gave me great trouble, and which tired me to such an extent that, if the question only affected me personally, I should certainly have yielded to the unjust demands made upon us. But it was a question of the rights of the Institute, and I should have erred greatly had I given way owing to my own physical fatigue. However, with the help of Jesus, and through the goodness of His most loving Heart, which does everything for me, I obtained the victory necessary for the Institute, after all the troubles which have already affected it. All that happened, however, was with the consent of the Divine Goodness, which allows us to be afflicted in order to make us more worthy of the singular graces with which He deigns to favor our small and beloved Institute, which is not worthy, certainly, of so many signal favors. After thanking God, we should also be grateful to those persons whom Our Lord thus allowed to trouble us, and to pray from our hearts for them. And since true friends are realized in the time of need, I was able to count as such many eminent Cardinals, who love with a paternal heart our beloved Institute. This was proved by the sacrifices and trouble they undertook to defend truth and uphold justice. How they are enlightened by the Holy Ghost! Amongst these were the Most Eminent Cardinals Parrocchi, Vannutelli, Rampolla, Agliardi, Steinhuber, Cretoni, and other Cardinals and Prelates whose names would take too long to write.

The audience of which I have already spoken closed the whole affair with great success, and then I went to the Novitiate of Codogno, where with one hundred and fifty Sisters I made my Annual Retreat lasting ten days. During that time I was able to take that spiritual rest which I had been waiting for so long, and which was also necessary to recruit my bodily health, which had suffered greatly. It might have been said that I should not be able to undertake another long journey, which, before its completion, will have taken me a distance of about sixteen thousand miles, not to speak of other obstacles which frequently occur and are not always pleasant, though, of course, always acceptable as coming from Him Who gives wool in measure as required by the cold, and Who even with the ice and the snow conserves the heat of the earth, "*Qui dat nivem sicut lanam.*" Though the spirit of the Institute and the works of piety it inculcates are sufficient to keep us united to God, nevertheless, a spiritual retreat now and again is a necessity for our souls which are destined to climb the mountain of perfection, as true Spouses of Jesus Christ and as Missionaries of His Divine Heart. "I will lead my beloved into the solitude, and there I will speak to her, heart to heart." Jesus Christ Himself frequently retired alone into the mountains and into the quiet Garden of Olives to converse with His Eternal Father in the silence of the night. In retirement and solitude we are disposed to speak with God confidentially and to beg Him to fill us with His grace. It is in Retreat that we learn the multiform and precious ways of prayer. It is there we learn to pray, whether it be by means of the tongue, good works, or sufferings. It is there one acquires the spirit of interior prayer so sublime and rich with merits, for it is the interior spirit that raises us up at every moment and in every work to God. It is in Retreat that the soul learns to give internal glances at the beauty and goodness of God. These glances are like a melodious prayer, pleasing to the Divine Heart of the loving Jesus.

God is a most pure Spirit, and He loves, with a special love and very dearly, pure and immaculate hearts, and their loving, simple looks please Him. When can we better simplify and purify our spirit than during Retreat? The soul learns to love God as He should be loved, so worthy of all our love. Then, also, these internal aspirations, however short, leave incredible power within, and are very profitable to us and give great glory to God. The soul learns that there is no necessity to look for her beloved outside her own being, and that she can find Him within herself, as on His own throne and in His tabernacle. The soul drinks in large draughts from that wonderful spring, the Wound of the Sacred Heart of Jesus. It is in Retreat that the Missionary learn what is required in order to become rich for eternity, and acquires at the same time a loving and continual purity of intention. Oh, how precious it is! The most vigilant in this exercise of the inner life have the richest graces in this life and the greatest glory in the next. Yes, my children, God is the beginning, the center and the end of all our daily actions, and whilst as Missionaries of His Divine Heart we give great and continual glory to God, we also acquire for ourselves at every moment immense treasures of grace. Whether we work, eat, teach or sleep, or voyage, let us do all in the name of Jesus and in that of His Divine Heart.

Remember always, and impress it also on all you have to instruct, that purity of intention in our actions is the life and the value of the same, and is the way to open up the inexhaustible mine of the incalculable good which we shall Find written in the Book of Life.

It is in Retreat that we learn to humble ourselves and to earn the precious gem of humility. If we become careless and ignorant in our spiritual life, we think ourselves better than we are. But, in solitude we are enabled to understand well what the Beloved Disciple meant when he admonishes us and says, "If we say we have no faults, we deceive ourselves, and the truth is not in us." Our misery is indeed great. Ignorance, blindness of intellect, pride of mind and heart, inclination to vice, repugnance to virtue, readiness for evil, and sloth in doing good—all of these are a sufficient motive for humbling ourselves in the most pure presence of God, and confessing that we are truly dust and ashes: nothing in fine. Let us weigh carefully, dear children, what a great misfortune it is not to have humility, for the lack of this precious pearl places a wall of bronze between us and God. If we are not humble, we shall derive no advantage from the ways that lead to humility, for whatever may be our fault against humility, though it appears small, it does us a great injury, for faults against humility are severely punished by God. Be, therefore, watchful, children, and guard that precious and holy humility, for none of the lovely works of piety prescribed by the Holy Institute can be carried out without humility, and your many and good prayers will not be helpful to you without a humble heart. We must pray much to obtain this great and precious gift of humility, for we must be humble if we want to be heard. Mary, our tender Mother, teaches us this by her example, because if God loved her for her virginity, He loved her more on account of her humility, as Saint Bernard affirms. Many often complain of not being heard, though they pray much, but, if they become humble, as Jesus desires, and practice humility, then they will be heard quickly, for the key which opens the celestial treasures is humility. Let us please God, children, and give glory to Him. Let us console the Adorable Heart of Jesus by becoming truly humble. Let us practice always and in every event great simplicity and humility, which is the glorious chain which unites us with God. No, you cannot stand without Jesus, He is for you a blessed necessity. The soul yearns for its Creator, its Center, its Beginning, its Beloved. Remove, then, any impediment produced by the want of humility, and then nothing will hinder you. Your wings will be free, and you will fly with all the vehemence and ardor of which the soul is capable unto your Treasure, Who will allow you to taste an anticipated Heaven which is the sure novitiate of eternal life. The peace and joy which God infuses into the humble soul exceed all understanding. Therefore, how much you should treasure the holy Annual Retreat, the Monthly and even the very short Weekly Retreat, when you retire to read over again the lights and resolutions which bring great advantages to you. But I must tell you that besides coming out of the Retreat feeling very well as to personal advancement, I had also the pleasure of seeing the Sisters also much better and much more enriched with precious gifts from their loving Spouse, Who, pleased with the fragrant odor of their holy resolutions, seemed to surround them with a beautiful white cloud, with a shadow of His Holy Humanity, so much so, that I thought I was with heavenly creatures instead of with poor earthly pilgrims. Being assured, therefore, that the Divine Blessing would always accompany them to whatever House they were destined, I left Italy without anxiety and very tranquilly.

On the 25th August I left Codogno, and on the 26th August I left Milan for Turin. There I thought I should be able to get the tickets cheaper from the Mediterranean Line Company through the recommendation of His Eminence, Cardinal Ferrata, who was anxious to help us in our Mission work, but the excellent Rector, Monsignor Vigo, of the Church of St. Julia, met us with a rather jubilant air, saying the tickets could not be had and that I should have to stop at his house. We had the great pleasure of meeting Monsignor Radini Tedeschi, who was engaged in the final stages of his work of organizing the celebrated pilgrimage to Our Lady of Lourdes, and so we were able to take some part in the homage and devotion to Our Lady by preparing the books with the names of those who were to act as leaders of the pilgrimage, and who so energetically cooperated with that great client of Mary Immaculate, Monsignor Radini Tedeschi, who is well known for his great faith, irreproachable life and singular attachment to the Holy

Father and to the Holy See. Our tickets arrived the same day that the pilgrimage set forth, and so we took train to Paris, accompanied by the blessing of the Archbishop of Turin, who gave us and our voyage his blessing, after he had already blessed the pilgrimage. Monsignor Vigo, not satisfied with lodging us for three days, continued his kindness by giving us a hamper of good things and by accompanying us to the station. La Signorina Jaggi, sister of our dear Sister Maurizia, remained in our company these few days, and then accompanied us to the frontier, in company with Sister Maurizia and the Reverend Mother of the House of Codogno, in order to help us to get through the Customs. Signorina Carolina Jaggi is a beautiful soul, and would do anything in her power to relieve us of any trouble, and, more so, because she is soon to become a member of the Institute.

On the 20th August we arrived in Paris, where a very generous and great personage awaited us. It was Monsignor Chapelle, Archbishop of New Orleans, who, forgetting his own dignity and merits, deigned to come to meet us at the station, and then conducted us to the house in which he was staying, and thence to the Sisters of Sion, whose hospitality he had procured for us during the time we were to remain in Paris. At the same time we visited Madame de Mier, who offered us her house, as she thought it would please her younger sister, who is finishing her studies with us. We could not refuse such an offer, especially as, this lady being very ill, our refusal might have given her pain. So we accepted it, and for a month her house was like a Convent. Everything was at our disposal, parlor, dining room, servants. Great silence was observed, for the lady was very ill, and only left her room to come to table, not to eat, but to keep us company and to see that we had everything necessary. She, in fact, studied how to make each day more pleasant for us.

But whilst I am writing to you of Paris, *The Umbria*, the Cunard vessel on which we are traveling, is making great headway, and seems to be almost flying. The weather is beautiful, the sea very calm, and the wind favorable. We might expect such lovely weather in the months of August and September, but not at this time of the year. So everybody is naturally surprised at seeing what a favorable crossing we are having. Occasionally the waves swell up. Then suddenly, as if by magic, clouds of mist are formed that obscure for the moment the rays of the sun, which dissolve at one time into very fine rain, and at another into enormous drops. Thus the salt water, coming into contact with the fresh rainwater, becomes calm and composed, so much so that we do not seem to move. I sometimes shut myself up in my cabin and sometimes remain on deck, and so am able to write with little trouble the sort of diary you asked for. Sister Frances is well and accompanies me everywhere. At the table she orders what I can take, which I myself certainly could not do, as I do not know the names of English foods, just as I also do not know those of our own country, accustomed as I am to take what is placed before me. Sister Frances is a very good traveling companion. She is always in good humor, and though simple as a dove, is not by any means ignorant, but, withal, prudent and cautious. She is very quick in managing things, and studies in every way to spare me trouble, performing everything openly and with great charity. She has many good qualities and that spirit which at all times ought to distinguish a true Missionary. She is kind to everyone, affable but not affected, and so leaves everyone edified. The world has no place in her heart, nor does it leave on her any impression that might damp that fervent love which draws her near to her dear Jesus. As you know, she does not speak Italian well, but she does her best to make me understand what she wants to say by turning the words this way and that. The other day, for instance, she wanted to say "cauliflower" in Italian, which is *"cavol-fiore,"* but her rendering made it *"fiore-cavalli,"* "horses' flowers." By expressing herself in this roundabout way she was doubly charitable, for she gave me the opportunity of a good hearty laugh.

How admirable is God in His works! He finds followers everywhere, and in the midst of a country where Protestantism reigns. He, through the goodness of His Heart, forms beautiful and generous souls who serve Him with great fidelity. There was a time when Our Lord went through the streets of Jerusalem drawing souls to Himself by His Divine looks, but, today, it is by His spirit and His loving Heart that He draws souls to His following and inflames them. My Jesus, how good Thou art! I shall never cease to speak of Thee and Thy Divine Heart! I shall never tire of proclaiming Thy praises, so that Thou risest every day like a bright and ardent lamp and run as a Giant in every country, enlightening souls, warming up hearts, drawing them into the fold of Thy Church and helping them to follow Thee more closely. Pray, dear daughters, pray much for the conversion of England. It breaks one's heart that this country does not possess the true Faith. England has all the qualities that make it worthy to be a portion of Christ's fold. Her only fault is that of having but half of the Faith, and no longer being allied with the only Head which forms the perfect union of the Church with Christ. Our Lord Himself said so: "He who does not enter by the door of the fold shall not have salvation." The door of the fold is the Catholic Church and union with the Head who represents Jesus Christ. It is faith in Christ, a pure, simple faith, not half a faith, but entire faith, that faith which embraces in its universality the revealed Word of God, which is necessary to enter the true Church. Such a faith makes us living members of the mystic Body of the Redeemer. In fact, of what avail is it, children, if Protestants lead naturally pure, honest lives, yet possess virtues which lack the interior impulse of the Holy Ghost? They may well say "We do no harm, we lead good lives", but, if they do not enter the true fold of Christ, all their protestations are in vain, because a really good life is that which is so formed and ordered as to lead to the Way that is Blessed and Eternal. Without this admirable order and relationship a good life is of no value. These poor people do not enter the door of the true fold of Christ, because they do not know Christ perfectly, or, at least, do not accept in their entirety His Sacred Commands.

8th November

Today the weather is more gorgeous than that of yesterday. The sun shines, the air is warm, the sea tranquil and smooth, and of a beautiful blue hue, whilst the vessel sails swiftly and quietly. My companion arose this morning as bright as a bird. Having said our prayers, we went on deck, where we spent our time, praying, reading or writing letters, just when we felt like it, and speaking to those who approached us, amongst whom were some Protestants, to whom we quietly suggested some religious ideas which we hoped might serve as the seed of a knowledge of the Truth. I must not, however, forget to turn back to Paris, with the thought of what the good Jesus inspired me to do whilst passing through that city. For seven years I had nourished a secret desire to open a House in Paris, but the strenuous life of our American Missions always prevented me.

Now, however, on passing through Paris again, an irresistible force held me back in the capital. I first visited Montmartre, as this seemed to me quite a natural thing to do, and I felt driven onwards. There I received Holy Communion, made an hour's adoration before the Blessed Sacrament, Which is always exposed in that temple for the salvation of France, and, as I looked at the beautiful statue of the Sacred Heart which stands over the altar with its arms extended, It seemed to say to me in mute but eloquent language, "Here I want you, here I will protect you, here, though you will have some difficulty, you will succeed." Having finished my visit to this great Sanctuary, built by the offerings of the whole of the French people, I felt a still greater impulse. So I went to the Cardinal Archbishop, but was unable to see him at home, as he had just left for the country. I was told to talk to one of the Vicars General. The only one I found was Monsignor Thomas, an excellent and exemplary Prelate, who, however, certainly inspired by God, thought it well to make certain objections, and represented to me how difficult that was which seemed so easy to me. However, instead of losing courage I felt more determined than ever. I seemed to realize the interior awakening of a great feeling of gratitude towards this excellent Vicar, who, by thus making the way somewhat difficult for me, gave me the opportunity of beginning, with the cross, a foundation which I had so much at heart. And it was really a cross for me, because, while the difficulties thus presented did not deprive me of the hope of opening this House, so long-desired, nevertheless they meant the delay of the realization of my long-cherished hopes. Moreover, I desired to arrange everything in fifteen days, so as to have time to go to England before leaving for America.

The delay was certainly a great obstacle to my plans, for I had business in England which required my presence there not later than the middle of November. I thought I heard the words of the eminent Cardinal Vicar ringing in my ears, "Disembark in England and found a House of the Institute there, and you will do great good." For me these words were like a precept, but the delay in France was an obstacle to my going to England, and caused me such great sorrow as to prove a real cross to me. I seemed to feel that I could embrace any other cross rather than this, but everything was arranged by God to render me more worthy of this blessing, without which there could be no success. In the meantime, the most Eminent Cardinal Richard, to whom Monsignor Montagnini had spoken on behalf of the Apostolic Legate, gave me instructions to open the House, about which he himself was quite satisfied. About the same time a letter arrived from Cardinal Rampolla, Secretary of State, Rome, who, in the name of the Holy Father, asked His Eminence to render what effective help he could in favor of the projected foundation. The matter would have been settled at once, but for the absence of the approval of the Vicar General, Monsignor Thomas, but even for this I hadn't to wait long, as an unexpected and gracious letter, full of those sentiments of piety which distinguished him, came from the Monsignor, in which he gave me as much satisfaction as he had previously given me trouble. Shortly after, when visiting our Houses in Milan and Rome, he told the Sisters that even whilst he was putting difficulties in my way, he felt interiorly as if he ought to say, "Go, found a House, and it will be blessed by the Sacred Heart."

The last difficulty was the choice of the place, for, not knowing the city, I might easily have made a mistake. Instead of the modest position I was about to choose, His Eminence the Cardinal, through the Vicar General, advised me to go to the Parish of Saint Pierre du Chaillot, between the Squares of Etoile and Il Trocadero, the most aristocratic locality of Paris, which I should not have chosen myself. We found a house in Via Dumont d'Urville, No. 20, and though it was one of the most modest houses in this distinguished quarter, it was very costly, and I should not have taken it, except under obedience to the wish of the Eminent Cardinal Archbishop, who encouraged me. "Obedience," I said within myself, "carries victory and works wonderful prodigies. When the House has been opened, the means to sustain it will follow." We did not, however, know where the means were going to come from, but the Sacred Heart, who always provides and cares for us, knew where they would come from.

The house itself being too rich in its appointments, we chose the servants' apartments for the Community as dormitories, the porter's room for the Community Room, the kitchen for the Refectory, leaving the best rooms for such lady boarders as might come. And, seeing what

I had done was God's Will, and in obedience to the Pope, whose blessing is always fruitful, we had one boarder very soon. On the day of the great Saint Michael the Archangel, the special Angel of our Institute, which he guards with a body of Angels and Saints, and called by me our great Crusade, the House was opened, and about the 1st of October the Countess Spottiswood Mackin, an American lady of excellent dispositions and with a big heart, came to us. No sooner was she with us than she felt strongly inclined to help in a special manner the Missionary Sisters of the Sacred Heart, and used all her efforts to bring us into contact with persons who could help us. She herself helped us, and, not satisfied with that, she organized a concert under the patronage of the Princess Eulalia of Spain, who accepted the honor very willingly, being only too happy to help the Missionary Sisters of the Sacred Heart in their new foundation. She, the Countess Spottiswood, arranged the affair so well by reason of her excellent and energetic personality and her beautiful disposition, that one would imagine she is capable of putting a whole country into movement when it is a question of assisting those whom the Holy Father favors.

With all her energy, she maintains a great simplicity which enhances all her other good qualities, and as simplicity is the sister of humility, so she listens to every word I say and obeys me like a child, being willing to make any sacrifice in order to conform with the requirements of a Religious House, and in order to make herself worthy, as she says, of doing us a little good, See, my dear daughters, how admirable is the Providence of that Most Adorable Heart, Who knows how to help His little Missionaries when they know how to abandon themselves to Him! But this is not all. On the 1st of October, His Eminence Cardinal Richard returned to Paris, and, through his Vicar General, made known his desire to see me. On the 4th October I went to His Eminence, and his kind reception left a lasting impression upon me–the impression of a most holy soul inspiring me with a great veneration for him. He treated me as a real father would, and gave me a letter not only formally approving the foundation, but making it very conspicuous in the letter that I had been recommended to him by the Holy Father, Leo XIII. He not only helped me in his capacity as Archbishop, but gave me a large offering which was recorded in a book, which moved others to follow his example, for the recommendation of the Venerable Archbishop had the efficacy of a command in respect to many other generous persons.

What do you say now, my dear daughters? Are you not astonished at the goodness of the Most Adorable Heart of the most loving Jesus? Let us acknowledge Him as our most powerful Advocate and Ruler. He is always in the presence of His Father, pleading our cause. Our cause is in His hands; in the Wound of the Side of the most clement Jesus. He never abandons those who have an upright heart, who trust in Him and hope in His Divine Heart. He is our sure Refuge in trials, and at the opportune moment He gives us His powerful and loving help. He scatters with His breath the designs of our adversaries.

Remember, daughters, that our trust in Jesus is our very life, and we must always hope in Him and in the goodness of His Most Adorable Heart against every hope. It may at times appear that He overlooks the evil that we suffer, but, no. He is awake. He watches over us and all our interests. It is He who brings forth the lilies of the valley and the flowers of the fields, but He thinks more of us, as we are the elect portion of His Divine Heart. Why? Because we are consecrated to Him as His Spouses, desirous to please Him always, and because in a special manner we are dedicated to Him as Missionaries of His Divine Heart. Yes, my daughters, as long as you have the grace to combat faithfully under the standard of the Missionaries of the Sacred Heart, you will always walk under the protection of a special Providence. But an exact fidelity is necessary to merit such a protection. You are certainly resolved to be thus faithful, but you must also supplicate the good Jesus to place His seal upon your arm so that you may never need to lean on human creatures and to put a seal on your heart, so that you will love Him only and will work for Him alone. Ask Him to seal with His Holy Name all your thoughts, words and actions, all your sufferings, your joys and aspirations. Beg Him to live always in you and you in Him, so that you may always be one with Him, that you may always glorify Him, and not bear in vain the noble and enviable title of Missionaries of His Divine Heart.

November 9th

Our voyage continues, as it began, just as quiet and calm as if we were on a calm lake. Last evening, in the company of my dear traveling companion, I remained on deck near the stern contemplating the beautiful spectacle formed by the phosphorescence. The steamer was one bright light all around, and the waves seemed to reflect the moon. My companion looked round, but the moon could not itself be seen at this moment. It was as yet invisible. Her surprise increased, as she could not account for the bright light coming from a sea so dark in color. The atmosphere was moist but loaded with health-giving qualities, and so we remained as though with our mouths wide open to inhale what the good Providence of God sent us. It strengthened our lungs, and I was happy, as I wanted my companion to get still stronger. We sang the *Ave Maris Stella*, and the quiet waves seemed to re-echo our voices and to modulate them in a curious way. It seemed that the heavens opened for the Angels to join us, and that Mary, Queen of all Saints, spread her mantle over us to give us ample protection. I, however, feel urged by sentiments of sincere gratitude, to again return in thought to Paris to tell you more about the people there who were so good to us. It happened that His

Grace the Archbishop Chapelle, had been to Lourdes to compose a pastoral for his diocese at the feet of Mary Immaculate, in whom, full of great faith, he places all his trust, but, though he had left for the wonder-working Sanctuary of the Pyrenees, he gave me, as before, all the help he could for the new foundation, and on his return came to congratulate me on my success and to give solemn Benediction in thanksgiving. Having seen the book in which His Eminence Cardinal Richard had written, he also added his own recommendation. This is a real adornment of the book, because it came from a heart so full of zeal, a zeal that renders him worthy of the Episcopate. Amongst other things, he said it was a matter of great satisfaction for him to be able to help our Institute, that it was very dear to his heart, and that it was his duty to help me as much as he could, the Holy Father having made a special recommendation of the Institute in the last audience he had with His Holiness in the month of August.

His Holiness, Pope Leo XIII, possessing great insight of character, recognized the merit and value of His Grace, Archbishop Chapelle, and created him Apostolic Legate at Cuba, Porto Rico and the Philippines. This clear-minded Prelate is already working day and night in Paris so as to make the treaty of peace fruitful and to preserve entire to the Catholic Church the populations of these territories. Monsignor Chapelle is now at an advanced age, but he works like a young man, and could take wings when it is a question of consoling the august and venerable Pontiff, so great is his joy. The Holy Father made no mistake in the choice, because the good Prelate has done great things in these few days, and it is not surprising that things go well with him, because he is a beautiful soul, all of God, working in His Holy Name; certainly, God supports him by His graces. If we feel our hearts, sometime, pierced with thorns at the sight of these terrible times, for it seems as if hell itself has been let loose with all its fury, we may be consoled when we see such men as Archbishop Chapelle working with so much energy to repair the injury done to the Church and to her beloved children. The wise Leo has said, "*Defende nos in prælio contra nequitiam et insidias diaboli.*" It was for good reasons, also, that he wanted the whole world to repeat it. Yes! The furious enemy of those redeemed by Christ, Satan, who, with pride, insults the noble people of Israel, will be conquered. He, the cruel enemy, advances with rage against us in every direction, but we'll conquer him, if we trustfully repeat, "*Defende nos in prælio.*" The enemy comes to us with the sword and spear and the shield, but we, like the shepherd David, made according to God's Own Heart, go to meet him without fear, in the name of the Lord, with peace and confidence, and enclosed within the Heart of God. Let us have confidence, dear daughters, unlimited confidence, and, like brave champions, we shall weaken the strength of the enemy and conquer him, and make everything redound to the glory of God and the consolation of His Divine Heart.

In Paris the time seemed to fly. On the eve of Saint Teresa, after having finished the preparation of our little chapel, the Rector of St. Pierre de Chaillot came to celebrate Holy Mass and to reserve the Blessed Sacrament. It was a great feast day for us, and we thought everything had become more beautiful and grander with the coming of our Beloved into our home. As Jesus had deigned to come, so with Him all other good things would come. Nothing else remained for me to do but to leave Paris, feeling sure that everything would follow all right. But, as the days flew by and between one thing and another, wishing to have everything in perfect order, the end of the month arrived before I had noticed it. During these latter days the second curate of the parish came to say Mass. The first curate, Father Chesnelong, having returned from the country, also came to visit us and afterward said Mass. He congratulated us on having opened a House in the parish, and encouraged us greatly, offering us his best wishes and help. Monsignor Granito di Belmonte, the Legate's Secretary, who did so much for us, came also to say Mass.

With the blessing of everyone, I left Paris on the 27th of October, nine p.m. for America via England, for, although there was no time for me to work in England, I felt I wanted at least to visit this country, where I longed so much to do some good.

The evening before, Monsignor Bishop Patron, Superior of the Franciscans of the Holy Land in Paris, a man of patriarchal goodness, obtained for us a reduction in the cost of our tickets. Three Sisters went in advance to the station to arrange everything. When I got there the Sisters came into the carriage with me, and as no signal was given that the train was about to start, the latter moved out of the station without our noticing it. The doors were closed hurriedly, and the train moved on for another hour. It was impossible for the Sisters to leave the train.

At first I felt upset owing to the late hour, but soon we were quite happy at the thought of being together for a few minutes more. The distance was going to be great and the separation still longer. At the first stop the station-master came to tell us we must not worry, and that in a few minutes another express train would come along and convey the Sisters back to Paris. In fact, at midnight they were already at home, as told me in their letters which reached me in England. At one o'clock I had fallen asleep, tired out with the work of preparing the luggage for the Missions, when I was suddenly awakened by being told that we were at Calais. We got out of the train in haste to get on board the steamer. The place was as bright as day with the light of the lighthouse, the brilliancy of which was as bright as if emanating from the sun. The sea was very smooth, and with the swiftness of lightning the boat conveyed us in an hour's time to Dover, where the train awaited us to take us to London with an equal swiftness. I wanted to admire England, which I had longed to visit, but I was absolutely fatigued, and, being alone with Sister, I took up a comfortable position in order to sleep or rest. I was told in Paris I should not reach London until nine a.m., but about five-thirty I was awakened by being asked for our tickets, and was told I was in London and that within ten minutes we should arrive at Victoria Station, our destination. I felt so worn out that I would have given anything to be able to rest longer. My limbs were aching a great deal, but it was no use, as I had to leave the train presently.

Having left our luggage at Victoria Station, we went to the Jesuit Church, Farm Street. We received Holy Communion, and on leaving the church went to see the venerable Superior, for whom Father Frigeri had given us a letter, He received us with that paternal goodness which is traditional with the Jesuits. He was interested in our work, and gave us a letter of recommendation to the Sisters of Mary Reparatrice, who were to lodge us for three days while we remained in London. They did not live far off, and I thanked God, for I felt I could not have taken another step. We saw the Superior, who received us with great kindness and gave us a very good breakfast, which Sister Frances ate with a sharpened appetite. As far as I was concerned, I needed rest rather than food, but I dissimulated and tried to keep going. As things turned out, in fact, rest was out of the question, for the Superior told us that the rooms were full and she could not accommodate us. The good Reverend Mother, however, gave us the addresses of two other Convents and sent a young lady to take us by the shortest and surest way. I thought of Mary and Joseph in Bethlehem, as I undertook the journey, but my legs would not move, so much so that I thought I had lost all power of motion. I decided to take a cab and visit the Bishop of Southwark, from whom I felt sure of receiving the help I needed, as he had been a friend of our Institute for two years. The journey was long owing to the cabman not knowing the residence of the Catholic Bishop, and so we arrived at the episcopal residence of Monsignor Bourne at one p.m. He was not at home, having left for the Seminary thirty miles distant to prepare the students for their ordination, which was to take place the following day. Zealous as he is, he himself wanted to prepare these new Levites for the great mission which awaited them. We met his worthy Secretary, however, who received us with great cordiality, as if we belonged to the same household. He ordered our dinner, and in the meantime sent word to the Sisters of Retreat asking them kindly to prepare a lodging for us. At four p.m. the good Father accompanied us in a cab to the Convent where we were about to stay.

I had hoped to go to bed as soon as I arrived, owing to my immense fatigue, but these good Religious, who for the first time were entertaining strange Sisters, especially Italians, surrounded me. They wanted me to talk about Rome and the Pope, so that before I could realize it, the clock struck seven p.m., and then we had to go to supper. At last they took me to my room. It was now eight-thirty p.m. I did not go to bed, but fell upon it, more dead than alive on account of the soreness of my limbs, which seemed dislocated. I was so exhausted that I could not sleep. The next day was Sunday, and I was anxious to go to the Community Mass at seven a.m., but I could not move. Sister Frances went to the chapel. The Sisters, seeing that I was not present, became alarmed. They came to my room to see if I was seriously ill, and appeared somewhat frightened, not being accustomed to receive Sisters of other Congregations. One of the Sisters, entering the room, threw the windows wide open and came to examine me. "Oh," she exclaimed, "she is like a baby asleep!" I accepted this pretty compliment. "Sisters," I said, "be patient, I want to rest a little longer, then I should like to receive Holy Communion, and afterward shall go to hear Mass at some chapel near at hand." At ten-thirty I went to the chapel, where the good

Chaplain, who also was a Religious of the Holy Retreat, gave me Holy Communion. Then I partook of a little coffee, and the Sisters accompanied me to Mass in a chapel near at hand, which serves as a school during the week and a chapel on Sundays, as in Brooklyn, where we have more than six hundred children. I went to Mass, but could hardly move my legs, and had to ask my companions to walk more slowly. In the meantime, I began to feel better and to walk better. I was glad, as this was not an opportune moment to get ill. After dinner I rested till Vespers. The following night I slept peacefully, and the next day I felt quite bright. So, after breakfast, I went out with my companion to see London. The first thing I wanted to do was to buy a trunk in place of the one I had left at Victoria Station. It had been given us in Paris, and had burst open during the journey. It was necessary to buy a new one, as we could not have continued our journey without danger of losing our effects. With this initial experience in shopping, we began to learn something about prices in London, which to us appeared fabulous. As everything is big in this great city, so also are its prices.

Leaving the Sisters' House to go to the center of the city, where all the commerce is transacted, we entered a small station. Having taken our tickets, we stood with many others in what appeared to us a room, waiting to start, when suddenly we felt ourselves descending into the earth. Then there was a stop, and we found ourselves in a large subway, lighted by electricity. People began to run as if they were running for their lives, and without saying a word. In London everybody seems to move about in silence. So, we too followed and took our places in the train, or, rather, trains, for there was a line of carriages which could not be counted in the light, for it was like night so deep down. We had hardly got into our compartment when the train moved off, and, as quick as lightning, we found ourselves in the center of the city, having gone all the way underground. At the station we entered a lift, though owing to its large size it did not seem to be a lift. Then we rose and came out into the daylight. We went around admiring the great edifices, which are really beautiful. When we asked people the way, they not only answered kindly, but even offered to carry our bag and umbrella. We asked one man the way, and, after pointing in the right direction, he apologized at not being able to accompany us, saying he had urgent business on hand. We entered a shop about six times the size of that of Bocconi of Milan, to buy something we needed, and were treated with great kindness and courtesy. We were offered chairs and shown whatever might interest us. In other countries they speak of nobility and courtesy, in London they practice it. In one shop where we were unable to get a trunk, the manager had us accompanied by one of his clerks and gave him instructions to help us to get what we wanted. Similar examples I could cite by the hundred. This is how they treat Sisters in England; and God, Who considers as done to Himself whatever is done to His servants, will bless this nation and give it the grace of entering into the One True Church.

November 10th

The weather has been beautiful and the days most gorgeous as we have proceeded, but today it is so cold that we cannot stay on deck. Fortunately, we are able to stay in our cabins, and very comfortably also, as we are not troubled with the smell of pitch, which is so disagreeable. We need not go to the common room. We spend a happy time, praying, reading and practicing languages. Sister Frances, who thinks she is already very clever at Italian, teaches it to others and amuses us with her mistakes, which she makes with so much grace and personal enjoyment. The other day they asked her nationality, and she said she was Italian because she belonged to an Italian Institute. One of the officers, sorry at seeing us always shut up, would come or send for us whenever there was anything new to see, especially when a steamer was in sight. This he did to mitigate the monotony, which he thought must be trying for us. But we were not in the least inconvenienced, because we were united with our Jesus and doing His Holy Will. We had Heaven in our hearts. The immensity of the ocean, with its most clear and vast horizon, raises our minds to Heaven. It seems as if the sky, with its clouds of singular beauty, touches the waters of the ocean. All this helps to raise one's mind to the most beautiful contemplation, and seems to bring us to the door of Heaven, and to enable us to hear the echoes of those holy and sweet words which the Church repeats with great jubilee, "Alleluia, Alleluia." Holy Mother Church never tires of repeating these words, as though to give us here below a foretaste of the harmonies of Heaven.

Let us return to London again, where courtesy and politeness reign supreme. It was midday, and, as my companion was hungry, I looked around to see if I could find an hotel, when I discovered one with an Italian name. We went in and asked for something to eat, and were received with great cordiality. They made such a fuss, that one would have thought we were relations. They put us at a nice little table, all by ourselves, and served us *à la Milanese*. It was a great pleasure to meet these Italians, who are a credit to their nationality, for they are good Catholics, loving their religion and practicing it. It happened to be a day of abstinence, and they offered us whatever we could eat in the circumstances. The day flew by very quickly, and, seeing that it was near sunset, we went to the station from which we started in the morning. This was easily reached, as the Underground runs throughout the city like a labyrinth. We took our tickets as in the morning, descended by the lift, and were in the train in no time. Having passed two or three stations, I remarked to my companion that I thought we had made a mistake, as our station did not seem to come round, and it was difficult to find one's bearings in the Underground. Sister Frances encouraged me by saying that, having been all round the city, the journey seemed longer, and that we should soon arrive at the correct point. I remained quiet for another few minutes, and said another decade of my rosary, but, not feeling convinced after having passed two other stations, I asked the conductor where we were. Our surprise was great when he saw our tickets and told us we were very far from our destination.

We had to leave the train, and after descending, crossed a bridge to take a train going in the opposite direction. We then stopped, after some time, at a station, which we were told was quite near the Convent at which we were staying. We inquired where the Convent was, but nobody seemed able to tell us. Night was coming on, and the darkness was great, as the moon, surrounded by clouds, looked more like a lamp going out, while its light rather bewildered us than showed us the way. In the end I was obliged to take a cab, but even the cabman had to ask continually where the Convent was situated.

On August 2nd, we left London to go to Manchester where some friends awaited us, and where Sister Frances was able to see her relatives before leaving for the Missions. Before leaving London we saw Monsignor Bourne, Bishop of Southwark, and bade farewell to the dear Sisters of the Retreat, who had become very attached to us and wanted us to stay on longer. At nine a.m. we were at Victoria, where we gave orders with regard to our luggage. The porters were going to weigh it to ascertain the cost of transport, when the clerk gave them orders to take it as it was to the train. "The Sisters," he said, "can go as they are," and he gave me a ticket to reclaim the luggage at the end of the journey. I was astonished at the courtesy shown me, and interiorly implored blessings on this country of England, which I soon should love to call, if possible, the "Land of Angels."

Editor's Note: This letter and also Letters 10, 11, 12, and 13, are incomplete.

10. New York to Havre

September, 1899

September 2nd, 1899

My dear Daughters,

Peace be to you, and may it accompany you everywhere and always.

"L'alme belle e fortunate
Sol Gesù può far beate
Senza Lui di un denso velo
Coprirebbesi anche il cielo."

How lovely and sweet it is to undertake a sea voyage when one is tired and worn out with the labors of the Missions! The day was fixed, the cabins were secured, and September the 2nd came all too quickly. I had to work day and night during the last forty-eight hours to settle certain affairs, connected with the Mission, which required a great deal of my attention. I had to prepare the luggage at night, hence I was worn out when I got on board the steamer. As soon as I had finished waving my handkerchief to the Sisters, I sat on a chair, and fell asleep. When I awoke I could not persuade myself that I was alone with Mother Virginia. It was only then I realized that I was far away from the Sisters and felt the sorrow of separation from them. It seemed to me that I had still a word to say to one Sister, to give advice to another, to suggest something to a third, but already the immensity of the ocean had isolated me from everyone, while the rainy weather seemed to make me feel sadder. Reflecting upon my vocation as a Missionary, I remembered that I ought not to allow sadness to take hold of me. So I entered into the Heart of Jesus, where I saw all the Sisters, and though I could not speak to them, I asked the Sacred Heart to tell each of them what I had forgotten, or what I had not time to say. Great was my pleasure at the thought that the Sacred Heart would inspire you with the good resolution to do what I want you to do, and to add to it His Grace, and thus facilitate the exercise of those virtues which give to true Missionaries of the Sacred Heart that energy which makes them zealous for the salvation of souls. Vast and fruitful is the harvest that the good God spreads out before you, and you can extend your zeal all over it, gathering every day abundant sheaves. You are the fortunate Spouses of Jesus; you are therefore made the queens of all the treasures of the King. Keep in mind that souls were redeemed by the Blood of Jesus, and therefore you must do all in your power to lead them to the Divine Heart. Work with fervor. Love will enable you to work with fervor and fruit. In your actions, your words and your sufferings, seek always the greater glory of God, and even perfection to which you must incessantly aspire will be animated by that most noble end—the glory of God. Unite all the powers of your spirit, work, pray and suffer. Do continual violence to yourselves, ever mindful of the words, "*Omnia possum in Eo qui me confortat.*" Have great confidence in God; let your confidence grow greater every day. You are poor creatures, and so you must lean on the Creator. You are weak and miserable, hence you must rely on the Divine Omnipotence. Yes, my daughters, lean on your Beloved, because the soul that abandons itself to the Most Adorable Heart of Jesus in everything it does, is not only sustained but even carried forward by Jesus Himself.

September 4th

This was the second night I had spent on board, and still the fatigue, which had not as yet abandoned me, left me somewhat indisposed. I awoke many times, and it took me several minutes to realize where I was, for I still imagined I was in New York, and that it was time for me to get up to go on with the work of the Missions which I had begun, and which you, with indefatigable zeal, should continue. I was even unsettled by anxiety, but, by the grace of God, I did not allow it to conquer me. I consoled myself with the thought that the work was well protected. I wish now to speak of my last Mission, in which, with the approval of His Grace, Archbishop Corrigan, I opened a School at "Five Points," where the Protestants work with great ardor, especially among the poor Italians.

The devil has made use of every strategy against me for several months past, even setting the most ridiculous obstacles in my way, but I hope to conquer, and my hope is supported by the indefatigable zeal of Archbishop Corrigan, who desires the School and supports it. However difficult a work may be, I always place it in the Adorable Heart of our sweet Jesus, and thus I rest sure and tranquil, even though I am far away, for I know well that He can do and complete the work I desire for His glory. When I am on the spot I shall work with might and main, but when Obedience calls me away to work elsewhere, I must leave without anxiety the previous work, trusting in Jesus that He will give help and energy to the Sisters who have to continue the work which I have left interrupted. Oh, the law of love is so beautiful and amiable! He has given it Himself to His creatures. But we cannot love Him if we are not first loved by Him. Having given such a law, He has communicated to us the grace with which to love Him. What shall we not do, then, for love of a God so amiable and generous towards us, that He has called us to follow Him closely and to continue His Mission on this earth? Let us correspond to His Love. Let us be generous, remembering always that the salvation of many souls is entrusted to our charity. We can do nothing of ourselves, for we are poor and miserable, but if we have faith and trust in Him Who comforts us, then we can do all things. Let us open wide our hearts, let us help those souls lying under the yoke of the king of darkness. Let us break, by the fire of ardent Charity, the heavy chains that bind these poor souls to the terrible slavery of the devil, and we shall see that our efforts are not in vain. Let us fall at the feet of Jesus, and, sorrowing over the iniquity of the world, supplicate the Divine Heart to open the treasures of Its infinite Mercy. Then let us begin anew, never allowing ourselves to be overcome by fatigue. Difficulties should never frighten the Spouse of Christ, but render her stronger and more steadfast. Do not be discouraged by repulses and contradictions, but always go forward with the serenity and strength of the Angels, keeping to your path despite every contrary influence. When things are easy, everything appears to smile, but difficulties prove where there is fidelity and constancy. Remember, daughters, you are the tutelary Angels of the earth, therefore you should always be ready when holy obedience calls, to fly over the vast fields which charity lays before you. Let your lives be a perennial sacrifice of yourselves in behalf of the human race. Let your joy consist in working much and praying much. Always renew your offering as victims of expiation and reconciliation between Heaven and earth. In contradictions and difficulties, bear in mind how Our Lord let the Apostles work all night in vain, midst the storm to try them, so that they might accustom themselves to suffer adversity, and not grow faint in the midst of persecutions they would meet in the course of their lives, but, rather, resist and go forward whatsoever the difficulty might be. And you, dear daughters, who are destined to continue the Mission of the Apostles, enter often into yourselves, amidst the retirement and silence which your rules allow. Look into your souls. See how you behave in moments of adversity and prosperity, both of which form the two storms of our lives. Greater is the storm of prosperity than that of adversity, but in either you may be shipwrecked. Examine yourselves well at the two examinations of conscience every day, which are exacted by your rule. See if you allow inordinate affections to predominate, and if you behave as you should when exposed to winds contrary to your spiritual welfare, no matter how much they serve to flatter your imagination and desires.

I wish you were all on board with me today. What a spectacle! An horizon so vast gives one an idea of immensity; wherever one turns to look, all is tranquillity. The steamer is traveling at great speed, but we hardly notice it, as the elements that surround us are so quiet that the steamer cuts through the waves with ease. One would almost think we were sailing through the sky, the waves being of such a pale blue that they resemble the skies.

This is a beautifully spacious and comfortable steamer–*La Touraine*. I have not seen another which provides so much comfort and convenience. It is like a small town, with its streets, avenues and squares. Magnificent rooms, parlors, studios and apartments with every possible comfort, help to make up this floating "town." The personnel is very good and kind. The Captain on board is a king and a father also, he acts in both capacities–he is as majestic as a king and as charitable as a father. Seeing that our cabins were situated in London Avenue, some distance from the dining room and the stair leading to the decks, I asked him to change them, and, to our great surprise, he gave us a luxurious apartment with two beds, on the top deck, the best and most comfortable. Near us is a wonderful parlor with a balcony, which is under the lamp which lights up the salon and dining rooms. This parlor is at our disposal, and no one is allowed to enter unless we wish it. It is here that I am writing. Mother Virginia keeps me company, sitting on a deck chair or lying now and then on her bed, free of seasickness, from which up to the present she has greatly suffered.

The passengers are a select class of people. Many are Spanish, some Americans and Italians and a few French. We have on board an Augustinian Friar, a French Priest, an Italian Priest, an American Priest, several Sisters, an Ursuline, a Marist and four Sisters of St. Joseph of Cluny. The priests and the first two Sisters sit at the same table with me, and help me very much, as I do not know which of the dishes offered will best suit me, for I'm like a fish–I feel better on sea than on land.

September 5th

Last evening, just before supper, the Captain came to see us, and we asked him what kind of weather we were likely to have during the night, as we had noticed a change come over the sun during the day as if it were late autumn, and we felt the atmosphere growing colder and more trying to bear. The Captain said he could not say, and so we concluded something new was about to happen. We also asked the staff, but, despite their kindness, they would not tell us the truth, faithful to their rule of not making known any probable danger to the passengers beforehand. We all went to table, but, after the first course, everybody, one after another, left, as the steamer swayed from one side to the other. We were naturally upset. Mother Virginia fled to her bed; it is the only place for her when the steamer rocks. At our table, only the Marist Sister and I remained until dinner was over, and then we took a walk on deck, thanking God for having made us such good sailors. But the rocking increased and the air turned colder, so I thought I would go to bed also. About nine-thirty the silence was broken by the foghorn. This is a sign of great fog, and is blown to call the attention of other steamers which may be coming in the same direction, as it is impossible to see them amidst such dense darkness. The movement still continued, but, fortunately, it was of a rolling character rather than a pitching one, but the quite unusual activity of the crew frightened us as well as the other passengers. Coincidently, the points of our meditation spoke of the storm which tossed the Apostles, and so we became quiet at the thought of the beautiful words of Jesus to His beloved Apostles, "*Habete fiduciam,*" and "*Ego sum, Nolite timere.*" In fact, having our beloved Jesus with us, why need we fear? He is the Master of Creation, and all creatures obey Him. He is the source of every good, of every consolation, so we have every reason to remain perfectly serene. I had a small statue of the Redeemer, which I held up towards the sea with great faith and asked Him to bless the waves, at the same time saying to Him, "*Ne discesseris a me, intende in adjutorium meum.*" Then I went to sleep quietly and trustingly. Shortly after the foghorn stopped. This was a sign that the fog had disappeared. Though the rolling continued, I had no fear, although we were passing Newfoundland, where the weather is always bad.

The life of the Saints in Heaven is a life of love and praise; such should be the life on earth of a Religious, so much favored by our Heavenly Father. Our whole lives should be employed in Thanksgiving, because at every instant we receive infinite blessings from the Most High. Saint Paul always recommended thanksgiving to the Faithful, and to the Corinthians he wrote, "All things are for you, so that abundant graces may redound abundantly unto the glory of God by the thanksgiving of many."

The greater number of men give thanks to God only after having obtained a grace, but the spirit of Jesus Christ, by which we should be animated, teaches us to thank Him first, because the benefits we receive are continual and at every moment. This is the best disposition you can have to move the Divine Heart in our favor. It is a great comfort to me when in some Houses where they make Triduums and Novenas to obtain a favor from Heaven, I hear added to the prayers, *"Agimus tibi Gratias."* Then I'm sure the prayer will be heard. Yes, my daughters, thanksgiving is a perfect act of love, because in it we have no other interest than the glory of God, the pleasure of God, the complacency of God. When we ask, we are moved by our own interest, but when we thank, we are moved by more noble and more perfect sentiments. Let us repeat, children, let us repeat the hymn of thanksgiving which, like a blessed and ardent arrow coming from our hearts, will fly to and wound the Heart of our most loving Spouse and Benefactor.

September 6th

What a terrible night we have passed! The steamer seemed to jump and fly out of the water. At other times we thought it would capsize. Everything was on the move. It seemed as if we were going to fall out of our beds, we had not a moment's rest. At dawn there was a little calm, and then we tried to rest our tired limbs, which seemed bruised after the continual and by no means gentle rocking. Having been accustomed to quiet voyages, I did not know if this was a dangerous storm. So, about midnight, hearing the crew and staff moving about, I rang up the steward and asked if it were necessary to prepare for any emergency, but he said there was nothing to fear, and to remain quiet, as there was a good sea. Though I could not believe that the sea was good, as the effects were quite the contrary, yet the cool and pleasant air of the steward made us feel reassured. If there had been moonlight, it might not have been so bad, but the night was very dark. At nine a.m. the rocking began again. I was still in bed, for I could not get up, and the stewardess asked if we wanted some breakfast. I told her to bring us some coffee. It was the first time I had ever had anything brought to my bed, and the poor coffee reached me at a very bad moment. No sooner had it been poured out, than cup and coffee pot, by a sudden jerk of the steamer, were scattered over my bed. I was forced to get up whether I liked it or not. Poor Mother Virginia would also have liked to get up, but this involuntary rocking took away all her strength, so that she could hardly move without feeling sick.

September 7th

The wind has not ceased yet, and the steamer is tossed about as if it were a mere shell. The sea, however, is calm, and this contributes to our feeling much better, giving us the opportunity and pleasure of doing some good. On deck, we contemplate the vast horizon, and in the immensity of the ocean we see reflected very brightly the attributes of God, especially His power, His wisdom and His goodness. How great and admirable is our loving God in His works! He made everything, made it for us, and great should be our gratitude. It ought to be an immense source of comfort for us to remember the many favors we have received and by which every hour of our lives is marked. We should often in spirit adore the Hand of the Sovereign Donor, for every grace is a special act of the love of God. This vast multitude of graces should not render us indifferent or negligent in showing our gratitude, for the multiplicity of them does not diminish their value, but, rather, increases it and makes it more valuable.

Let us frequently consider the graces with which we are continually surrounded through the immense goodness of God. Let it be an incentive to warm our hearts with holy gratitude, which in turn will inebriate us little by little with Divine Love. Be assured, dear daughters, that if you are faithful in expressing your gratitude in the loving service of your God, Jesus, Spouse of your souls, will work in you new prodigies of graces and blessings.

The flame of the love of God will not die in you, for it is like fire. The more it spreads and increases, the more it requires to be fed. Love is the fountain of grace, and grace has a sublime power of attraction. Love is industrious, and becomes, by way of superhuman effort, like unto the most pure gold of perfection. It conquers sorrows, persecutions and difficulties. May the good Jesus love us accordingly and accompany us always with every grace. Often you complain of being far away from Jesus. That is not so–He follows you everywhere. Be faithful. Leave the common ways. Walk swiftly in His footsteps, and, sanctifying yourselves, you will save many souls who will follow your example and listen to your words. If you love God with great fidelity, it will follow that all your actions, sufferings and affections will be marked with the Divine Seal, so that your fidelity, your loving work, which, in its beginnings is like a small stream, will grow in its admirable course and became like a broad river.

September 8th

Beautiful, tranquil and gorgeous is the morning. It is the birthday of Her who, with Jesus, forms the great joy of Heaven, and the happiness of their children on earth. Happy are those who love Mary. What goodness, what tenderness does not this blessed Mother show us! Her thoughts are all for us, whom she calls her children, and we are hers in a special manner, for she is the Foundress of our Institute, and it is through the goodness of this Divine Mother that we are the Missionaries of the Sacred Heart. Our

Mother of Grace has us written on her virginal breast. Often looking down upon us, she delights in us, and is pleased because she sees in us the image of her Beloved Son. With greater joy she looks on us when we are faithful to our holy vocation and seek to closely imitate her celestial virtues. She rejoices when we love much and work much for Him, for the love of Jesus is an ocean of unending light, and when it lives in us it renders us as beautiful as the Angels. In order to be faithful and constant in Divine Love, let us try to remain always under the mantle of our most tender Mother. She is the Dove of Paradise, and in her conception crushed the head of our infernal and deceitful enemy. Look upon Mary and imitate her. Having corresponded faithfully with grace, she arrived at such a sublime degree of perfection, that she became the most wonderful prodigy of celestial virtue, and surpassed in sanctity all the Angels and Saints. Oh! dear Mother, on this beautiful day you seem to show forth in a most particular manner your beauty, your purity and your sanctity. Turn towards us your most loving eyes, which give joy to Heaven and consolation to the earth. Shower upon us thy blessings, the most beautiful flowers of thy most precious virtues, that, under thy protection, thy children may preserve themselves and grow beautiful, odoriferous with celestial perfume, and merit to be one day transplanted into Heaven, where they will be with thee a pleasing incense to the most holy Heart of Jesus.

I take up my pen again now, and it is three p.m. I wish you could only see the blue of the sky, and how vividly the sea reflects it, just as if the sea were the sky itself. The vast horizon gives us an idea of the vast sovereignty of our celestial Queen and most loving Mother. But what have I said? The vastness of the immense seas vanish. The splendors of the sky are eclipsed and the richness of the earth disappears before the splendor of our celestial Queen: "*Fecit mihi magna qui potens est.*" Yes, God has done great things in our Mother because she was faithful to the grace that He invested her with. What happiness is ours to have such a Mother as the Foundress of our Institute! Yes, she did found it, because, whilst I was wavering, not knowing whether God wanted this work, so many others were also praying to the Virgin of Grace. I also prayed to her, and after many prayers Bishop Gelmini commanded me to act. Bishop Bersani, with his sweet character, induced me to obey without delay the command I had received, and Monsignor Serrati helped me with great fervor and energy, so that I found myself so implicated in the work that I could not withdraw. From our Holy Mother Mary came forth the Institute of the Missionaries of the Sacred Heart. She is, therefore, our Mother. What have we to fear?

September 9th

Our good Celestial Mother has quietened the waves. At her command the sea became more and more beautiful. It really looks like a sky of most beautiful blue, and its tranquillity gives one an idea of the soul united with Jesus Who preserves peace of mind and makes everything easy and possible. The steamer is traveling at a great speed, though we don't notice the movement, and yesterday did four hundred and twenty-seven miles, and is doing still more today. At a distance we can see great fishing boats, and the sea looks so much like the sky that the boats appear as if suspended in the air. The faces of the passengers have now lost the look of sadness they had during the past stormy days. They are happy and contented, but it is not the weather alone that contributes to their state of mind, but the thought of this being the last day of the journey. Tomorrow friends will meet friends, and merchants will receive their merchandise, which they have perhaps calculated will bring them great riches. We, leaning on our Beloved Jesus, have always remained serene even in the stormiest weather. Some priests on board would say often to us, "But you are always happy, like those who have a clear conscience." I do not know if we really have a clear conscience, but I do know we trust the Most Sacred Heart of Our Lord Jesus, and, leaning on Him, we do not fear, knowing well that He has a special care of us, and that not one hair of our heads shall be touched without His permission.

2nd December, 1900

My dear Daughters,

May the balsam of the sweetness of the most Sacred Heart of Jesus penetrate into your souls, and render you worthy to bear the title of the Missionaries of the Sacred Heart of Jesus.

Nel viaggio novel T'invoco e grido:
Nel tuo bel Cuore qual Colomba ascosa,
Deh! mi guida O Gesù, pel mare infido;
Vado e mi mostro sempre fiduciosa.
E tu, mio caro Ben, fra pioggie e venti
Spira al mio cuor fiamme d'amore ardenti:
Io bramo, il sai, che del tuo Cuore il fuoco
L'essere mio si strugga a poco a poco,
Lasciando infitto, al tuo sereno sguardo,
Nel cuor delle mie figlie un dolce dardo.

It is just a year ago today that I arrived at our House in Milan at midnight, after having left Spain, where our foundation was so wonderfully blessed by Jesus, in the goodness of His Divine Heart. It was the vigil of my and our Patron, Saint Francis Xavier, and the next day, as you may imagine, there was a great feast, a true family feast. Tomorrow will also be the beautiful feast of the great Apostle of India, but none of you, my beloved daughters, will be able to keep the day with me. Only the somewhat muffled roar of the waves will typify the echo of your prayers, which, said with such filial affection, will surely reach the mystical staircase which leads to the throne of the Most High. The good God, moved by your supplications, will send a choir of Angels to guard this beautiful boat, *Alphonsus XIII*, on which I happen to be traveling for the first time, and I have firm hopes that, after a prosperous voyage, we shall arrive safe and sound in the port of Buenos Aires, where our dear Sisters have been awaiting us for such a long time.

I embarked with Sister Anna and Sister Michelina at Genoa, on the 30th November of this dear Holy Year 1900. On the morning of that day there was a great rush, as the Spanish Transatlantic Company notified us, through the kindness of Monsignor Romero, titular Bishop of Jasso, that they would sail at eleven a.m. The Archbishop of Genoa, having so kindly favored us by celebrating Mass, gave us his heartfelt blessing, and withdrew in order to allow us time to finish our final preparations for the voyage. At a quarter to eleven, accompanied by a good number of Sisters and children, we arrived at the port. Hiring some boats, we reached the *Alphonsus XIII*, which was some distance up the bay, and almost on the point of sailing, as we thought. We ascended the gangway, one after the other, and on entering the salon found His Lordship, Bishop Romero, who, having returned from Rome after a pilgrimage which he had led, had hurried to get on board in order to arrange three places for us. He received us just as a father would. Our pupils took possession of the piano at once, and gave an improvised reception in honor of the Bishop and the good Captain. It was a pleasant surprise to both, and put all the passengers, who had the pleasure of assisting at the short entertainment, in good humor. But eleven a.m. came very soon, in fact, it was nearly twelve a.m. when the sound of the cannon off the fort of Genoa was heard. So, with the thought of a speedy departure, I bade goodbye to the children and Sisters, who reluctantly descended the gangway to go into their boats. The waving of handkerchiefs was very brief, as, in the midst of the vessels that always lie in the port of Genoa, they soon disappeared out of sight. We were all called to table, and we feared that once away from the table we should feel the effects of the boat rocking, but the vessel was still immovable, being secured by immense anchors. We took advantage of these moments to put our cabins in order, but about four p.m. we asked why the boat had not set sail, and were told, to our great surprise, that not until the dawn of the next day would they raise anchor, as, owing to the bad weather, the men had not been able to work during the night, and so the cargo was not complete. I at once made up my mind to send a dispatch to our House in Genoa notifying them of our delay, and had hardly taken up my pen, when I perceived Mother Augustine and Mother Lucia, who, having gone to the U.S.A. agency to arrange for the prospective voyage of the Sisters, heard we were still in port. It was quite a wonder that they did not try to walk the waters to see us again. After having exchanged joyous feelings, I asked the Sisters to go and fetch the Reverend Mothers of the Convents of Codogno and Rome, and with the best of wills they went, only too happy to share their pleasure with the Community. Shortly after, Mother Augustine with the two Superiors appeared. The Captain, moved by the affection of the daughters for their Mother, said they could remain all night. The Sisters did not need to be asked twice, and so, though they will never have a Mission outside Italy, they passed at least a night on board ship. The consolation we experienced at being reunited that night, when to all intents and purposes we should have been separated, you may imagine better than I can describe.

December 3rd

Feast of Saint Francis Xavier! What a great day! It seemed to me that we could not be better placed for keeping his Feast than on the ocean waves which this indefatigable Apostle braved so often, and, who, in such a few years, brought so many souls into the bosom of the Catholic Church. I will say nothing of the life of our dear and holy Patron, for you know it better than I, but I will ask you how it was that he became such a great Saint and worked with such tremendous zeal? Only because he remembered the words that Jesus Christ used to say to those whom He called to be His Apostles. You know these words so well. "*Sequere me:* follow Me, and imitate My example." These beautiful and important words He said also to us, and, fortunately, we have listened to Him, and have given ourselves up to God with great generosity of heart, consecrating ourselves to Him in the Religious life. But everything is not yet complete. We have also to render ourselves perfect disciples in the school of Jesus Christ, reproducing in ourselves all the beautiful and precious virtues of the Divine Heart. Let us imagine we are like Saint Francis Xavier, and always keep our Divine Lord before us, beholding His mild gravity, His quiet amiability, His unalterable evenness of temper. In thus copying his Divine Model, we shall see how he worked, walked, spoke and taught. Let us think of the perfection that accompanied every act, and let us force ourselves to imitate Him at all times and in every moment with the fidelity which is possible to us.

This beautiful Feast Day we mostly passed in the port of Barcelona. We thought we were going to hear several Masses, as on December 2nd, but we ran the risk of not having even one, as nearly all the priests went on shore. However, the admirable Providence of God, Who watches over us, wished to console us by way of a special favor. The only priest who had arranged to celebrate on board, arose quite early to say Mass, as he intended going to visit the city after. But he could not find the key of the case in which he kept his sacred vestments. It happened that we had just got up, and met the priest at his wits' end because of the lost key. He was, indeed, about to take breakfast. "No, Father," I said, "Look again and you will find it, because we want to hear Mass to celebrate the Feast of our Holy Patron." So he went to make another search for it, and he found it where he least expected it, to his great joy. He said Mass at once, and we received Holy Communion and so completed our preparation of the previous evening. We regarded this as a pleasant surprise from our Holy Patron, who, from the beginning of our Missions, has never ceased to show his admirable generosity towards us. If you could only see the sea! How beautiful it is! It presents such a charming tranquility, and my two little companions, who suffered so much the first days, are as well as if on land. They eat, take walks on deck, work and perform all their acts of devotion, as if they were in the Convent. They are practicing the Spanish language, so that when they arrive at the Missions, they may not be totally ignorant of the tongue spoken there. We are at table with Monsignor Isaza, Bishop Coadjutor of Montevideo, his Secretary and other priests, who know a little Italian and like to hear it spoken. They always speak in Spanish to us so that we may learn their tongue. The Bishop delights in speaking Italian to us, as he wishes us to enjoy the description he gives of his visits to the various Sanctuaries he has recently visited, and this, together with the news of these different countries, affords us a source of great pleasure. Even Bishop Romero always speaks Italian to us, and takes care of us like a father. From the beginning of the voyage, he did all in his power to obtain a separate cabin for me, but at the port of Barcelona a family came on board which had the number of my cabin. I thought, then, I should have to give it up and adapt myself to the circumstances and go with the Sisters, but he, without my knowing it, saw to the matter, and, before evening, came with the Captain to tell me they had given another cabin to the new passengers, and that No. 4 cabin would continue mine. Wonderful, indeed, it was, for a large number of passengers came on board at Barcelona,

December 4th

Yesterday, at five p.m., the steamer raised anchor again. It was a great day for one incident or another, passengers coming on board, others leaving it, and others again coming to greet their friends. We expected to see no one, as the Sisters of Bilbao had so much to do in preparing for the first Mass which was to be celebrated on the Feast of the Immaculate Conception. Nevertheless, a surprise awaited us, for about three p.m., on going to table for some refreshments, as is customary on this steamer, we saw two priests, who on account of their venerable appearance drew our attention. All looked and asked who these priests were. "Perhaps they are Jesuit Fathers," was the exclamation. The inquirers turned to me also, but I said I knew no one in Barcelona. In the meantime, the two priests came very near us to greet a lady, when one of the Fathers recognized me, and I recognized him at the same time exclaiming, "Oh, Father." He almost re-echoed in the same voice, "Oh, Mother, are you here also?" He was the Provincial of the Scolopi whom I had met seven years previously when I went to Buenos Aires to establish the first foundation. He is a man of fervent spirit, and greatly aided me during my first difficult moments. The other was the Reverend F. Miracle, who was in very poor health when I saw him in Buenos Aires, but now appeared so well restored in health, that I had to look at him twice before I could recognize him. Then he went to find Reverend F. Terradas of the same Congregation, who had just returned from Panama, where I met him six years ago. From him I had news of our Sisters of Panama, where they are suffering from the revolution and civil wars that have been going on for such a long time in poor Columbia, in addition to the diseases that affect the country, such as yellow fever, typhoid, smallpox, and sometimes, though not so frequently, *"La peste bubbonica."* For three consecutive years they have suffered all these ills. But God's wrath seems to be appeased now, though the war still continues.

The admirable Providence of God has so far preserved our Sisters from all ills, and, besides being able to continue their work in the Academy, Schools and Catechism Classes, they also make scapulars of the Sacred Heart, with the word "Cease" on them, to give to the sick and the soldiers. The scapular works wonders, and every letter we get from our Sisters gives us news of the prodigies thus worked and obtained. Faith! What wonders it works! Many say that these people are superstitious and that their faith is not deep. But I say it is very good, and that their faith is rewarded with greater prodigies than elsewhere. They believe with simplicity, and this is one of the wisest qualities of the true believer. They are ignorant, it is true, but they have good reasons for their belief. God has infused the faith into their souls, and they show every goodwill to become instructed. No! The faith of the people is not to be despised. One may not be able to express why he believes, he may not know how to defend his belief, but he does know the reason of his faith. How many illiterate souls, by reason of the purity of their hearts, have raised themselves to God in sublime contemplation, thus showing that those mysteries that are superior to science and to the mind are not superior to the greatness of the human heart. No! The mind does not understand the mysteries of our Holy Faith, but the heart, that has the gift of faith, feels rather than understands that they are the mysteries of love. Yes! The Holy Trinity, the Incarnation, the Holy Eucharist are mysteries of a God of Love, of a God who is a Father to us, Brother, Victim and Food. These mysteries are proofs of an infinite love. The heart feels the truth because it must be infinitely loved. Oh, faith! Oh, Most Holy Religion, what great good you have brought to humanity! Appearing amidst the darkness of ignorance, you have crushed error, you have secured both for reason and for truth a place that they can never lose.

December 5th

At dawn this morning we arrived at Malaga. The steamer stopped quite near the land, and all got out. So I, also, thought I would like to make a little visit to the town, and, as everyone was buying the raisins of Malaga to take to Buenos Aires, I also secured a box as a memento of the place. But I had better luck than the others who went into smart-looking shops to get theirs, where they had to pay more for the box than for the raisins. I, however, fixed my eye on a donkey which was descending a near mountain, loaded with boxes of celebrated grapes of that mountain. In the evening everybody returned with their beautiful and elegant boxes, and I with my rustic box, which contained an abundance of raisins, and less costly. At table someone offered us a bottle of Malaga wine, and I, wishing to reciprocate, sent to the cabin to get one of the bottles that Mother Augustine had placed there. They asked if it was Malaga wine. "Yes," I replied, "it is in Malaga." They enjoyed the joke, drank the wine, and were surprised at its exquisite taste, particularly the Bishop of Montevideo. They could scarcely believe that such good wine came from Piedmont.

December 6th

Whilst at supper, the steamer saluted Malaga, and very slowly steered towards Cadiz under a serene sky. The quiet sea and pleasing temperature seemed to be atmospheric conditions more suited to pleasure-seekers than to people going out to work on the Missions. Our good Jesus plays with us and treats us as children, always compassionating our weakness. It means that we ought to endeavor to be generous, if He wants to try us with bad weather, though we are inclined to think He is always going to give us good weather. Resigned, however, to the Heart of Jesus, resigned to everything that pleases His Most Holy Will, we feel greatly consoled and experience an anticipated Heaven. We arrived at Cadiz this morning at five a.m. The steamer stopped, and this made it easier for us to go to the chapel and hear Holy Mass and receive Holy Communion. We wanted to go ashore, but the steamer was too far from land, and I thought it better not to go, as I had not got over the cold which I caught at Genoa while on deck saluting the Sisters. With the cure I'm using, my cold will soon be gone. Even here I am able to use the milk-cure, though the milk, of course, is not so fresh and tasty, as, on board, condensed milk is generally used. There was a time when I could not even bear to look at tinned milk, but forced by necessity to try it, I find it quite good. They told me it was even better than fresh milk, as it is like sterilized milk.

December 7th

Yesterday so many new passengers came on board that we could scarcely move. The steamer is full and all the cabins are taken except one which the good Captain left for me. I have changed cabins as many times as we have found ports to stop at, because the new passengers who come on board have booked these particular cabins, and I have had to give them up, for they were mine through kind favor. Today is the third time I have had to change in this way, just like those who go to Rome from the hundred cities, and change houses every month not to pay the rent.

December 8th

This morning, before the break of dawn, the glimmering rays foretold that a bright light would arise to illuminate us with its splendor and raise our souls to noble and higher sentiments. So I could sleep no longer. It was the precious aurora of the day of the Immaculate

Conception, and it seemed to me that the most meek Dove, our most pure Mother, had turned her gaze of special predilection to greet us amidst these wild waves, and with her voice, which carries away one's heart, invited us to rise and praise her and to put ourselves securely under the mantle of her maternal protection. Thinking of our dear Mother, I forgot all about fatigue. Going quickly to the chapel, we heard the first Mass. At the second we received Holy Communion in company with Maria Santissima, and so where we could not merit for ourselves, she, who is called the Immaculate, well merited for us. Oh, how beautiful is Mary Immaculate! God Himself created her worthy of Himself, all beautiful, all pure, all noble, all glorious! Oh, how beautiful is our Mother! The three Divine Persons love her singular majestic beauty. Mary is the greatest and the most glorious work which came from the hand of the Omnipotent, after the Most Holy Humanity of Jesus. Mary, amongst pure creatures, is the closest and most perfect image of God; the arm of God, the wisdom of God, the goodness of God are reflected with visible splendor in this privileged creature. She alone renders more glory to God than all the angels and saints taken together, and the fragrance of her virginal purity exceeds the purity of all the angels. *"Tota pulchra es, Maria et macula originalis non est in Te."* How beautiful is Mary! How amiable is this most noble creature! She is the manifestation of God on earth. Through her God will be known, adored, loved and blessed in the world, and so, rightly and in a special manner, Mary is the Mother of the Missionary of the Sacred Heart, who has for her scope the sublime mission of instructing her people in the knowledge and love of our Divine Redeemer, who, in the infinite goodness of His Divine Heart has deigned to call us to so sublime a vocation. What shall we fear, daughters, if Mary Immaculate, the pure Dove of God, is our Mother, our Refuge, our Hope, the cause of our joy? In God, dear daughters, let us put all our strength, our hope, as in their Principal Cause; in Mary as in their secondary cause.

In God, as the prime cause of all good, of all graces. In Mary, as the salutary aqueduct through which we derive the most pure waters of His Divine Goodness and Mercy.

Today we had a number of Masses. I arose at four-thirty a.m., and at five a.m. I called the Sisters. I went immediately to the chapel for the priests had already begun to celebrate the Holy Sacrifice. After seven low Masses, we had a Solemn High Mass celebrated by the Auxiliary Bishop of Montevideo, who also gave a beautiful sermon on the Immaculate Conception and on the meaning of such a dogma, proclaimed by Pius IX, so great and so famous. He showed how strong the American people were in their belief in the Immaculate Conception, even before it was defined as a dogma, and dwelt on the sublime words of the Angel Gabriel who saluted Mary. "Hail, full of Grace." She is, indeed, a singular Virgin, the Co-redemptrix of the human race, the true Mother of the living. In Mary everything is great, providential: the mission of Mary in the world has a character all its own. She is like a resplendent sun, her light is immensely powerful, her splendor is heavenly, her beauty is divine. Mary lived more in God than in herself. She was more where she loved than where she lived, and therefore her intellect was more limpid and clear than those of the Seraphim, her will being fully conformed to the Divine Will. In her beautiful soul all is light, beauty and harmony. Her body is most pure, immaculate; her purity is angelic. She is most faithful, and abandons herself entirely to God; her intention is always pure and most perfect, her love of God most fervent. It was her strong, continual and interior love that made her surpass not only the love of all the Saints, but even that of all the Seraphim. Her humility was most profound, she always sought seclusion, and kept secret from everyone, and even from herself, her highest gifts. Her charity for her neighbor was like a sweet balsam; all the miseries of the world seemed to find a place in her heart so sweet and merciful by its very nature. And today, oh, daughters, what are we to say of the characteristics of Mary? Her innate inclination is to diffuse everywhere her graces, to console all, to lead all to the knowledge and love of Jesus Christ. Oh, how beautiful and majestic does Mary appear! She is truly the holy and mystical city of God whose glorious foundations are on the peaks of the most sublime mountains. But I should never finish talking of Mary, because everywhere we behold her beauty, her power and her majesty. Of her the sea speaks by its immense extent. The waters, with their blue and transparent colors which, like crystals, reflect the colors of the most precious, rare and resplendent stones, are in their mute language like an open book recording the virtues of Mary. I should be happy if I could raise your hearts and souls towards Mary, and infuse in you a strong hope, a firm trust and a true devotion to that sweet and most loving Mother. When your weaknesses tempt you, run to Mary, invoke Mary, look at this beautiful Morning Star, who by means of her splendor disperses all darkness. If you are in danger, if your hearts are confused, turn to Mary, she is our comfort, our help, turn towards her, and you will be saved. Follow her, and you will not mistake the road that leads to Heaven, for Mary is the Gate of Heaven, and you know it well, for you never tire of singing every evening, "*Felix cæli porta.*" Blessed are you, who follow with fidelity this beautiful devotion of singing every evening in praise of Mary, the *Ave Maris Stella.* I never, even on the sea, forget to render this pious praise to our most loving Mother. After dinner I go with Mothers Anna and Michelina to the far end of the deck, and there we give vent to our voices, and, uniting them with yours in spirit, we sing the *Ave Maris Stella* and say our prayers. Afterward we enjoy ourselves by looking at the traces which this colossal steamer leaves behind it, as it cuts through the water so rapidly and so majestically. What a beautiful sight!

December 10th
Yesterday was Sunday, and the Feast of the previous day was repeated. There were several Masses, and then a Solemn High Mass celebrated by

Monsignor Romero, who explained the Feast with that facility which is his particular gift. Speaking of the answer given by Jesus Christ to the disciples sent by John to ask if He were the expected Messiah, or if they were to await another, he dwelt on the last words, "and to the poor the Gospel is preached." Here he brought out the great energy with which Our Lord pronounced these words, giving to the poor more importance than He attached to the power to cure the lame, to give sight to the blind and life to the dead. From this, the preacher showed how necessary it was for the rich to take care of the poor, for masters to give time to their dependents to fulfill their religious duties and to have them instructed in the truths of our Holy Faith. Let us hope the forceful words of the Prelate did not fall on dry stony ground, for the attention and devotion with which the passengers and the staff assisted at the Holy Sacrifice of the Mass was really edifying, Mass was celebrated in the deck-salon where the passengers were, and underneath in the dining room, where the whole ceremony could be seen. The Captain, Officers and Crew assisted. It was a most inspiring sight, especially for myself, as it was the first time after twenty voyages, that I had the happiness of seeing Holy Mass celebrated on a steamer. Every evening, at seven p.m., a bell is rung for all to come and recite the Holy Rosary. The statue of Our Lady of Mount Carmel in the salon is uncovered. The Captain is always the first on the scene, and it is most edifying to see how fervently he prays. How good this Captain is! He is just like a father, he has a good word for everyone, no one asks him anything in vain. He comes every day to ask how we are and if we need anything. He is a man full of faith, observing God's law. He enjoys great peace of mind and communicates it to others, gently inducing them also by his example to observe the law of God, that law that has been imprinted on our souls by the hand of the Most High. How sad it is to see those who, through their own fault, have allowed the darkness of incredulity to gather around them.

We have occasion to feel great sorrow in seeing men who, after abandoning the Catholic Religion, after having rebelled against Jesus Christ, reach the precipice of Atheism, Pantheism and Materialism. "There is no God," the first say. "There is no difference between good and evil," the second say. "There is nothing better than to accumulate riches by all possible means, and to give way to pleasure," exclaim the last. By means of these insensate theories they have upset the world, and many have lost their own good sense and reason. From such errors have come all the misfortunes that affect the present and menace the future. Oh, daughters, let us render the homage of our fidelity and love to our most loving Jesus, Who with ineffable mercy has deigned to enrich us with all that is necessary to obtain our temporal and eternal felicity. We are the children of God. Let us try not to degenerate from such a high and sublime dignity, and let us see that our heart, our soul and our life be always and entirely consecrated to this merciful and good Father. Let us pray that we and all creatures may give glory to God in time and eternity, that His most holy law may reign and govern us and all men from one end of the Universe to the other.

Now, we are all quite well. I never told you when I was not feeling well, but, now that it is all over, I may as well tell you. From Cadiz to Teneriffe I was obliged to sleep in the Sister's cabin, as there was not one unoccupied owing to the increase in the number of passengers. The Captain was very upset, and the Bursar, who at first seemed very indifferent, came and told me that as soon as a Colonel and his family disembarked at the Canary Islands, he would see that I was well accommodated. In fact, just as we arrived at the Canary Islands, at six p.m., they hurried to put the cabin in order for me. It is very nicely situated in that part of the steamer where the rocking is little felt, and there is a porthole to the west which I can open at pleasure. I have to keep it closed from four a.m. to seven a.m., as the sailors clean the ship during these hours and throw water about heedlessly. The water often enters through the portholes, and causes much inconvenience to those who are not expecting it. I always close the porthole before I go to bed, as I prefer to put up with the heat than to receive a surprise visit from a fish. I know the inhabitants of the Gulf Stream, but I am not too friendly with them. We had another stop in the Gulf of Santa Cruz off Teneriffe, just in front of the peak of the same name. When I studied geography as a child, which, together with history, I like better than all other subjects, and read of the peaks most celebrated for their height, I longed to see two especially, that of Miranda and that of Teneriffe. The first I thought I saw while going from San Sebastian to Bilbao, and from Bilbao to Victoria, which journey I liked very much. I was told, however, that it was not exactly there, and that I should have to go more to the west. If God spares me, I shall see it when I go through Spain, where they expect me on my return voyage. Now I shall see Teneriffe Peak at last, when approaching Santa Cruz. We perceived at first a beautiful mountain, cone-shaped, of a good height, and then other smaller ones of the same form. They looked like the Pyramids of Egypt. I almost thought I was passing through the Red Sea. It was a great joy to all the passengers to see such a beautiful sight. We longed for the steamer to stop, so that we might contemplate this grand panorama, not made by man but by the Hand of the Supreme Maker. Instead, the boat sailed on with an extraordinary rapidity. You would almost think it had taken wings and had become a flying fish, simply because our good Captain had promised to reach port before evening, and at any cost wanted to keep his word; so he increased the speed of the ship's engines. In fact, we reached here just before the sun had entirely disappeared. As we arrived, the dinner gong sounded and, though reluctantly, we had to go to table at once, so as not to keep Bishop Isaza, who presides at table, waiting, and also to be present at grace. Whilst we were dining, night came on as rapidly as it does in Central America, where twilight is unknown. There was no moon either, so we saw nothing. The Captain offered to take me ashore with the Custom officials, but as it was night, I did not accept the kind offer. We went on deck instead, and not far distant we could distinguish the Peak of Santa Cruz, which was lighted up with electric lamps, and we also saw some steamers which had either entered the port before us or were about to enter at the same time as ourselves. Amongst them was the *Duke of Galliera*, lovely in form and lighted up with a hundred lights.

I have never traveled on that steamer, but I have done so on the *Victoria*, a sister ship of the same Company. Of this vessel, there remains only the wreck near Genoa after the disaster of 1898, when it was destroyed by fire. Its passengers were fortunately all saved, as well as the crew, by seeking shelter on the *Alicante*. Five of our Sisters were the last to leave the ship at the Captain's bidding, who did all in his power to save it. The fire took place in a cargo of sulfur, which it was impossible to extinguish. That terrible disaster might have taken place in mid-ocean, where rescue would have perhaps been impossible, but the loving Providence of God, Who watches over His creatures, did not allow such a tragedy to happen, Our Sisters had with them relics of Saint Vitallione, and the Holy Martyr showed the power of his protection by rescuing everyone from danger, together with the cargo, except the sulphur. The disaster was caused by some youngsters having hidden themselves in the hold in order to have a free passage. They had not the means to pay for their passage, but they did harm to themselves and to others. It occurred to me to tell you this, because on the steamer *Alphonsus XIII*, on which we are traveling, there were hidden seven youths, from eighteen to twenty years of age, who took advantage of the night during which we stopped at Cadiz. But the good Captain and the Bursar, who are wide awake, and interest themselves in everything, found them as soon as we left port and imprisoned them. When we arrived at the Canary Islands, they were handed over to the custody of the police at Santa Cruz of Teneriffe to be sent back at the first moment to Spain, where they will be cross-examined as to whether they sought a free passage because they were unable to defray the expense, or because they had committed some crime and were flying from justice. The two Bishops, Monsignor Romero and Monsignor Isaza, as soon as they knew the unfortunates were imprisoned, went to the Captain to obtain their liberty. It was not difficult to obtain some clemency from this good Captain–Captain Decampa. The good Prelates, in the meantime, gave them some money which alleviated a little the merited punishment.

That evening after dinner we found a store opened on the deck as if by magic. It had been arranged by some young men from the Canary Islands, who came on board to sell wicker chairs, small and large, and so nice that everyone was tempted to buy one. They also offered shoes, laces, embroidery, silk shawls, woolen vests, etc., and they did a good business, for the passengers bought lots of things. A lady wanted me to help her, so I chose one I liked, a table-center, very well made. What was my surprise when I found out that the lady had bought it to make a present of it to me when I call on her in her own house. I shall not tell you the name of this lady now, but later on I shall have to speak of her, as she intends to do something great for the Institute. As soon as the lady had satisfied her purchasing propensity, we withdrew from the market, for we could not remain amidst such confusion. In the morning we got up with the desire of going on deck to enjoy the wonderful sights of these mountains, but we had first to go to the chapel to hear Holy Mass and to receive Holy Communion. The Masses succeeded one another, and we heard them all on behalf of the souls of Purgatory, and so the time grew late. The steamer raised anchor, steaming at a great rate, so much so, that when we went on deck we were a great distance from land, and only the top of the Peak of Teneriffe could be seen. It appeared to follow us with all the majesty for which it is renowned. It has a very pointed peak like the peak of a volcano not yet fully open, and on either side of the slopes there extend, in the shape of a tail, other mountains which seem to be its offspring. This is a feature of volcanoes, which nearly always have other mountains dependent on them, and in whose prominence, it would appear, they find vent.

On the day after we had left the Canary Islands, the luggage was placed on deck to satisfy the requirements of the passengers, so that they might get what they wanted. Those who embarked at Genoa were the last served, as their luggage was down at the bottom of the hold. However, when the bell rung for dinner, I asked the Head Steward to please watch for my trunks as I wanted to open them. The man told me I could rest assured, as he would see to them, When I came up, lo and behold, the man told me he had seen to all my trunks, and had sent them down again. Whether I had not explained myself sufficiently, or whether he had misunderstood me. I do not know, but he thought he had done me a great service. I said, "My good man, I wanted to open them." At this stage the Bursar came forward and asked me if I would like to go down to open them, which offer I accepted at once, but in the short intervening space of time they had piled up so many on top of mine, that it was impossible to see them, much less to open them. Several sailors offered to remove the great pile in order to extract mine, but I hadn't the heart to make them go through so much trouble and fatigue, so I contented myself with my small stateroom trunk, lending the Sisters some of my own clothes. Providence, which watches over us like a loving mother, kept the weather cool. All had thought that the heat would be suffocating, especially near the Equator, and for some hours it was indeed such. But the rest of the voyage was more of a pleasure trip than a tiring voyage.

12. Buenos Aires to Genoa
August, 1901

From the bay of Buenos Aires, August 22nd, 1901

My dear Daughters,

May the good Jesus be with you all and comfort you. May He accompany us on your voyage and conduct us to port. Amen.

Nel Cuor dolcissimo
D'immenso amore
Io voglio chiudermi
In tutte l'ore;
Da Lui vo' attingere
Pace e conforto
Ch' Ei farà scendere
Nel mare e in porto.

We embarked on the 22nd of August, but I have not begun to write until today, the 28th, when we have just left the port of Santos. The day I left Buenos Aires I was not feeling well, and your farewell and that of the children had really overcome me, and I remained in this exhausted state for a good while. Having said goodbye to the three Sisters who were at the farthest end of the bay, I went to my cabin and to bed. My bones were stiffened with pain, and I hadn't the strength to move the smallest object. I wanted to put my cabin in order, but I had to leave it as it was, for I could not stand. Two days later I felt better, and well enough to go ashore at Santos, though it was raining. I asked the way to the church, and those whom I interrogated wanted to know if I was looking for the *"Igreja."* I was afraid of being directed to some schismatic church, so said "No," and went on. On asking others I got the same reply, so at last I understood that the word meant Catholic Church. Some offered to go with us to the Parish Church, which they call the Mother Church.

When we arrived at the church we found Solemn High Mass just beginning, accompanied by drums and trumpets, which took the place of an organ or harmonium, neither of which the church possessed. In the meantime we asked a priest to give us Holy Communion at the Altar of the Blessed Sacrament, and thus comforted by the Food of Angels, we returned to the steamer, sure of a happy and prosperous voyage. It was raining, and we got quite wet. Had it not been that we wished to receive Holy Communion, we should not have gone ashore at all. We had two umbrellas, but when we reached the church that of my companion would not close, so we left it open without any one taking the least notice of it. One good man turned to me and said, "It is our curate who is celebrating Mass, he is very good and we love him very much." He spoke to me in Portuguese, and I understood him fairly well, as it is a language which, one might say, comes midway between the Italian and Spanish languages. I could do nothing else but congratulate him. When we had finished our devotions, we went to the sacristy to ask the curate's blessing. He received us with singular kindness. He wanted to entertain us longer, but we had no time, so said goodbye, accompanied by his blessing, which seemed like that of a patriarch. I wanted to visit the town, but there was no carriage to be had, so we returned at once on board.

The steamer then departed, and in two hours' time we reached Rio Janeiro. It was about two p.m., and I should have loved to visit the town, but the steamer stood out a great distance from the land. Moreover, the sea, as usual in this place, was very rough, so I thought it better not to undertake the double journey there and back, especially as I wanted to go and receive Holy Communion the next morning, which I did not want to miss. The captain had told me they would remain in port until the following day at two p.m., so the next morning we went on shore as soon as possible. They had offered me the ship's boat, but I should have had to wait until eight a.m. So I decided to hire a boat, trusting to the Providence of God to carry me safely through the agitated waves and over a distance lasting half-an-hour. In fact, we reached land quite safely, and turned towards the first steeple we could see. We lost sight of it, however, as we passed through the narrow streets and between the houses. So we asked for the "Igreja," having learnt the name at Santos, and everyone with great kindness pointed out the way to us. We entered the first church we saw, it was called the Candelaria; it is beautiful, rich and kept in great cleanliness. The altars are of very fine colored marble. On the High Altar there is a statue of Our Lady with the Infant Jesus. This Madonna is called Our Lady of the Candelaria or Purification. I took pleasure in counting the candle sticks on the High Altar, which were grand and in the form of a pyramid, and were placed at the foot of Our Lady. They were fifty-two in number. Perhaps the number had some meaning, but, not knowing the language, I was unable to ask why the candlesticks should be fifty-two in number. As soon as we entered the church we went to the Altar of the Blessed Sacrament which was along the nave of the church, next to the High Altar. Above it hung a majestic, monumental Crucifix, under which was a painting of Calvary.

Several Canons were reciting the Office, and two altar boys were seated near the Canons. I called one to tell him that I wanted to receive Holy Communion. He spoke to one of the Canons, who answered that the Office would last two hours, during which no one could receive Holy Communion. I could not wait, so I asked the boy to show me the way to another church, which he did very willingly. Saluting the Blessed Sacrament, I was just on the point of leaving when I met a priest and told him I should like to receive Holy Communion, but that I could not wait for two hours, and would he please show me the way to another church? "No, no." he said, "Stay here. I am going to say Mass at which you can receive Holy Communion." In fact, as quickly as he could, he came and celebrated Mass at the second altar of the church–the Altar of the Sacred Heart which was beautiful also. As the lovely benches of the church did not reach so far down as this altar, the sacristan came forward with two lovely cushions for us to kneel upon. I was astonished at so much kindness, but it was in keeping with the dignity of the whole place that great courtesy should be shown to visitors. Having made our thanksgiving and had a look round the church, we went out, and as my companion and I were now very hungry, I sought a café where we appeased our hunger, and then, taking a cab, we visited the town, which is partly built on hills. We went to that part called Saint Anna, as they told us the Papal Legate resided here, but, meeting a priest, he told us the Legate was at Petropolis. We lost no time, and descending halfway, we met the Vicar General, who asked us at once if we had seen the Bishop. "No," I said, "for I did not know he lived here, and I have no time to go back." I gave him my visiting card to present to the Bishop. He took it very kindly, said he would present it at once to the Bishop, and that he would ask for a special blessing for the prosperous continuation of my voyage. I felt very sorry I could not return, but there was no time. From this grand hill you can see the whole town and the bay. I should have loved to go to Petropolis, but it was three hours distance by rail, so there was no possibility of my going, Rio Janeiro is really beautiful! I like its smiling hills, its spacious squares and pretty gardens. I shall say nothing of the churches, as you have an idea after my description of the Candelaria. The Canal which enters the bay of Rio Janeiro is charming. What beautiful cone-shaped mountains! One of these owing to its shape is called the "Sugar Loaf." These and others are so formed that they seem to rain abundance on the country. Even at Santos the same impression is made, though Santos is not so much favored by nature. It is simply a road to St. Paul, which city everyone praises for its beauty. Brazil is certainly richer than the Argentine. They say it is not healthy, but I think that applies only to the lower and marshy parts of the town, which, if cleansed and put in order, would not suffer from contagious diseases. There are some very narrow and dirty streets in Rio Janeiro, and the water which runs in the gutters, instead of cleansing like water does in the streets of Paris, rather helps to infect the town, for it looks more like slush.

At Buenos Aires the superintendent of the "Veloce" Company had given us two lovely cabins, one for the Sisters and one for myself, opposite each other and in the best possible position, as they were on the west side of the steamer, where one never feels the contrary winds. We could always keep our portholes open and always have fresh air. At Santos a large number of new passengers came on board. The steamer was quite full, and there was no more room, but some recommended by the superintendent and others by influential persons, managed to get on board, and thus passengers in excess of the proper number were accepted. I feared a little, but, as our tickets were endorsed "Reserved Cabins," I remained tranquil. The day was almost over when I perceived the Doctor approaching me. On behalf of the Commander he made a request. He said I had every right to refuse the favor about to be asked, but, as it was a very special case, he wanted to know if I would allow a lady, the wife of a chemist of Saint Paul, a Venetian, to sleep in the same cabin with the Sisters; she was traveling for family reasons only, and her husband asked as a favor that she might be placed near the Sisters. He made the request so courteously that it was impossible to refuse him, and so I consented. And I am not sorry that I did so, for the lady is very good, courteous and refined, so much so, that one finds pleasure in her company. One would think she formed part of the Community herself, everyone admires her and respects her.

After we left Rio Janeiro, the sea was very rough or "bravo," as the Spaniards say; indeed, it was so agitated that one would think it was really "bravo" (angry). At night, especially, it frightened me, as it was the first time I ever made such a long voyage on such a small steamer as *The Piemonte.* When we left Buenos Aires we were never tired of praising it, as it did not make the slightest movement, but since it took on board a cargo of twenty thousand sacks of coffee at Santos, it has never given us a moment's peace. It may have been the wind or the cargo, but the fact remains that since that day the rocking never ceased, and so momentous was it that one expected the steamer to capsize at any moment. Not being an experienced sailor, I thought my fear was justified, but the day after I asked the Captain, and all my fear disappeared. Other disasters might happen, he said, but not the capsizing of the boat. The Captain said the worst disaster of all was fire, but, he added, that even in the case of fire there were many ways of saving oneself, the boat being built in such a way that it could be isolated into three separate parts in case of such a danger arising.

13. London to New York

August, 1902

My dear Children,

Oh! quanti bei manipoli,
Che sparsi son nel campo
　　Senza temer inciampo,
Con Dio raccoglieró.
Mon mi sgomenta il viaggio,
　　Neppure la procella;
Sempre da buona ancella
L'ufficio mio faró.
　　Gesù! quel caro Dio
Mi accende in fondo al core
　　Il palpito d'amore
Spronandomi ad oprar.
Su dungue, figlie care,
　　Sempre per me pregate,
Il divin Cuore amate
　　Che il cuor puó inebbriar.

On board the *Etruria,* of the Cunard Line, my thoughts fly to you, my beloved children; you, who afford me so much comfort, and, though I am tired and worn out, nevertheless I write you, for I know you are anxious to have some news, and it is a great pleasure for me to satisfy your desires.

I arrived in London on August the 5th, after having visited our House in Paris, which, like a steamer guided by a good pilot, is spreading its sails and navigating prosperously in the midst of the terrible storm that at this moment is agitating all Religious Institutes in France, causing them great consternation. I could not have done otherwise, for this brave Pilot, this Omnipotent Pilot, is the Heart of Jesus of Montmartre, to whom I confided in a special manner our interests in France. From the height of that happy hill, where He is honored, He benignly looks at His children and defends them from the wild billows that assault and threaten to destroy all that savors of Religion; in a word, everything animated by God's charity. It is a real miracle that the House still exists. The Sisters near us, and even the Sisters of Charity have been sent away from the schools. They could not get the better of their enemies, though the people rose up to defend them, guarding their houses night and day. We, as foreigners, have few friends in France, and I did not ask even these few to defend us, but I placed all my confidence in that sweet and amiable Sacred Heart of Montmartre, Which in the end is destined to save the whole of France, and will cause to arise from this storm much good and new fervor that will render France worthy of her honorable traditions.

So, on the 5th I left Paris, and taking the line Calais and Dover, arrived in London. It was a fine day, but a greater sight still presented itself to my vision on my arrival as the sun went down. A sight I had never seen before appeared playfully in the heavens. Some clouds resplendent with gold formed a glorious throne, in the midst of which shone forth an extraordinary light, surrounded by twelve shining stars which sent forth sparkling rays. It seemed to be the throne of the Queen of Angels. I then saw Our Blessed Lady wearing a beautiful diadem, with the Child Jesus on her knees stretching His Arms out in the act of protecting us. Though it was but the playful movement of the clouds at the setting of the sun in England, its happening just as we reached London gave us great pleasure, and it seemed to augur a special protection from Heaven over our foundation in London. My two companions, Mothers Flora and Albertina, were very enthusiastic about this beautiful vision. At the station we were met by two Sisters, who had been sent in advance to secure accommodation for us, as owing to the approaching ceremonies of the Coronation of King Edward and Queen Alexandra, it was difficult to find lodgings in the great metropolis, where there were already assembled representatives from every part of the world. In fact, the two Sisters found us a place with the Servite Nuns, with whom we remained a fortnight; and in the meantime we visited His Lordship, Monsignor Bourne, Bishop of Southwark, who, like a good friend of our Institute, opened the way for us, so that in a short time we were able to find a house on one of the hills of London, and in a big parish where as yet there was no Religious House, thus offering good field for us. I wrote to the Propaganda to obtain the decree required for a foundation in England, and got the answer very quickly, so that when we entered our new convent we could say that the House was established with full ecclesiastical approval.

The morning of the 23rd was very rainy and we had to leave about ten a.m. We set out to take the twelve a.m. train for Liverpool. You may ask why it took so long to go to the station, but you would not be surprised if you were in London and saw the vastness of this metropolis. If you take a cab for an hour's journey, it is always wise to set out two hours in advance, as the traffic of London is so great, that you never know when you will reach your destination.

At twelve a.m. we boarded the train, which flew through towns and fields at such a speed that at four p.m. we arrived without a stop at Liverpool. We left the train to embark at once on the *Etruria*. In a very short space of time she raised her anchors and rapidly set out towards Ireland. The next morning we arrived at Queenstown, Cork, where the steamer stopped for half-an-hour only to take on board passengers, vegetables and fruit, and then set sail at once, so that in a few hours time we were already on the high seas. My companions were quite well, but after breakfast on the 24th they began to suffer from stomach trouble, and for the whole day they had to keep to their cabins on account of sea sickness. Mother Flora thought she was really going to die. Mother Albertina acted the same way. I sent them to bed, and there was no way of getting them up again. It was only this morning about eleven a.m. that they seemed to get the better of the sea. Today the good little Sisters, persuaded that the sea was all right, have come on deck to enjoy the fresh air, and are feeling better. The sea is not so bad, but it is a little rough and choppy, producing that rocking which is trying to those who are not accustomed to the sea, and who do not love, as I do, the sea like the fish. I feel better when there is a little movement, and storms seem to give me an appetite. "God tempers the wind to the shorn lamb."

He has made me, in the goodness of His Divine Heart, a Missionary, and has confided to me far-distant Missions, and though I have habitual ill-health, I feel better at sea.

But in the meantime I fly to you in spirit, rejoicing greatly at seeing you gathered together to carry out the Spiritual Exercises for the Annual Retreat. "I will conduct my beloved into the solitude, and there I will speak to her heart." Blessed are you, my dear daughters, who hear the voice of your Beloved, Who helps you to appreciate more and more the sublimity of the Religious state to which, through the sheer goodness of Our Lord you have been called. Oh, yes, the Missionary of the Sacred Heart bears the seal of God, and proves to all that her election to such a state comes not from nature but from grace. His Divine Will, the extension of the Kingdom of Jesus Christ, is all that concerns us, so that the luminous and glorious motto of the Missionary of the Sacred Heart is always and everywhere–"All to the greater glory of the Most Sacred Heart of Jesus," and in difficulties, *Omnia possum in Eo qui me confortat.* Always appreciate the great gift God has given you by calling you to Holy Religion. He alone, the Master elects, calls and destines His Creatures to the noble state, the high dignity of becoming His Spouses. Yes! God alone, through His Divine goodness, chooses for His glory a weak, fragile creature. No, it is not nature that can claim supernatural graces and gifts of grace, but the goodness and benignity of God, who raises nature to a celestial life. It is not nature that renders herself superior to her strength, but Divine Grace which condescends to human weakness and thus manifests the absolute authority of God over us, while it discloses again His infinite mercy and goodness by raising us poor human creatures to the Divine nuptials. Dear children! It is only by an ineffable condescension that God deigns to strengthen our fragile clay, to sanctify it, to purify it, and to render it capable of becoming a precious instrument in the Religious House, in the Church, both

Militant and Triumphant. At the end of the Retreat you will have the good fortune of renewing your vows. This renewal is a new promise of a sincere and generous offering which we make to our Divine Spouse, and it is a real glory to be dedicated and consecrated to Him. To renew our vows is to renew our Profession, to offer to the Lord the new fruits of the same tree, and to burn on the same Altar of our heart new grains of incense, in the odor of sweetness, to the Divine Heart.

By the renewal of our vows we confirm ourselves in good, increase our fervor in piety and devotion, make ourselves more energetic in the discharge of our duties, cling more closely to the most amiable Heart of Jesus, love more tenderly the Institute to which we have been called. This renewal recalls to our minds the immense benefits received, and enriches us with new benefits, new graces, new blessings and new merits. By the renovation of our vows we cancel our faults, negligences, omissions and all the imperfections we have committed, whether they be against our vows or against the Holy Rules. It not only cancels and destroys in us these stains, but strengthens all our acts of virtue. Oh! what an immense benefit does the renewal of our vows bestow!

Every time we renew our vows, it is as if we just then and there took our holy vows or made our Profession, increasing again and again the glory of God and our merits. All works that refer to God directly never become old; our most loving Lord is His infinite goodness always looks upon them with that same complacency with which He regarded them when they were performed for the first time. In every work God always considers our will, which should be always firm, constant and persevering in serving Him faithfully until death, just as we promised on the day of our Profession.

How this, my dear daughters, should animate us to frequently renew the act of our total consecration to God, or, at least, every time we go to Holy Communion!

How much it helps us to remember our first Profession made at the end of the Novitiate! Do you remember it? What a grand day! It was really the day of the Lord!

"Hæc dies quam fecit Dominus; exultemus et lætemur in ea." At that moment we experienced how lovely it was to consecrate ourselves to God, and how Jesus had been awaiting us so long. We tasted the ineffable sweetness of the Religious life. Our souls were filled with gifts typical of a new Baptism, all of Divine fire. The joy of the Holy Ghost, that so abundantly inundated our souls on the day of our Confirmation, copiously filled our hearts with celestial joy on the day of our first Profession. On that solemn and never-to-be-forgotten occasion we drank large draughts from the Most Holy Wounds of the Divine Redeemer. The heavens lowered themselves and approached the earth. The Divine Lamb, in the extreme amiability of His Divine Heart, exulted with joy at celebrating with us the mystical Espousals. Remember always, dear daughters, that our Espousal with Jesus was the work of the Holy Ghost, Who united us with our dear Jesus when we pronounced our Religious Vows. At that moment we felt ourselves raised up to a new power of the knowledge and love of our dear Jesus. The books of the Incarnate Wisdom were disclosed to our intellectual eyes, and then it was we understood new truths, new doctrines regarding our Religious Vocation and our special Mission, predestinated to eternal glory, through the observance of our vows.

Then it was we entered the Promised Land. Divine Grace opened out to us its treasures, and we received from our beloved Spouse full faculties with which to enrich ourselves at our pleasure. Regenerated on that holy day into a holy and blessed new life, we were by a celestial wave purified by Divine Grace, sanctified and reformed. We became new creatures, living images of our Creator, in a word, on that memorable day we were sealed by the Hands of God as His inheritance and property, now and forever. But what merits had we that we should be favored to enter the House of God? On the contrary, how many demerits that should have excluded us! Nevertheless the good Jesus did not look at our unworthiness, but only at His own Infinite Goodness. He really loved us, and did good to us, introducing us into His Holy House, sharing with us all His treasures.

Do you remember, daughters, the vision of Jacob? Whilst journeying, he saw a ladder that reached from earth to Heaven, and the Angels were ascending and descending upon it. Awaking, he exclaimed, "This is the House of God, the Gate of Heaven, and I did not know."

The passage from the Religious Community to Heaven is very short. Oh, blessed, a thousand times blessed, are those who live in the House of the Celestial Father, because they will praise and glorify Him for all eternity.

Remember, however, dear daughters, that it is not enough to live in a holy land to be holy; rather, it is necessary to live saintly, according to the Rules, and in the actual exercise of virtue. One cannot be called holy who merely belongs to a family of Saints, if he does not walk in the footsteps of the Saints. Our Divine Master, our most loving Spouse Himself, tells us so, "Not those who say Lord, Lord, shall enter Heaven, but those who do the Will of My Father." And what is the will of our Celestial Father in our regard? We have to comply with His Will expressed in the Holy Rules, in our Holy Vows, and in other obligations proper to the Institute.

If you want to become Saints, dear daughters, you must esteem your Holy Rules and regard the observance of them as the price of your eternal predestination. Be prudent virgins, always keep your lamps lighted with faith and the fulfillment of the laws professed. Be faithful, and observant, both in the greater and the minor Rules, for the most loving Jesus has prepared for you incalculable riches.

Remember always, dear daughters, that the Holy Rules are like a precious treasure which the loving Jesus gives His Spouse, so that she may grow continually in merit and in virtue. They are an inexhaustible mine of graces and blessings. They are fountains from which gush forth the perennial waters of life and salvation. They are the mystical chains of the solid gold of charity which are like sweet ties ever drawing us closer to our most loving Savior. In the observance of the Rules, you will find, my daughters, a superhuman strength to combat and to conquer all your enemies, you will find peace, joy and all spiritual riches. If you become really observant, you can say in truth you have found every good. In your Holy Rules only does your perfection consist, and in vain will you look for your sanctification outside of the road traced for us by the Holy Ghost. Remember that every point of the Rule has an immense importance for you, and it is for this reason I always exhort you to be ever faithful in both greater and minor regulations. Remember the story of Samson, whose strength was in the hair of his head. When his hair was cut by Delilah, he became weak and fell into the hands of his enemies. This fact teaches us clearly that all the strength of a Religious is in the observance of the Rules, even the minutest, figured by the hair. When a Religious forgets or despises the observance of the Rules, she loses the vigor of her spirit, her strength, her virtue, and then falls into the hands of her enemies, who are ever ready for her ruin. If our Holy Rules do not bind under pain of sin, except when they are despised, it is nevertheless true that every voluntary transgression, however small, is a disorder in

God's House, and inflicts a new wound on holy observance. Moreover, it is a lack of correspondence with Divine grace, a sorrow to the Most Adorable Heart of our most loving and sweet Jesus; it is a degree of grace and glory lost. Saint Teresa was right in exhorting and inculcating the exact and minutest observance of the Holy Rules and timetable, because the diligent and observant Religious will not only walk in perfection, but will fly along the path of good, and in a short time will find herself rich in virtue and merits.

27th

It is already the 27th August, and since last night the foghorn has been continually sounding, as there is a dense fog, and there is danger of our meeting other steamers, which might mean a great disaster. In spite of all this, the Sisters and I slept quietly, reposing in the Most Sacred Heart of Jesus, who, through our Superiors, has sent us on this voyage, assuring us that He would be our Pilot, our Guide, our sure Refuge. At seven-thirty we left our cabin, but owing to the dampness and fog we could not remain on deck, so we went to the music room, and each one did her own work there. Mother Flora painted a pretty card for the Captain who was so kind to her. Mother Albertina copied music and went through some pieces, and I finished my letter to you, speaking to you, my beloved daughters of the observance of the Holy Rules which will make you holy and blessed.

At nine a.m. we went to table for breakfast, but the Captain, who always goes also when we go, is not with us this morning, as he has to remain on the bridge. It is always dangerous in these great fogs. Perhaps he may not even come to lunch, as it is already midday and the fog is as dense as ever. Amongst the four hundred passengers there is a man by the name of Valdobrandi, a tourist by profession, who voyages with an American Company, and who has made the round of the world. He is a very nice person. Having noticed that we eat little, he comes every day to explain the menu to us, and so encourages us to eat everything. There is also an Italian Doctor called Cucchi; he rather needs to be comforted by us, as he has suffered very much from seasickness and is very timid. He is traveling for a Bologna Society of Doctors, and is going to the Tropics to learn about the diseases in those places. The poor man didn't eat for three days, but, encouraged by Mr. Valdobrandi and by us, he is feeling better.

28th

This morning again we had fog, but it didn't last long. The sun soon broke through, and we have a most beautiful day. The sea is as calm as a lake. Yesterday the fog was obstinate, today it lifted at once, and we could see in this the figure of a docile soul which allows itself to be overcome by the grace of God, the Sun of Justice, whilst a rebellious soul resists all the most beautiful graces, and becomes hard and exposes itself to great danger. Blessed will you be if you are animated by the spirit of Obedience, because that precious virtue makes your way sure. In Obedience all is light, splendor, grace, health, joy and peace. Love obedience, my daughters. Remember, a true Religious is always and in everything obedient. She knows no delay, she never puts off till the morrow what has been commanded today, being always ready for whatsoever is ordered. The truly obedient soul performs exactly and entirely all that has been commanded. She does not do her work in part, but entirely and completely. She does not offer half of the Victim to her Celestial Spouse, but she offers it whole and entire, and so the whole sacrifice is acceptable and rises with a sweet odor to Heaven. It is, indeed, a heavenly sight to see a Religious obey cheerfully with a spirit of joy, whilst on the contrary it causes pain to see another who obeys with laments and difficulties.

The good Religious conforms her judgment perfectly to that of her Superior. She thinks as her Superior, hence the intellect and judgment of a good Religious are in all things conformed to the intellect and judgment of the Superior, as the pious will can bend the intellect, as Saint Ignatius observes, in things that are not self-evident. You, my dear daughters, want to become holy and perfect. Behold the shortest and surest way is to give yourselves cheerfully to the exercise of obedience. Do not look and consider the qualities, gifts and ways of the Superior, otherwise you will exchange the Divine for the human. See in the Superior only the authority of God. Blessed will you be if you know how to obtain from God the true spirit of obedience, to merit such a beautiful grace, do all in your power to obtain it. Obey promptly and exactly, not only her who is greater than you, but submit willingly to your equals and interiors. When you work, pray, eat, recreate yourself, do all in the spirit of obedience, trying in all things to deny your own will, and conforming it to that of your most amiable Spouse, Who is always looking at you and all you do for His love, and observing the manner in which you do it. If you do everything in the spirit of holy obedience, you give new splendor to even the most ordinary tasks which you perform for the Community, because of obedience that accompanies every act is even greater than the work itself.

The great people of the earth have their coats-of-arms, or shields, which remind them of their illustrious ancestors, or of some of their glorious deeds, and I would love that the Shield of the Missionary Sisters of the Sacred Heart should have written on it very clearly the beautiful and really glorious words which Jesus said of Himself, "*Ego quæ placita sunt ei facio semper.*" Obedience is a revealed word, a ray of living light that descends upon us from the Father of Lights, a manifestation to us of His Divine Will. God does what He likes with obedient souls, they are the delight of His most adorable and sweet Heart. To all obedient hearts

God communicates willingly all His lights, His gifts, His most precious graces. On these He causes to shine the light of His face, and fills them with happiness and delights of every kind. You, dear daughters, are Missionaries. You must render yourselves capable of gaining many souls to the Heart of Jesus. So try and acquire the true spirit of obedience, because it is through such obedient souls that Jesus accomplishes on this earth His sublime designs and great works. The good Jesus likes to stay with obedient souls, and guides them with His wisdom. He illumines them with His light, He comforts them with His grace, and makes them arbiters of His inheritance. Yes, daughters, she who is obedient to Jesus and acquires a true spirit of obedience, obtains that all creatures become obedient to her, and so she conducts them to the Kingdom of Jesus Christ. But I should never finish talking of the holy treasure of obedience that will make you blessed, so I conclude by exhorting you to recall well the words of the angelic Saint Thomas, that it is obedience that makes the Religious, and that of the three Vows it is the first and principal, for by the vow of poverty we give our goods, by the vow of chastity our own body, but by the vow of obedience we give our whole being, which is certainly much more, as the soul with its powers is by far more excellent and more noble than riches and the body. Be victorious, my daughters, but in what way? By being truly obedient, for obedient souls triumph over their enemies.

It is the afternoon of the 28th. The sea looks more beautiful than ever, and my companions are charmed. Several dolphins follow the steamer, to our great amusement. Some passengers asked Mother Albertina to play the piano. This she did and pleased them very much, they saw that Catholics can be sociable when occasion presents itself. An English Protestant lady, a great writer and a contributor to the *Chicago Tribune*, came to me afterwards, and in the course of her conversation, showed a secret desire to become a Catholic. She remarked that she would go on writing until the Anglican Church became Catholic again, for England is the nation which has given the Church more saintly Kings than any other country. It was very strange to hear her speak in that strain, but she is an intelligent person, and if she works on the right lines she will do a great deal of good. She wanted the address of our House in Rome, so that when she returned she might visit us and seek some Catholic Priest to instruct her in the Catholic Religion. If the Sacred Heart would only bless us so much as to give us such a conversion, the suffering of this voyage would be very little to endure. To the Sacred Heart of my Jesus nothing is impossible. He is the Master of Hearts. He can change them in a moment as He changed that of Saint Augustine, the great Father and Doctor of the Church, whose feast we celebrate today.

14. On the Occasion of the Inauguration of the House in Denver

November, 1902

Denver, Colorado, 18th November, 1902

My dear Daughters,

Yesterday, in the presence of His Lordship, the Bishop of Denver, a large number of priests, amongst whom were several Jesuit Fathers, and a select audience, including the flower of the Italian Colony, the new Mission of this capital was solemnly inaugurated, and His Lordship blessed the School recently opened for the education of Italians in this city.

A few months ago, Monsignor Matz, the Bishop of Denver, met two of our Sisters, and, having grasped a little of the spirit of the work of our Institute, was desirous of having a foundation of ours in Denver. He wrote to me at once, and accompanied his request by such pressing exhortations showing all the good the Institute could do, the necessity of our work in that country, the vast field, as he put it, that the

Missionaries would find in which to exercise their zeal, etc., that it was impossible to refuse the offer.

I knew the conditions of the country, which in a few years had made rapid development, and I realized His Lordship's assertions were quite true. I had not the heart to refuse him the work of the Institute when the greater glory of God was in question. After mature consideration, I consented to comply with the wishes of His Lordship, and we arrived here two or three weeks ago to launch the new foundation. The opening took place yesterday, and was solemnly inaugurated and blessed by the Pastor at whose desire we had come to Denver. On our arrival in this city, the Sisters found a vast field of labor. Though our work extends to every class, without regard to nationality, nevertheless the number of Italians is very great, and this renders our Mission all the more necessary. A School is needed for our children, in order to prevent them from going to the public schools, where they do not receive religious instruction, this being given only in the parochial schools. Apart from the children, the adults think only of gaining their living, and forget all about their souls. There are to be found here young people, up to thirty years of age, who have not made their First Communion yet. There are marriages which have not been blessed by the priest, children not baptized. In the mountains, hundreds of workmen are to be found oppressed by work, living far from the church, where Mass is seldom celebrated, who have not approached the Sacraments for many years, but they are in such good dispositions that they only need encouragement, and if we go to them with Christ's charity, which is all to all, they will, as good sheep, return to God and listen with docility to the voice that calls.

It will not be long before the Sisters will have the pleasure of preparing for the beautiful and consoling functions which are enjoyed in Louisiana and in other States, where they teach the Catechism to the poor peasants and prepare them for Holy Communion, which perhaps they have not received for more than fifty years. Here also they will prepare in a small hut, or sometimes under a tree, an Altar, the canopy of which is the sky and the walls of which are the beauties of nature. Here, in the midst of this poverty, Jesus, docile to the word of the priest, descends into the hearts of these poor people, whom He loves so much. At other times it is the Bishop himself who, in this immense temple of nature, having for his throne the trunk of a tree, for a carpet the green moss of the mountains, or the green grass wet with dew, administers the Sacrament of Confirmation to his children, on whom from Heaven God looks with complacency.

To begin our work, we opened a School at once, to which two hundred children came the very first day. Yesterday we had the pleasure of having it blessed by our worthy Bishop of Denver. He is a man after God's own Heart, full of charity, zeal and sacrifice, for the good of the sheep entrusted to his care. The most Sacred Heart of Jesus has inspired him with such confidence in the work of the Missionaries of the Sacred Heart, and with so much affection for them, that we feel we have a father in him, one who will help us and second our efforts, and offer us new fields in which to do good.

Like a good father, he himself desired to bless our children, so we had to prepare a reception for His Lordship. You may imagine how happy we were to offer our tribute of gratitude to our good Bishop. Everything seemed easy, despite the shortness of time at our disposal, the difficulty of polishing, as it were, those little mountain stones, our children, who certainly possess hidden gems of the best quality, though at present they are rather rough and unpolished. We must admit, however, that they surprised us by their brightness, docility, good nature and lovely simplicity. The children worked a whole week with might and main and with growing anxiety as the day drew near.

It was lovely yesterday morning to see them arrive from all parts, notwithstanding the snow, on which, like a beautiful white mantle, the sun's rays sparkled and covered the earth. They were dressed in white, and they took their places in the center of the old church, which is now converted into a schoolhouse. The two side aisles were crowded with their parents. Just in the center was erected a stage, artistically adorned with the Papal colors, and in the midst of which hung the portrait of our immortal Pontiff. How could he be missing from our gatherings and festivals? It is he who protects our Institute so much, who loves us so much, and who renders our work fruitful by his blessings, and in whose name and at whose command I feel encouraged to undertake any work, assured that, leaning on the rock of the Vatican, I have nothing to fear, but, on the contrary, have in that protection a pledge of celestial favors.

Now this sight was quite new to the Italians of this city, and one could perceive the purest joy in their countenances, as well as in that of the Rector, who moved about amongst his parishioners with his face lit up with smiles. The good Jesuit Fathers Pantanella and Gubitosi, who help so much in this Mission, were equally delighted as well as the poor parents, who underneath a modest smile hid the pride they felt as they watched their children file out in order to the music of a march and take their places with a discipline that squalled that of our other Schools which have been long established. The hall presented a beautiful and consoling sight, which struck me as being the first-fruits of a Mission which will develop under the fructifying patronage of the Most Sacred Heart of Jesus.

A few minutes after ten a.m. the bell announced that the Bishop was approaching the School from our House, which in his kindness he had visited in order to see me. In a few minutes the carriage drove to the School, where the good Bishop, accompanied by a number of priests, entered the hall. With quick step, and smiling all over with kindness, he saluted the children and their parents in their mother-tongue, our Italian language, which he speaks well. He also speaks English, German, Spanish and French. The children, who had been taught to make a profound curtsy to their Bishop, as was becoming in the case of one in his high position, understood from his sweet and familiar salutation that he was indeed a father among them, and so they greeted him with great enthusiasm. As he confessed afterward, the good Prelate was greatly surprised to see so many children gathered under the protecting wings of our Holy Mother the Church. His heart was filled with joy, and, as he said, he understood the sentiments of Jesus better on an occasion like that, for when Our Lord was surrounded by children, He spoke these words, "Let little children come unto me, for of such is the kingdom of Heaven."

He took the above words as the text of his address, which he delivered after the children had finished their concert, which they performed quite nicely, considering the short space of time the School had been opened. It was in the course of his address that this great Prelate revealed the goodness of his heart and the uncommon mental gifts with which he is adorned. Speaking to the Italians present, he showed them the necessity of giving a Catholic education to their children, of the advantages imparted to their children by learning, not only the language of the country, but the mother-tongue of their parents—the sweet Italian language. He spoke of the necessity of learning different languages in this country, where there are people of so many nationalities, and where a man is, according to the saying of a celebrated

Jesuit, as many times a man as the number of the languages he speaks. He spoke highly of our beloved Italy, its genius, its art, its culture. He praised the work of the Italians in the Eastern States, referring to their strong constitution and the energy with which they work and how much the world expects from them. He spoke words of encouragement to the children, praised their behavior, their singing, their recitations, and, like a good Father, exhorted them to be good. For the Rector he had words of deep appreciation, encouraging him to build a new School at once. If his prophecy comes true, we shall, before the end of the scholastic year, have double the number of children. To the Sisters he spoke kind words, as to children devoted and grateful to him. He assured them, as he did at the start, that they would have an immense field of work. He assured them also of his interest in them, and promised that he would always assist them. And, in truth, I believe that the Institute has really found in the person of Monsignor Matz not only a good father, but also a zealous coworker who will always lend his aid and facilitate and increase opportunities for us to work for the good of our neighbors. The School has now begun its regular course, and the Sisters are also working courageously in the neighboring towns.

The diocese of Denver comprises a large territory, being the only one in Colorado. The area of this State exceeds that of Italy. One-third of the land is a plain, whilst two-thirds comprise the mountainous regions of the Rocky Mountains. This is a high chain of mountains, the highest peaks of which are 14,500 feet high. As the name explains, these mountains are immense masses of rock, colored with the most beautiful tints of the rainbow. They present a most enchanting view, and form one of the great natural beauties of the United States. If one were to see this scene painted, those enormous masses that appear to hang by a thread, with the railway cars running zig-zag between the folds of the mountains up to the highest peaks, and then precipitating themselves down into the valleys below, and running through the gorges called canyons, whose walls are inaccessible, and, because of their marble-like, colors and beautiful forms seem like an enchanted castle, one would imagine the whole thing was simply a creation of the painter's brush. These surprising shades of color are formed by the various elements of which the mountains are composed. Every kind of metal, amongst which gold, silver, tin and lead abound, is found here. The mines form almost the exclusive industry of this part of the State.

In these deep caves far away from the light of the sun, absorbed in hard work, immersed sometimes in the boiling water which emerges from the mineral springs that abound here, many thousands of miners spend their lives. Whilst the Companies amass millions, the greater part of the miners work hard, and, by indefatigable digging, seek a precious vein which may prove a fortune for themselves and family. Often, after many years of hard labor, they receive a very small reward by way of compensation for their strenuous efforts. At times when fortunate enough to find a vein (which is found among the rocks of granite and quartz in the crevices produced by volcanic eruptions, and by which the volatile metal is transformed, having been deposited by the work of Nature in incalculable far distant ages), the ways and means are wanting with which to develop it, and so the poor men remain as if they had found nothing, and as if they were just beginning their task. They live, however, absorbed and intent on gaining worldly goods, forgetting the good God.

They are fortunate in those villages where the priest goes once a month to celebrate Holy Mass. In the meanwhile there is a spiritual famine, and you may imagine how great is the need of spiritual help. Our Sisters have begun their rounds. They have descended nine hundred feet into the mines, being lowered in a cage hardly large enough to contain them into a shaft about only one square meter wide, and cut obliquely in the rock. The compressed air introduced into the mines makes respiration possible. They have also walked at times several kilometers through narrow tunnels at the same depth, speaking a word of comfort to these poor creatures and reminding them of the eternal truths. It is not difficult to touch on the subject of hell as they walk through these dark tunnels where breathing is difficult, where the only available light is that of a few tallow candles, a pale idea, it is true, but still very expressive of the eternal darkness.

The Sisters, who are performing this Mission for the good of others, find it also advantageous to themselves, for they realize what the world does for temporal gain, and the thought of this fills them with greater zeal to work for the glory of the Sacred Heart and the diffusion of our Holy Religion. To work for the extension of the Kingdom of God on this earth, there is no necessity to go in search of veins of gold, for the smallest act sanctified by a pure intention, and in our case by Holy Obedience and performed according to the spirit of our Institute, is the purest gold, and deposited where thieves cannot steal. Oh, how fortunate are the souls who are called by God to religion! Let us love our vocation with our whole heart. Let us thank God constantly for having conferred upon us so great a gift, working always with zeal in whatever field obedience places us, not counting our sacrifices, bearing in mind that we do very little, and that on the great Day we shall know the truth of the words of Jesus Christ, that "the children of darkness are more prudent than the children of light."

Returning to what I was saying, the passion for gold which absorbs so many lives and ruins so many souls, has, in this State, rather contributed to the benefit of the inhabitants of the boundary State of Utah. They are for the greater part Mormons, a sect which practices polygamy. Not tolerated in the other States, they migrated to Utah. Providence, who never fails its children, moved by the prayers of the good offered in behalf of these Mormons, disposed that the latter should be drawn by the prospects of gain in the mines of Colorado, which are considered richer than those of California. Hence many of these Mormons have left their own State and abandoned their sect. The laws of the United States do not countenance, but rather condemn, the Mormons, and they are precluded from the higher offices of the State. So much so, that when an attempt was made to place one of them in one of the highest offices of the State, a general outcry of indignation arose, especially among the women, who revolted against such a degradation, regarding the whole thing as a violation of the most sacred rights of womanhood secured them by Christianity.

He who is faithful to God is faithful to his country and to his family, and the more the fear of God animates the citizens of a country, the greater and the more respected will the nation itself be. Moreover, as it is said that nations are formed on the knees of the mother, it follows that the more the mother is venerated in the family, and the more she herself conforms her conduct to that sublime model that we have in Her, who, repairing the faults of Eve, raised the status of humanity, so much the greater will be those future generations who will form the glory and the prosperity of their country. These principles, my dear daughters, you should teach in your Schools, because, as educators, you must not only form good Christians, but good citizens for the State, which we wish to be great and respected.

And here I address myself not only to you, but also to the good young ladies in Rome who are studying in our College, and who will shortly be called to educate others. Make them understand what the Church and Society expect of them.

The world is poisoned with erroneous theories, and needs to be taught sane doctrines, but it is difficult to straighten what has become crooked. It is in your hands to form new generations, to lead them in the right direction, to instill into them those principles which are the seed of good works, though for the moment they may seem hidden. The impressions of childhood are never obliterated. We shall be indebted to you, if the youth whom you educate, when grown up, become the pride of the family, of Society, of the State, and, especially, the honor and support of our Holy Faith. I have had already great consolations among the Alumni of Rome, and I am expecting to receive many more, being convinced that these good young ladies are doing good and will continue to do so. The great amount of work I have found in the Western State will prolong my stay longer than I had expected. It is not time lost, however, so accompany me with your prayers and sacrifices, so that all our works may prosper to the greater glory of the Sacred Heart of Jesus. For if the whole world is obliged to love and make reparation to this loving Heart, Which beats only with love for us, how much more so should the Missionary, who bears His name, and who, with the love of predilection, has been chosen to imitate Him and to promote His interests, he permeated with the spirit of love and reparation. We all know the greatness of our vocation. Let us be careful not to make ourselves unworthy of it by putting a limit to our love, to our sacrifices for Jesus, for the Missionary should never say, "I have done enough." Nor ever shrink from difficulties, for not being able to do it of herself, the Missionary can, nevertheless, do all in Jesus, for she has her motto, "*Tutto posso in Colui che mi conforta.*" Grow more and more, day by day, in virtue, always according to the spirit of the Institute, and may God's blessing descend upon you and may you increase in numbers, for the crops are abundant, the harvest is great, but the reapers are few. The days fly, souls are being lost. Death is approaching more quickly than we realize, and then the time for work is over.

Work, then, while you have time. Work with energy, and especially with the spirit of sacrifice, for it is this that forms the true Missionary. This storms the Heart of Jesus, and draws from It, as it were, the most precious graces for those souls who are the hardest and the most obstinate in resisting His love. Work with an apostolic spirit which offers everything, actions, prayers and sacrifices for the conversion of souls. Seek amongst your acquaintances, above all, among those who wish to do some good for the glory of God, souls who will cooperate with us and give material help for our Missions. Saint Paul, in one of his letters to the Philippians, speaks of his predilection towards those who are generous and help with their offerings, and he calls them coworkers of the Gospel. How many beautiful souls there are in the world whose hearts are filled with zeal and with the love of God, and who are distressed at the thought of so many about to be lost. They wish to do something to save souls. Not being able, on account of their position, to consecrate themselves to this great Apostolic work, they timidly keep repeating to themselves, "Oh, if I could do something for those souls," and they proceed no further. Teach them that, without leaving or neglecting the obligations of their state or country, they can become Missionaries of the Sacred Heart, and that they will find themselves among the number of those who enter Heaven followed by a number of souls saved by them. But how? you will ask.

The first condition is prayer. Saint Teresa helped the great apostle of the Indies, Saint Francis Xavier, by praying and sacrificing herself in the solitude of her cell. The second condition is to help the Missions entrusted to the Institute by offerings. God's judgments are very different from the judgments of the world. The world judges from appearance, and gives honor and glory to those who do not merit them. God sees everything, even our most sacred thoughts, and knows how to trace the origin of that small offering which did so much good, and which therefore may have been the first and real author of the good done by the Missionaries of the Sacred Heart in far-distant lands. What is given to the Missionary is given to God, because given for the benefit of the poor and the abandoned. If it is sweet to deprive oneself in order to give, how much more consoling, is it not, to give to God from Whom we have received everything? He will not allow Himself to be outdone in generosity, He who is so good and magnificent! Banks fail, thieves steal, the moth destroys, storms ruin possessions, but the money given to God is placed in the Divine Treasury, where it repays a hundredfold.

Continue, my dear daughters, to procure the greater glory of the Sacred Heart, in which I leave you, so that He may inflame you with His Divine and Holy Love.

Yours most affectionately in Jesus Christ,

Frances Saverio Cabrini

My dear young Ladies:

I hasten, before the close of the scholastic term and before you leave for your homes, to thank you for your very welcome letters of Christmas and Easter, which you wrote me after the Retreat you made during the carnival season. It is, as you already know, a great pleasure for me to learn that you are progressing in your studies, in your designs for the future and in your aspirations. It is true that now and then the Reverend Mother informs me as to your good conduct, but it is a greater pleasure for me to read in your own words, and, if I may say so, between the lines, of the workings of grace in your souls, and to contemplate how the precious seeds of virtue sown in your souls, developing into graceful little plants, will one day grow to a perfect height, and have their boughs weighed down under a load of precious fruits. This great interest I have in you is a natural outcome of the singular affection I bear you as the favorite children of a great family which the Sacred Heart has confided to my care. I regard you, not so much as soil, whereon, with my dear

Sisters, I strive to implant a Christian education, but rather do I consider you as coworkers, destined one day to associate your lives with ours in the great enterprise of the Salvation of Souls.

How great, noble, exalted, is the mission you are called to accomplish in this world! To you, Our Divine Lord addressed the words He spoke to His Apostles one day, "I have chosen you so that you will bear fruit and that your fruit will remain." Reflect a little with me on the predilection of God for you in this call, "I have chosen you," not "you have chosen Me." In fact, He did not wish that during your studies you should be exposed to the poisonous atmosphere of the world. He has drawn you into His own House, so that you could breathe into your souls its salubrious atmosphere. There you prepare yourselves for the mission you are to fulfill in Society. To many of you, already, we may say, despite our great regret at parting from you, "Go and bear fruit," for you are already fortified against the world's dangers by the solid instruction you have received. But what fruit will you bear? However small your experience is of the world, still you see that the multitude is insensible, forgetting God. But how much good cannot a wise teacher do to repair this, the greatest of evils, if to her mental culture and her intellectual gifts she adds that of a soul solidly founded and frankly Christian and religious. She knows as the immortal and lamented Pontiff Leo XIII, said, that we cannot renew Solomon's judgment on the child by the cruel and unjust separation of the intellect and the will. She knows that while she cultivates her mind, she is bound to direct her will at acquiring virtue to obtain the last end. She knows that those who have not received in their early years the impressions of Religion, grow up without having even the slightest idea of those high truths which alone can awaken in them the love of virtue and the control of the passions. She then makes her sweet influence felt in the school, aided by the grace of the Holy Ghost, and silently mold those young hearts which, soft as wax, are ready to receive impressions. Here you perceive the great responsibility of those who neglect their duty, for it is difficult to eradicate these early impressions. This is the fruit which you are called upon to bring forth in the Church, with this difference, however, that whilst a simple teacher has only to instruct her class of children, you have the responsibility of educating the future teachers, and consequently have a wider field wherein to sow your seed, which will thus spread more rapidly and bear more fruit. As such you are associated with the great work of the Christian Apostolate. Thus you enter the ranks of those generous champions who at the command of our great Leader and His Vicar on earth, fight bravely to restore the world to Christ.

How far the world is from Him who is the Way, the Truth and the Life, is better understood by one who has to travel so to speak, from one end of the world to the other.

A few weeks ago I was at Seattle, the capital of the State of Washington, in the extreme west, where we opened a Mission. This city, recently built on Puget Sound, with all the comforts of its sister cities, has such a charming position that it might be called the garden of the United States. Indeed, here it is distinguished by the name of Queen City. It might very well also be called the City of Twenty Hills–the town, in fact, does spread over twenty hills. A most beautiful panorama crowns it. Whilst the snow-capped peaks of the Rocky Mountains on one side, and the Olympic Mountains on the other, remind us of the North Pole, the green hills bathed by the sea are perfumed with lemon and orange blossoms and rich with splendid vegetation. In February we actually gather strawberries. It is a continual spring, though we are fifty degrees north latitude; and this is due to a warm stream that comes from Japan. The dark green background of the virgin forests furnishes excellent building wood in abundance.

This town reminds one very much of Southern Italy, in its nature so beautiful and fertile, whilst it presents a good field of work for the Missionary. We found Italians who for the last forty or fifty years have not seen a church. They do not want to go to the English speaking churches which they believe to be Protestant. Our first care was to build a small, simple church, just big enough to contain them all; it is close to our School and Orphanage, which are built on a hill. On the slopes and valleys beneath are scattered the houses of the Italians. At the beginning we had no bell, so the Sisters used to go in twos to call them from the different hills. These poor people would answer the call and follow the good Sisters who lead them to the church. When the first signal is given of the service, they all come running to the church, so much so, that when in Lent they come for the Stations of the Cross, some of them often have time to make the Stations three times over before the service actually begins. Though these Italians have been so many years away from God, still I found the Faith well rooted in them, even in their very bones, as it were, though sometimes latent. Therefore, by means of a little kindness and courtesy it is easy to bring them back to God. It is very touching to see men of advanced years cry with emotion at seeing an Italian church in which they hear the Word of God in their mother tongue, and where they are reminded of the old country, so long left, and the ever-dear impressions of childhood–the steeples, the squares, the feasts, the solemn processions in their native land. I expect much from this Mission.

During my sojourn in Seattle I was asked to open a Mission in Alaska. You know this region from the description you have read, probably, but it is much more interesting when you hear about it from people who have lived there. This peninsula is not far from the State of Washington. From Seattle our Italians embark for Alaska in search of gold, which they say is found there; an expectation which, though it has proved fatal to some, still continues to deceive others. The natives of Alaska are supposed to have come from Lapland. I should think it will be very interesting for the Sisters who are going there to visit their igloos. Their system of building is very simple. They need no architects or masons. With a few planks of wood which the sea waves, guided by the Hand of God, throw up in quantities on the coast of a country where there is perpetual snow and ice, these Eskimos build their roofs and walls, which are supported against the side of the mountain. Then they pour water over the huts, and this freezes at once. This operation is repeated until the walls attain a thickness that renders them inaccessible, even to icy winds. The Eskimos pass their lives in these huts, which are more like dens than houses, and they enter them by crawling through a low narrow opening. They stretch themselves out on skins, in which they dress themselves, and they oil their bodies against the cold.

In the summer, at ten p.m., the sun is still shining, and in winter, at three p.m., it is dark night. The sky often favors them with the meteoric display that appears at the Pole. Now and then, by a mirage similar to that seen in the African desert, one sees suspended in the air an entire city, which is supposed to be the far-away city of Petersburg. Their manner of taking food is very strange. If you are invited by some great personage, such as the head of a tribe, you must not imagine you are going to eat a piece of salmon or roast cod fish, of which these coasts abound. In front of the head of the family you see two plates, one with the dressed meats and the other empty. Now his work begins, and this must be very hard, for he chews all the food which is given to the guests. When this has been done, it is placed on plates and handed around accordingly. This ceremony over, all the guests eat of this well-prepared dish. This story was told me by a Jesuit who passed many years there. This holy Religious added that this was not the worst thing done there.

The white people, however, have begun to build houses and villages there, so if any of you wish to join the Sisters who are going there, you need not live in ice huts. Communication with other countries is interrupted for long periods. Only twice during the winter is the postman, dressed in skins and shod in iron-bound boots, seen making his way with difficulty along the road covered with eternal ice. The letters are sewn up in his coat, as it is too cold for him to have his hands exposed. We see now what sacrifices are made to get gold, or to make some earthly gain–efforts which often fail. Is it not right that the Missionary should remember that in these far-off countries there are souls to be saved, and that she should be ready to sacrifice herself for love of them? And is it not the duty of all who love God and His glory, to pray and to offer some sacrifice for those souls who have been bought by the Most Precious Blood of Jesus Christ?

The journey from Seattle to Denver is very interesting. One passes through cities all so different from one another. In Utah I saw the lakes and the mountains of salt of a transparent milk color. But more interesting still is it to see the Indian Reserves. The territories where the United States Government confines the Indians are called Indian Reserves, as the Indians are not allowed to live with the whites. They are allowed in the towns now and then to sell their merchandise.

Some time ago, when hatred still existed between the Red man and the White, only one Indian woman, Angelina by name, was allowed to enter the city of Seattle, and I will tell you why. Amongst the many idols that the Indians adore, some of them have truly repugnant appearances. Now it happened that the white men carried off one of these, and it still stands in a square of Seattle. This idol represented a deformed gnome, and, with other smaller monsters, formed a column. The Indians were so exasperated that they swore to avenge the profanation and to vindicate the honor of their idol by the destruction of the town. But Angelina was a sweet, good-hearted woman, and did not want so much bloodshed. So, crossing mountains and valleys and risking other dangers, she entered the city at night. The white men, having been warned, were thus prepared to defend themselves against the attack of the Indians. So they never forgot the kindness of Angelina. She was therefore allowed the privilege of going into the town at any time, and of lodging at any hotel at the Government's expense. She was called the Queen of the Queen City. It seems a small thing to us, but to the Indians it was quite a big affair, of which even today they are proud. I have passed near the Reserve, called Cæur d'Alene, because of the ferocious nature of this tribe. Though they retain a few of their old habits, they are now more civilized owing to the progress of religion, especially through the Apostolate of the Jesuit Fathers. There is much to be done yet, for there are still many ridiculous and shameful superstitions amongst them. When an Indian dies, all the friends are called to weep over the corpse, whether they want to or not. They even have to chant their grief in a more or less monotonous strain like this: "You were very good, oh, oh, oh, you had a lovely house, ah, ah, ah." You may imagine what the rest of the chant is like, and continued throughout the dead of night. When the morning dawns, the Chief arrives. and they beg him to tell them if the deceased has gone to heaven or to hell. Then he commands them to fetch him a bowl of bread and water. They hold the strange belief that while the corpse is on earth it needs nothing, but if it goes to hell, it has to be provided with bread and water, as these items are not to be found in hell. If the dead is destined for heaven, it needs nothing, so it does not return to take bread and water. Naturally, the deceased does not return for its bread and water, consequently the tribe concludes it has gone to heaven, and makes merry over it, partaking of a great banquet. Poor souls! These are they for whom Christ shed so much Blood, who so much grieved His Heart in His sorrowful agony when He saw, in all the horror of His imminent Passion, the uselessness of His agony for so many souls. Oh, how bitter to the Sacred Heart was such a thought! How painful those stripes, thorns and nails of the Cross! If it were only possible for us to console the Divine Heart, to comfort Him, and to become victims for the salvation of souls that cost such a dear price! Such comfort we can give to Jesus. All of us can devote ourselves to this enterprise by means of prayer. Let us be generous in our little sacrifices to Our Lord for the success of Catholic Missions. Perhaps, one day, when we ourselves are gathered into the Eternal Tabernacle, we shall meet many souls who will tell us that they owe their eternal happiness to us.

The Indian woman, as in all those nations which have not received the light of faith, has to work while the man quietly smokes his pipe. The poor woman and mother of many little ones, who are too small to stand, is forced to tie her offspring around her waist in a sack, and in this unconventional way has to do her washing. If the baby cries, she moves it with a shrug of her shoulders and thus quiets it. This is the way the Indian baby is fondled.

See how grateful we should be to Christianity, which has raised the dignity of woman, reestablishing her rights, unknown to the pagan nations. Until Mary Immaculate, the Woman by excellence, foretold by the prophets, sighed for by the patriarchs, desired by the people, Dawn of the Sun of Justice, had appeared on earth–what was woman?

But Mary appeared, this new Eve, true Mother of the Living, elected by God to be the Co-Redemptrix of the human race, and a new era arose for woman. She is no longer a slave, but equal to man; no longer a servant, but mistress within her domestic walls; no longer the object of disdain and contempt, but raised to the dignity of Mother and Educator, on whose knee generations are built up.

All this we owe to Mary, and in the midst of the tenderness that naturally arises in our hearts for such a pious, amiable, good and condescending Mother, ever ready to listen to our prayers, ever ready to come to our aid, we must not forget what Christian society owes to her, and, consequently, what our obligations are to her.

Mary derives all her greatness from Jesus. If it was her boast that she became the Mother of the Redeemer, to her also, as the Holy Father has said, was consigned the office of guarding and preparing the Victim of the human race. Mary was the Mother of Jesus, not only in the joy of Bethlehem, but also on Calvary, where she not only contemplated the cruel spectacle, but rejoiced at seeing her Son offered for the redemption of mankind. Thus did she most worthily merit to become the Co-Redemptrix. If, then, we wish to reach the height of the importance of our Mission, let us banish all vanity and levity, and remember that we shall only be true women, when, by the discharge of the principal duties that are imposed upon us, we become the true educators of society, angels of the family and faithful imitators of Mary Immaculate. But what have you to do to imitate her? I should love you to look upon your Morning Star, Mary, and become so many copies of Mary Immaculate. Cast an interior glance on your Mother, and, if your eyes cannot sustain the vivid light that radiates from Her, listen to what St. Anselm says of her: "Mary was docile, spoke little, she was always composed, was never heard laughing aloud, nor ruffled or disturbed, she persevered in the reading of the Sacred Scriptures, in mortification and in the works of mercy."

Saint Ambrose says: "Her movement was not indolent, her walk not too quick, her voice not affected or sharp; the composure of her person showed the beauty and harmony of her interior. It was a wonderful spectacle to see with what promptness and diligence she performed her domestic duties, to which she applied herself with great solicitude, but always with tranquility and great peace. Her forehead was serene, and a modesty more celestial than terrestrial pervaded her every movement. Her words were few and always dignified, prudent and joyful. In Mary, all and everything was well regulated."

Holy Church in her earliest days appeared to be all concentrated in Mary, all hearts turned to her, all hopes after Jesus were placed in her. She was the Ark animated by God that contained the Law of the New Alliance, the living Rule of the precepts and counsels of Jesus Christ, the treasure of the wisdom and knowledge of God.

The difficulties of the primitive Church are just the same after twenty centuries, and it is not to be wondered at, for Christ has always been the sign of contradiction. And so it must be with His Spouse, the Church, in this vale of misery and tears. Do not fear difficulties. Let us raise our eyes to our Heavenly Star. Let us call upon Mary. She is to us what she was to the Apostles and first Christians. Let us honor this Immaculate Dove, and let us trust her with unlimited trust. The eyes of her soul and mind are turned towards us. Her eyes are sharper and more penetrating than those of the prophets and seers of Judah, more perfect than those of the Ecstatic of Patmos, higher than the angelic hierarchies. How admirable is Mary Immaculate! Let us abandon ourselves into her hands. She is, I repeat, our august Queen and Mother. Under her mantle we shall be safe.

At Denver I found the School, which I opened only a year ago, quite flourishing. The cheerful predictions made by the good Bishop on that occasion have been succeeded by realization, and now this zealous pastor wants us to found an Orphanage for Italian orphans, who are very numerous in Colorado, owing to the disasters that befall the poor miners.

In two days I made a rapid journey from the capital of Colorado through Texas, to Louisiana. Even here what beauties of nature are visible–a pale image of Him Who is the Eternal Beauty, and Who, to testify His predilection for us, has willed to spread them over the earth.

For hours we ran through very narrow chasms, called "canyons," which are renowned all the world over. They consist of perpendicular walls of inaccessible height which seem to touch the sky, whilst below the river flows in zig-zag fashion, alternately impetuous and calm, reflecting in its pure water of variegated colors the most wonderful rocks I have ever seen. It is impossible to describe them. A brush that attempted to paint them in all their reality would be considered bold. These rocks do really excite one's wonder, they even change color at different times of the day, and assume colors and tints that even the most skilled artist could not hope to reproduce. They are the work of the Immortal Artist, Whose existence men dare to deny and to forget while the powerful and wonderful works of His hands speak so eloquently.

The immense plains of Texas, the greater part of which, owing to the rapid extension of the State, is uninhabited, are most fertile, rich in vegetation and suitable for every kind of cultivation. These virgin lands are of a reddish color, full of life and promise, and seem to await our Italian emigrants, who go more willingly to the populous States of the north, whereas here, ease and a life more like that in Italy awaits them. There are some Italian colonies already, especially in Louisiana, where they are employed in the cultivation of cotton, rice and sugar, whilst on the outskirts of New Orleans they gain a livelihood by the cultivation of vegetables. In the latter town there are about thirty thousand Italians. You can imagine, then, whether you have not much work to do. The Schools hold seven hundred children, and, as our houses had not sufficient room, the Archbishop made us a present of another a few weeks ago. But I must think of the orphans, for they are increasing in number. I am engaged on this work at present. When I have finished here, I shall return to Colorado for a little while. Then I shall go on to Chicago, and from there to New York, to embark for Italy.

To my regret, I shall not find you at Rome on my return, for by the time you have received this you will already have entered on your exams, and these will be succeeded by the holidays, which will be for some of you the end of your scholastic studies. So this is a very busy time. But you have done your best. You have studied with diligence, so be calm and quiet and you will do even better. Have confidence in God and Our Lady, and they will help you to pass with honors. I wish you all the fullest success. You deserve to be crowned with success, for you are very good and of great promise. It is unnecessary for me to tell you to pray, as I know you do so, and that you pray from your heart. This consoles me very much, because prayer is the weapon which will not only defend you, but will help you at the present and throughout your life. It is the key of the celestial treasures, it is the channel through which grace comes to you. As long as you pray, you will be safe. Blessed Canisius says: "He who prays is on the road to Heaven." Never forget this shield, this powerful weapon, which will secure for you ultimate victory. In great success, pray, and you will take your success moderately, for pride comes before a fall. In defeat, pray also, and trust will return and you will become strong with the strength of God.

Pray for yourselves, for those entrusted to your care, for the world, for the Church. Make a practice of prayer, and if you reach that degree of sweetness of prayer which is found in intimate converse with God, you will never have discomfort or despair. Dark clouds will not trouble for long the serenity of your souls.

Obey the precepts of Jesus Christ. Pray, and pray always, and God will do His part in you, and will fulfill His promises. "Ask, and you shall receive, seek and you shall find, knock and it shall be opened unto you." And now, goodbye, my dear children. I shall not have the pleasure of seeing you, but when you come to Rome you must visit the Sisters, and then I shall have the pleasure of congratulating you on the Diplomas you have obtained and the progress you have made in knowledge and virtue. To those who will return after the holidays, let one say a heartfelt *"Au Revoir,"* and to the others whom I see leaving us I say regretfully, though with confidence, the words of Our Divine Savior, which are full of wisdom: "Go and bear fruit, and your fruit shall remain." May the Sacred Heart of Jesus bless you in all the vicissitudes of life. May the Divine Heart he for you always the door of salvation in which is found shelter, help and comfort. May the Mantle of Mary shelter you all. May she clothe you with her virtues, keep you under the shadow of her protection. I, seeing you entrusted to Jesus and Mary, shall fear nothing, but shall implore the blessing of Heaven upon you.

Yours most affectionately in Corde Jesu,

Frances Saverio Cabrini

New Orleans, May 31st, 1904

16. Letter to the Students of the Teachers' College, Rome

May, 1905

My dear young Children,

Several times I have sat down at my table to write to you, and, particularly, two months ago, when I received your letters which spoke of the Retreat you had made at the end of the carnival season. I intended to congratulate you on the expression of your good will to lay aside the futile, and oftentimes bitter, amusements of the world, and to give up your souls and faculties to the consideration of heavenly things. After those days of recollection, you opened the second half of the scholastic year which terminates with the fear of the examinations. I call it fear, for it is really so, as the thought of these examinations conjures up such colossal forms which develop fear.

My work for the last few months has so much increased, that I have not had a spare moment of time to write to anyone. Your Easter wishes awoke me to the fact that I had not even answered your other letters, so, in order not to be like the statue of Saint Philip that is always going to move but never moves, I must answer your letters at once.

I wish I had the gift of your style, so that I could express myself in such kind and elegant language as comes from you, but as I know that it is the heart that dictates your sentiments, so it is my heart that thanks you and blesses you, only as the heart of a mother can. You know well that you form a favorite portion of the great family that the Sacred Heart has given me, and I have a special concern for your welfare and pray for you most fervently.

You ask me to pray for your examinations, and I shall do so willingly. I know the Sacred Heart and Our Lady will obtain for you the grace to pass with credit.

From you I ask two things: first, continue to pray with fervor, as you have done so far. God alone has put into the mind of man this Divine spark of intelligence. The poet, the artist, the scientist, all owe to God the genius that makes them great, and the Church, amongst the glorious titles she gives to the Holy Ghost, calls Him the Spirit of Wisdom and of Intellect. It is meet, therefore, that we should draw water from the source, and so, after having worked on our part and studied assiduously, we must have recourse to Our Lord and expect from Him memory, intelligence and success. The celebrated Cardinal Ximenes used to place himself at the foot of the Crucifix when there were great questions of State in hand. When asked by his Ministers why he did so, he answered, "To pray is to rule." Pray, then, but not at great length, for you have no time except for prayer with fervor. The world of today is going back to paganism, and, in spite of its gigantic progress in science and commerce, has forgotten prayer, and hardly recognizes it any longer. And that has come about because, with pagan sentiments, man makes a god of himself and of creatures, and loses the idea of the relations that exist between himself and God. Our good God, who, as the child recites in the catechism, has created Heaven and earth, is almost banished from the world–there is no place for Him. Man has made an idol of himself which he adores, and so does not pray to, or adore, the true and only God. No wonder, then, that after superhuman efforts, nature, weak and impotent to fight any longer, or to attain what it seeks, abandons itself to despair, suicide and crime. Prayer would have obviated all this. Prayer is like an incense rising to Heaven, and draws exhilarating graces from Heaven. It strengthens the strayed soul, giving it back peace and calm.

Now, here is the second thing I would ask of you. Be calm and composed. Place all your trust in God. This is not presumption, as you have worked and studied hard all the year, so don't alarm yourselves. Study quietly. Pray, and confide in your Mother, Mary Immaculate, and all will go well. He who trusts in Her shall not be confounded.

We had, in the foundation of the Chicago Hospital, a visible proof showing how powerfully Heaven helps those who invoke with faith. We went to Chicago, after leaving New Orleans on the 10th February, where I bought some ground for our Orphanage. This now has a beautiful villa, facing some of the principal roads of the town, and extending into various parks until the grounds reach the crystal waters of the river Bayou St. John. When I arrived in Chicago to complete all arrangements in the hospital which was to be opened on February 26th, I found there were two months more work to be done. The date of opening had, however, been fixed, and it could not be changed. The President of the Hospital, the celebrated Dr. Murphy, whose fame is world-wide as a surgeon and the inventor of surgical instruments which bear his name, wished to be present at the opening of the Hospital. He was about to go to Florida on account of his health, and would not have been able to be present if the date was postponed, and would therefore have been obliged to forego such a pleasure. This I certainly could not countenance.

What a work! It is a vast edifice six stories high. Though it is solidly built of enormous stones, still the interior had to be brought up to date to meet the requirements of modern medical science and surgery. So there was needed a number of workmen, masons, carpenters, plumbers, electricians and decorators. But this was the least important of all. There was the organization of the start, which had to receive the sick the day after the inauguration. Only those who have experienced such a big task can understand what it all means. The Sisters worked day and night. The work seemed to increase instead of decreasing. People even remarked, "It is too much; it cannot be finished, there are too many difficulties ahead." But firm trust in the Heart of Jesus kept us calm, and amidst this tranquility the work was quickly and well done, so much so that on February 28th we were able to open the doors of the Hospital, and at the same time feel sure the critical eye of the public would have no reason to find fault or ridicule.

It was a great day for the New Columbus Hospital. We called it "The Day of the Lord," as it was all His work. Even a most clear sky, with a sun which made the blue waters of the immense lake Michigan sparkle, seemed to participate in the feast.

The opening of a Hospital, though it is a great event for the medical profession, does not awaken great sympathy in the public, as people shrink from these asylums of pain. Great, then, was the surprise of the worthy Archbishop Quigley, when he saw himself surrounded by 4,000 people who crowded around the chapel and reception rooms to hear him speak. Several thousand people were sent away, as there was no room nor any hope of their being accommodated at the ceremony. All agreed that there had never been such enthusiasm over the opening of a Hospital in the United States as there was on this occasion. It was the Lord's Day, the work of the Lord.

The morning ceremony was purely religious, and consisted of the blessing of the House by the Archbishop, followed by a long procession of people. There was a Solemn High Mass, with a sermon by His Grace the Archbishop. A pleasant surprise awaited the congregation at the close of His Grace's touching sermon, when the Archbishop read a telegram from His Holiness the Pope, who sent his blessing. You, young ladies, who are so privileged at seeing His Holiness so frequently and receiving his blessing, experience holy emotions in your souls. You can imagine, then, with what enthusiasm this telegram was received by the doctors and guests. It came as a heavenly message. It was as precious as the distance is great which lies between these shores and the Vicar of Christ. Not knowing how they could better express their gratitude, they asked me to send a telegram of thanks to His Holiness, which I did very willingly, as I was so pleased to see how well the Holy Father's precious blessing was received. As for myself, I look upon the blessing of His

Holiness as a pledge of heavenly favors, for I have always noticed that success attends every work which has been sealed by it. The hand of the Holy Father is never raised in vain. Blessed are you who are able to receive his blessing from him personally. Protected by such a powerful shield, have courage, for His Holiness' blessing will extend to your families, interests, studies and examinations.

At the dinner, the function was enhanced by a select musical program, interspersed with eloquent speeches by the most eminent persons present, i.e., Doctor Murphy, Chief Justice Brentano, and other distinguished personages and visitors.

The medical faculty of the city classify our Hospital as one of the first order. All agree that it is in a most charming position, and that its architectural features stamp it one of the best in Chicago. As for modern requirements of science, everything is of the latest. Every ward is governed according to the hygienic laws of modern surgery. There are several operation rooms, offices for sterilization, other rooms for electricity, X-rays, etc. Annexed to it is a training college for nurses, who, after three years' training, obtain their diploma.

The Hospital is situated in the vicinity of a park, with a splendid view of Lake Michigan. One might say that Nature, with its invigorating and oxygenated atmosphere, and the science of the doctors, who form the medical staff, go hand in hand to secure the well-being of the patients who, in this place of rest, come to seek their health and to recuperate their strength.

I believe it will please you to hear some of the points of Doctor Murphy's speech, which was a glory to the Church and our beautiful land.

He remarked that as our country was first in science and art, so also can she boast of being first in the field of Charity. Before the coming of Christianity, there were no institutions, no expressions of fraternal charity, like those of our modern hospitals. Even ancient Greece, with all its culture and civilization, ignored this noble sentiment and hardly took care of its wounded soldiers. But Christ came into the world, lighted the fire of Charity, and Italy had the glory of having the first hospital in Rome, followed soon after by one in the Campagna Romana. Some centuries passed before other nations followed her example in these works of charity, amongst which was England. The Holy Catholic Church did this work, and continued to practice it all through the Middle Ages, and there was no Convent that had not annexed to it an Infirmary, where the poor and the sick were succored.

Now the Columbus Hospital has begun its beneficent work for Society, and great numbers of sick seek its shelter and remain within its walls willingly. We have patients from Colorado and California. As soon as I saw the Hospital settled, I returned to these Western States, and now I am amidst the mountains of Colorado. Whilst I write, the President of the United States has arrived triumphantly in Denver, after being away for three months hunting bears amongst the Rocky Mountains. Ten fell victims to his gun, and he is sending the skins to Washington for his daughter, Alice, who asked for them. I have not been able to follow him and admire the wonderful birds which build their nests in the highest peaks of the Rocky Mountains, for this is not my mission, nor have I the strength to do so, but in this splendid State, which is named as they say after its multi-colored mountains, there are flowers and birds of the most brilliant and variegated colors. Let us thank God, who allows such rays of His infinite beauty and power to fall on this earth.

The citizens of Denver wish to name President Roosevelt honorary member of the Press Association of Denver. Do you know what kind of diploma was offered him? In the neighboring mines they excavated a quantity of gold which they fused in their big foundry. This was then drawn out into a shining sheet of the most pure and solid gold, upon which they engraved in silver (a product of Colorado also) the formula of aggregation. This was in turn studded around with the most precious stones to be found there. What a beautiful gift! There are like wonders in California, where I am going as soon as I have bought the ground for our Orphanage. Here it is the mineral kingdom which boasts of its wonders. There the vegetable kingdom opens another page of the book of the beauties of the Universe—a pale image of the Most High.

To Him, then, let us turn our souls, created by Him and for Him—those souls in which He has infused a great attraction for the beautiful and great, a proof of our high origin and the end for which we were created. Let us raise ourselves up from this earth, and, since we cannot fly from it, let us rise above the things of the world. The pure intention that we put into our daily work is the magic wand that changes it all into gold, and the Christian virtues that we practice blossom forth as so many odoriferous flowers, wherever we pass. And, whilst faithful to the Divine commands and to the teachings of Holy Church, let us discharge our duties, however humble, and the Angels will defend us from dangers and faithfully note our good works. They will accompany us to the sojourn of the good God, where our joy and happiness will be complete. I will not preach to you, my dear young ladies, for you have heard many sermons in past years in the College.

You know the way. You have the arms to combat with. So I will content myself by expressing the firm trust I have in my heart, that even after you leave the College you will show yourselves worthy of whatever state of life to which God has called you, that you will impart to others the lights you have received, always calling to mind that life is short, and that we have only one soul which will live eternally in the abode either of glory or of suffering, according as we have prepared for ourselves either the one or the other in this life. The thought of the four last things to be remembered made a Saint of Saint Teresa. May the holy and the tremendous truths of our Holy Faith strengthen you not only in the trials of life against the false illusions of the world that try to deceive you, but let them incite you to do as much as you can for the students of the Normal Schools who will be entrusted to your care, so that they may become not only cultured, but well founded in the maxims of that Holy Faith, which is the Ark, outside which there is no salvation.

God bless you now, in your examinations; in your scholastic career and in your state of life, so that you may render it fruitful to the Church, Country and Society.

Mother Frances Saverio Cabrini
Superior General of the Missionary Sisters
of the Sacred Heart

Denver, Colorado, May 9th, 1905

Chicago, February, 1906

My dear Daughters,

I was very pleased to receive your letters and wishes for a Happy Christmas, though I had hoped that this year, at least, I would have been in the Eternal City to spend the Holy Feast with you, and so be able to reciprocate your happy wishes in person; on the contrary, I must now convey them to you, a hundredfold, in writing. I confess that such noble and kind expressions of feelings on your part have given me great consolation in the deep regret I feel at finding myself still so far from Rome. Duty alone, which the Missionary must always put before pleasure, has kept me so long from Italy, but, believe me, immediately the little business which detains me now is finished, I shall not delay my departure a single day.

How many times have I thought myself almost at the end of my present Mission in the United States, when I have found new work to do, work that I could not have neglected without neglecting the holy interests of the glory of God and the salvation of souls. But now I am in a position to assure you that in a few weeks I shall be with you to rejoice in your virtues, in your progress and in your loving company.

I wrote to you from the summit of the Rocky Mountains, promising to tell you something of my journey to California, and I do not think you would be disposed to forgive me if I forgot my promise. Hence I steal a little time, at one moment from my Religious and at another from business to converse with you.

Regina Cœli Orphanage, Denver

I think I wrote to you of my work in Denver for the enlargement of the Orphanage we have in that city for the daughters of our emigrants. It will be enough for you to know that, with the help of the Sacred Heart, always ready to favor us, I have been able to acquire a beautiful property at the foot of the Rocky Mountains, standing upon a pleasant hill which descends with a gentle slope to the banks of the Rocky Mountains Lake. The house, to which a wing is being added, because space is already limited on account of the thirty orphans which are gathered there this first year, is surrounded by trees laden with fruit and enhanced by the proximity of the clear waters of the lake. To the west extends the imposing Rocky Chain with its summits covered with snow; to the east is the beautiful city of Denver. To the south and north are great plains, three-fourths of which include the territory of Colorado.

Meanwhile, seated in a comfortable carriage of the Santa Fe railway, which was taking me to Los Angeles, my glance swept across those immense plains which, around Denver, are dotted with the cottages of our Italian agriculturists, and which, further on, are uninhabited, there being immense tracts still of virgin soil. My thoughts flew to our emigrants, who, in such great numbers, land every year on the Atlantic shores, overcrowding still more the already populous city of the east, where they meet with great difficulties and little gain. In the west there is still room for millions and millions and its most fertile soil would offer occupation more congenial to the Italian emigrants, as well as a field in which to develop their activities and their agrarian knowledge, and to crown their efforts and labors with copious results.

This stream of population must have its course intelligently directed. I know that the Emigration Department is occupying itself with this problem, which is so important for the welfare of our immigrants in the United States. The solution, however, presents great difficulty, not only because of the four thousand miles which separate the Atlantic from the Pacific, but more especially because it is difficult to find good-hearted persons who will occupy themselves with the work and will not speculate in the sacred interests of the poor.

Poor immigrants are so often cheated by those who pretend to be their protectors. This deception is all the more cruel, because these so-called protectors know well how to color their private interests under the cloak of charity and patriotism!

During my journey I saw these dear fellows of ours engaged on the construction of railways in the most intricate mountain gorges, miles and miles away from any inhabited region. Hence they are separated for years from their families, far from the Church, deprived of the holy joys which in our own country the poor peasant has on Sundays at least. In Italy the peasant is able to put his hoe aside, and, in his best clothes, after having consecrated the morning to Divine Service and heard the words of the priest, who reminds him of the nobility of his origin and of his destiny, and of the value of work consecrated to God, has one day in the week to devote to his family and to honest amusements, and is thus able to resume his work the next morning with his mind invigorated.

Here the hardest labor is reserved for the Italian worker. There are few who regard him with a sympathetic eye, who care for him or remember that he has a heart and soul: they merely look upon him as an ingenious machine for work. It is true that here the Italian wins esteem because he is sober, honest, faithful and industrious, but how much real joy does he not give up in leaving his native country for foreign lands, without anyone to guide him on the road of true happiness, which does not consist in hoarding heaps of money, which, more often than not, cannot be enjoyed when misfortune comes. How much better his little field in his native country would be for him. What a great social and philanthropic work could be achieved by anyone who knew how to turn these hands, which waste their activity to the advantage of foreign countries, to the benefit of our own lovely land!

I do not mean to deny that there are advantages in these immense fertile virgin lands. They certainly offer the emigrants work and a comfortable life, but I trust that some really generous minds may arise who will take to heart the interests of the poor, and direct them well and conscientiously when they land on these shores.

I can assure you, now, that in my journey through our Missions, the evidence of the good that is being done by our Institutions for the emigrants is of the greatest comfort to me. That which, being women, we are not allowed to do on a large scale, such as helping to solve important social problems, is being done in our little sphere in every State and in every city where our Houses have been opened. In them the orphans, the sick and the poor are sheltered, but the good done by coming into contact with a great number of people, which such institutions of charity make it easy for the Sisters of the colony to get into touch with, is immense.

The relations between the Sisters and the people are very cordial. The poor people call them Mothers and Sisters, and they feel these words are not without meaning, for they know that with such titles hearts truly maternal correspond. They know that the hearts of the Sisters palpitate in unison with theirs, and that, having put aside all thoughts of themselves, the Sisters make their troubles, their interests and their joys their own. All this, however, is not our merit, but the fruit of the love of Christ and of the prodigious fertility of our Holy Religion, the true friend of the people, the light which guides them in the darkness, the house of refuge, tower of strength and port of safety.

While I am conversing with you, we have reached the Colorado Springs, the aristocratic city of Colorado, which rises out of the shadow of Pike's Peak, one of the highest summits of these mountains. The weak and consumptive are attracted here by the mildness of the climate, the salubrity of the surrounding mountains and the many and various mineral waters, which on every side spring up fresh, foaming and sparkling. The Indians, astonished at such a wealth of mineral waters, thought their god Manitou, an Indian word which means Great Spirit, lived in these mountains, and especially in the one called the "Garden of the Gods." On my return I will show you a view of this natural park, several hundred acres in extent, in which brightly-colored rocks are scattered in thousands and sculptured by Nature in the most strange forms, now imposing, now grotesque, sometimes austere, sometimes frivolous, as it were, presenting the strangest appearances. Here, a little further on, General Palmer, one of our good benefactors, possesses a private "Garden of the Gods," a real jewel of art, both as regards the palace he has built and the natural beauty of the rocks, which here form very high peaks, reflecting the most varied colors. Among the rocks can still be seen the nest of an eagle, which for years lived here as queen of the mountains. But a short time ago its young eaglet was killed, and since that day the noble bird has deserted the nest, to the great regret of the General, as may be imagined, as he had become very proud of it.

Leaving the Colorado Springs, we reach Trinidad in a few hours. This is an important field of various mines, especially coal, in which very many Italians are employed. Our Sisters visit them regularly, and to these poor people such a visit is like a ray of sun in the darkness of the bowels of the earth. They speak to them of their daughters whom they have under their charge, and of their families whom they have visited. They remind them of their religious duties, comfort them in the sadness of their miserable conditions, and always leave them happier, or at least more resigned to their poverty. The fatigues of the Sisters in climbing up the steepest mountains are rewarded by the smiles which light up the faces of these poor people on hearing the maternal tongue resounding in these dark vaults. Poor miners! Do you want to know what their life is? Those who work on a day shift, enter the mines at six o'clock and remain buried there till midday. They come out at twelve o'clock for a short meal, and go in again at half-past twelve to leave at five. Half-an-hour is spent in washing themselves and preparing for supper. When they have finished this meal, feeling worn out, they throw themselves on their little beds, to rise again the following morning at the sound of the whistle which calls them to work. On Sundays they smoke and sleep. This is the life they lead far from their families and separated from the company of men. They continue uninterruptedly year in and year out, until old age and incapacity creep over them, or at least until some day a landslide or explosion or an accident of some kind ends the life of the poor worker, who does not even need a grave, being buried in the one in which he has lived all his life.

Oh, if the voice of religion at least could reach all these poor people, and teach them to make holy and noble such fatiguing work, and to render it fruitful for Eternity, what a boon it would be for them! Thus you see the tremendous responsibility resting on those who take away the gift of faith from the working classes, for in so doing they rob them of every hope of the future life, banishing the love of God from their hearts. Take away the supernatural principles and dictates of our Holy Faith, and what remains but wickedness and the indulgence of every passion? Pray, my good daughters, that the number of Missionary workers may be increased, and that they may be really zealous and good-hearted, because the efforts of such are capable of arresting the materialism and unbelief which, like a most subtle ether, infiltrates itself everywhere, causing great, immense and irreparable damage.

Pray that all the docile Faithful may listen to the voice of the Vicar of Jesus Christ, Pope Pius X, who, conscious of these great evils which threaten to shake the foundations of Society, proposes to restore everything in Christ. Strong in the strength of God, assisted as he is by the Holy Ghost, he will not fail to fulfill in the Church the high mission to which God has elected him, but at the same time what fatigue he must suffer, what cares, what troubles must torment his heart, and preoccupy his mind in such an arduous task. At least let him feel that he is comforted by the love and obedience of his children, and let him find in each and everyone that cooperation which it is our bounden duty to give to him. This cooperation will make possible the fulfillment of the holy designs of the Pope and the arresting of the many evils which threaten to overwhelm the world.

Having left the large manufacturing city of Trinidad, the train enters the heart of the mountain district. As the locomotive ascends slowly, we are able to admire the beauty of the landscape. Every minute the view changes. We behold austere mountains whose summits are whitened with shining snow, hills quite green with pine trees and reddened by the colors of the rock and soil, sharp peaks which seem to touch the sky and on which the eagle alone rests, plateaus where the hardy goat back from his mountain excursions comes to browse upon the green grass in which they are so rich, and where the slow ox and the proud buffalo pasture together quite unconscious that in the neighboring glen the howl of the white bear resounds. Here and there silver streams descend among the rocks and soon become threatening torrents which, in rapids and waterfalls, follow their beds of many-colored rocks. The name Colorado was never better applied than to this enchanting country, to these most beautiful natural parks, where the hand of man could never add greater beauty than that with which Nature has enriched it.

In truth, here one exclaims spontaneously: How wonderful is God in His works! But, meanwhile, we have begun to descend the western slope, and, turning with a rapid run towards the Pacific, have crossed the frontier of New Mexico. This country is most interesting. Here the Indians still live in their pueblos, little villages constructed like fortresses on steep and almost inaccessible mountains. It may, indeed, be said that the rock itself forms three sides of the house. The front is hermetically sealed, having neither door nor window, so that only by means of a ladder and an opening in the roof can one descend into their little houses. It seems that these Indians of New Mexico, unlike the other more savage and hunt-loving tribes are a temperate, frugal, industrious race, and devoted to agriculture. It is with the object of safeguarding their provisions and the fruits of their labor from the rapacity of their neighbors, that their pueblos are built like regular fortresses. Looking out of the carriage of the train, I saw these poor Indians sitting before their hovels, in their picturesque costumes, making small baskets, at which industry they are very clever. When I arrived at Albuquerque, the metropolis of the Valley of Rio Grande, I was able to approach them, as they were arranged in double line under the arches of the station, offering to travelers the products of their industry. Some were selling terra cotta vases, daisy works and boxes cleverly constructed, while others contented themselves with offering garments, topaz of various colors and other little stones found in the Mexican deserts. The interior of the station contains a beautiful collection of Indian art, and the cleverest of the Indian people weave the famous Navajo blankets.

The Indian races are very numerous and varied. Some of them show an erect forehead and aquiline nose, with a proud intelligence shining over their countenance, whilst the penetrating eye reveals the hardiness proper to their race, not to mention their nobility and kindness of heart. Other Indian tribes are much inferior to these, and their faces denote an almost stupid dullness. The women especially, seem very fond of painting their faces in various colors in such a way as to resemble tattooing.

Many and various are their costumes, which I will not attempt to describe, because the illustration which I shall bring back with me will give you a better idea of them than my own description could. Just as I got off the train, some Mexicans and a few Indians crowded around us, delighted at seeing the Sisters. The Indians more timid than the others came forward gradually, offering me their little works. Attracted by the shining Cross, they asked to be allowed to kiss it. Whilst satisfying this innocent desire of theirs, I thought "How many among these uncivilized peoples do not yet know God, and are sunk in the darkest idolatry, superstition and ignorance, without anyone to do them a little good, and all for want of Missionary workers!" Oh! how the heart of the Missionary suffers when, kindled with zeal for the glory of God and the salvation of souls, she feels her very forces paralyzed by her powerlessness to enter into every place where the interests of God call her! These poor souls in the meantime fix their eyes curiously on one, and seem to say in their mute languages, "Why do you not come and bring the light of your Faith amongst us?" Oh, generous and Christian souls! Why do you not listen to the call of these distant brothers of yours? You do not lack courage, energy, intelligence or heart. Why leave hidden and buried so many beautiful gifts with which the Lord has endowed you, and not employ them rather for the benefit of those who do not know the true God? Why do you not reflect that these talents of yours, employed in the service of the Lord, will produce immense merit on earth and glory in Heaven? Thus spoke the poor Indians of Albuquerque to my heart. These Indians represent to me the numerous and scattered tribes of the west of the United States and a keen feeling of regret makes my heart bleed at not being able now, through lack of assistants, to remain amongst them and to apply myself to their spiritual and intellectual culture. The Missionary Sisters of the Sacred Heart, who work day and night in the United States, already number more than four hundred, but they are, however, only as a little blade of corn in a limitless field. Oh, may the Sacred Heart grant that, for His greater glory and for the salvation of souls redeemed by Him, many generous souls may come forward and enroll themselves in our ranks under the banner of the Sacred Heart! There is room for everybody, for every activity, for every talent and for every inclination. She who consecrates herself to Jesus as a Missionary Sister, willing to carry His name even to the utmost ends of the earth, sacrificing her dearest affection and even life itself, is a true heroine in whose heart the flame of love burns brightly. She does not stifle her own heart nor put under a bushel the shining light of intelligence with which God has endowed her. On the contrary, the flame kindled in her heart becomes a regular volcano of love which embraces everything. That gleam of light becomes a brilliant torch, causing darkness to disappear and erring souls to find their way. Happy the one who, at the tribunal of God, will be able to present herself followed by a great number of souls saved through her. The voice of God calls many, but not all listen to Him. For this reason very often we sorrow at seeing a great harvest lost for want of workers.

You, my good daughters, in your great mission of education, are the first cooperators in the Missionary works of the Sacred Heart, and for this reason you are especially dear to my heart in the great family which Jesus has given me. I expect much from you. Not only your native country and religion hope for great things from you, but all the world. To be a Missionary it is not necessary to go all over the world. The facility of transport and means of emigration today enable men to pass from one country to another with the same amount of ease as that with which they go out of their house into the garden. Every year we see thousands and thousands of our countrymen landing here. We see them in constant contact with irreligious and godless people. If every child that is entrusted to us in our schools is brought up in the fear of God, if we, moreover, train the little mind, we thereby educate the heart and instill into that child the principles of religion and honesty in such a manner that he will grow up a good Christian citizen. Is it not likely also that this pupil of ours may in turn become a teacher himself, and prove much more efficacious in his teaching, because familiar exhortations may often strike the mind more readily than sterile and academical instructions? The teacher who educates her pupils in the way I have indicated sows the mustard seed abundantly. This seed, according to the words of Our Divine Master Himself, will grow to a great height, and the Missionary will never know in this life how much fruit it will have produced unto Eternity. My good daughters! May your school be not only a school of literature, science, mathematics and history, but also of virtue, solid Christian morality, and you will have rendered a great service not only to religion but also to your country. Moreover, you will greatly contribute to make our country honored and respected by all other nations.

Now we have left New Mexico and have entered Arizona, or, to speak more accurately, the desert. Really the deserts of Arizona are not at all what we should have imagined them to be from their name, they are neither monotonous nor without life. They are immense territories intersected by chains of mountains, profound abysses, extinguished volcanoes, various colored peaks and mounts or gigantic forms, so varied that with a little stretch of the imagination they seem at one moment like castles with turrets and towers of defense, while at other times they look like colossal monuments adorned with an infinite number of columns and marvelous sculptures. The sands of the desert have already proved to be fertile soil for whatever the cultivator may desire to produce, i.e., if he has the courage to dig wells in dry sands and sow vegetables and plant fruit trees. The great heat of the country enables the producer to gather his products in the winter when they are dear. We are approaching California, the land of the giant in the vegetable kingdom, where the yuccas and shrubs and herbs assume colossal proportions. Here the cactus, which is called *Cereus giganteus*, reaches a height of sixty feet. But the greatest attraction of this desert consists in the Petrified Forest and what is called the Grand Canyon of Arizona, which is a tract of about one thousand square acres, which probably flourished on the shores of an interior sea, and in the evolution of time became submerged by the waters and is now covered by the sands of the desert. Here we find lying on the ground or springing up from the sands, innumerable trunks of petrified trees of different dimensions, some of them extending to ten feet in diameter. They seem to have been pines or cedars. Water has gradually filled up the cells with flints, manganese and oxide of iron mixed with other such substances, which have given them such beautiful tints as to elicit the warn admiration of the traveller. Under the action of the heat or cold, these trunks have become fractured so that they present the appearance of having been sawn by the hand of man into enormous disks. In their natural state these masses of wood do not possess very brilliant colors, but when they are skillfully worked, they justify the name of *jewel forest,* an appellation given to this wood because every particle of these trees can be and has been transformed into chalcedony, agate, amethyst, topaz, etc. One of these trees, to which I am referring, with its trunk still intact, has fallen across a chasm forty feet wide, so that it forms a kind of bridge. Its top and root are buried in the sand, which fact gives you an idea of its height. You will, surely, be curious to see a specimen of this beautifully petrified wood, and to satisfy your curiosity I will bring a piece of it on my return.

From this wonder we pass to another still greater, one which up to the present moment no one has been able to describe, viz., the Grand Canyon of Arizona. So I shall not even try to make you realize the beauties of it when gifted writers have found their task superior to their ability. The word *cañon,* from the Spanish, is used here often to indicate the gigantic gorges, mountains and precipices, call them what you wish, which the immense rivers of these countries have excavated in the course of centuries in these titanic regions. The Grand Canyon is an intricate system of canyons, more than six hundred feet in depth, one hundred and twenty-five miles in width and one hundred and eighty miles in length. Anyone venturesome enough to look over the edge of the canyon would imagine he was on the top of a very high mountain, instead of on the edge of a profound abyss, having regard to the stupendous panorama which is spread before him. It is a labyrinth of immense architectural forms infinitely varied in design. There is no reason to envy the pyramids of Egypt or the majestic mausoleums of the Pharaohs, decorated as they are with the most curious ornaments, when nature can produce these marvels, resembling sometimes lace or veil, and giving at other times a vision of festoons hanging from the rocks painted in a great variety of colors such as the hand that holds the palette can produce. Diaphanous tints of marvelous delicacy are also to be seen. The highest mountains which dominate this abyss, change their color according to the hour of the day; so that the rubies you see now change themselves later on into emeralds, while afterwards they become as brilliant as diamonds under the powerful rays of the sun, and like sapphires in the evening time. In the presence of such an imposing spectacle, man feels very small. In the eye of the Faithful, this is an image, though a faint one, of God.

Down the Grand Canyon, the ridges of which are about six hundred feet high, the train descends at high speed along the sides of the mountains, coasting, as it were, on the brink of precipices, until we arrived at the city of Needles, which is but a few feet above the level of the sea, only to ascend again immediately about three thousand feet. The position of this city, nearly buried between two very high mountains, coupled with the nature of the soil, all covered with lava erupted during past centuries by the neighboring volcanoes, makes Needles one of the hottest countries in the world, or at least in the United States. Really, the heat was suffocating. Not being able to endure the flaming heat, which entered through the small windows and even through the cracks or small openings in the train, I tried to shelter myself behind cushions, but in a few minutes they also became, as it were, red-hot.

Needles is on the confines of Arizona, and so is the gateway of California. The darkness of night soon enveloped the country, which is not very attractive; but the next day, as soon as the sun rose, the train was running amidst clusters of orange groves, hedges of eucalyptus, and the most beautiful green meadows and hedges of flowers. We were in California.

With good reason, this State is often compared with Italy, and especially with our so-called Riviera, and those who say it should be compared with the land of promise flowing with milk and honey are not mistaken. California is rich in gold, silver and every precious metal, amongst which are the famous mines of Tourmaline, which provide a stone which is now being used very much. But one of its principal attractions is its incomparable climate. Here there is constant spring. The sky is even more beautiful than that of Italy. It rains only two months in the year. There are hot days it is true, but in Summer the heat is tempered by sea breezes. The nights are very cool. When I left California in the month of December, the hills were already green and the trees putting forth their new buds. A beneficent fog, loaded with all the smoke and miasma of the city, rises every evening, but during the night is pushed slowly towards the sea by a current of fresh air which comes from the mountains. In the morning another kind of fog envelops the hills on which the city of Los Angeles stands. The sun takes some time to dissolve it, so that often it does not rise until ten a.m. This fog, which emanates from the sea, is of a transparent blue, and as it is driven by the sea winds in an opposite direction to that of the evening fog, the atmosphere becomes purified and remains limpid and serene for the rest of the day.

As far as the climate is concerned, the products of California you know better than I. Every fruit tree and every herb grows to immense proportions. Here we find gigantic trees in the trunks of which chapels are built and arches cut out through which motor vehicles pass to and fro. Here is the celebrated water-lily *Victoria Regia*, which you know from the description. Here is to be seen a trunk of *Washingtonia Regia* hundreds of years old. It is the giant of the forests, and fell by some unknown accident. Its immensity is such that a squadron of horsemen can ride over it as if it were a main street, or, better still, a parade ground, for military display. Here the geraniums grow to such a height that they form hedges which divide the various properties, and sometimes climb to a height of thirty feet and gracefully adorn the trunks of palms that line the streets and adorn the gardens.

The fruit have a special fragrance and flavor. Here, near Los Angeles, lives the celebrated naturalist, Burbank, who, adding new wonders to the wonders of Nature by his ingenious experiments and gratings, has produced new kinds of fruit and flowers, apricots and prunes without stones and grapes without seeds.

To the glory of the Church, I must tell you that Mr. Burbank, was shown the way to success by Abbot Gregory Mendel, who, half-a-century ago, in his Monastery in Austria, began the experiment which has made the name of the naturalist of California famous. What the latter now accomplishes is due to the ingenuity and skill of an intelligent Augustinian monk. From this we see how much we owe the Church as the cultivator of sciences and arts.

As soon as I arrived here I began to look round the town and its suburbs, in order to find suitable grounds for a School and Orphanage. There is not a hill or valley which I did not visit, and always with an increasing admiration of God's goodness, which is so clearly seen in this privileged country. Every valley is a natural sanatorium, where, by just remaining in the open air night and day, one is cured of some special disease, and there is such a valley for every illness, Those suffering from consumption have their tents placed at the foot of a hill. In these they sleep and live, and after some years find themselves stronger and more vigorous than ever they were. In other places those who suffer from asthma, nerves and anemia, likewise recover their health. The air acts both as doctor and medicine to all.

Los Angeles in 1880 had only eleven thousand inhabitants, now it counts one hundred and fifty thousand, and in the winter this number is increased by tourists who come to spend the season here. Whilst I was there, thirty thousand more were added to the population. It is only about sixteen miles from the sea, which is easily reached by an incomparable system of electric trains. The most elegant palaces, not to be found in other States, adorn the streets, while villas and parks extend from the brow of the hills to the plains. There is no house, however small, that has not a flower garden and palms give the city an elegant aspect. It was precisely on one of these hills that I found a place adapted to our work, and I can really say it was prepared for us by the Sacred Heart, for the palm trees in front of the house hide it so nicely that it seems like a real Convent. At the same time we are but a short distance from the town, and at the foot of the hill where our house is situated the Italian families live, so that the Sisters find themselves in a few minutes right on the field of work and are able to quickly reach the School that Bishop Conaty is erecting for us.

Whilst I was arranging to buy this property, I had the opportunity of visiting the Venice of America, as it is called. This place is situated in a most charming position on the shores of the Pacific Ocean. It is a small city built after the style of Venice. There are artificial canals and bridges, small copies, one might say, of the Queen of the Adriatic, and the canals are crossed by small gondolas.

Stone buildings are few in number, as are also brick houses in Los Angeles, but the houses made of wood are of exquisite workmanship. Therefore, except in the principal streets, which remind one of Italy, the city consists mainly of tents. There are thousands so lined up so to form streets of them, and they are as large as a good-sized room, well-furnished, lighted by electricity, and even the richest leave their palaces at least for a month to enjoy the freedom of the Pacific beach.

A restful and pleasant trip was offered to me by Mr. Banning, owner of the famous Santa Catalina Island, who granted us the passage on his motor boat. So much I had heard of this pretty island, that I could not leave California without being able to tell you something about it. There we went recently, on a sunny day, when the sky was cobalt blue and the ocean well deserved the name of "Pacific". The three-hours trip seemed very short, absorbed as we were in the sight of the ocean and sky. As we approached, only the outline of the rocky island could be seen—about thirty miles in length—but on entering the bay, the fog gently lifted like the curtain of an immense stage, revealing the enchanting scenery prepared by the hand of God. I thought I was viewing, in a dream, an earthly paradise. Against the background of a sapphire blue sky, rose green mountains dotted here and there by elegant villas, nestling among pines and palms. The air is so clear that distances can scarcely be measured, for the power of vision seems to increase. In the transparent blue waters the bottom of the ocean is easily seen, swarming with myriads of fish, among them the flying fish that suddenly darts in the air like an arrow, and dives into the waves. Seals, imported from Newfoundland playfully swim among the fish, which accustomed to their company, seem to pay no attention to their antics; as they are not frightened by men diving and swimming in their midst. Such is the harmony of nature reigning here. More friendly still are the aquatic birds, playing around and hovering over the fishermen. Thousands of sea gulls live in the bay of Avalon, flying, dipping or gently rocking on the waves. They roost on sail masts, on the edges of boats, on rocks. Any object rising above the waters is adorned by their elegant white forms. But a more enchanting sight may be enjoyed by taking a trip in a glass bottomed boat. I had heard of the undersea gardens of Santa Catalina and I imagined that through some optic illusion, produced by mirrors and lenses, people could see fantastic plants and flowers at the bottom of the ocean, and I did not think it worth while to take the trip; but what I saw surpassed all my expectations.

In the bottom of the boat there is an opening with a glass window, through which you can see everything in the sea. We had hardly left land when the sea, which appeared smooth and sandy at the bottom, gradually became full of rocks and then of green mountains. Between these were plains and valleys, all covered with green sea plants, which in some places reached a height of one hundred feet, waving to and fro with the movement of the sea. There was a never-ending variety of aquatic plants, some of which bore purple flowers, different kinds of fruit of delicate tints, fresh like the blossoms of Spring, and they were continually moved by the waters, as by a breeze. If the view of a land park is beautiful, I can assure you that a marine park is much more so, especially when you behold it inhabited by every kind of fish, including the goldfish, and its rocks adorned by shells of the most brilliant colors. After two hours of these wonderful sights we landed on the beach of moonstones. These are rough pebbles, and when cut and polished they are made up into various kinds of ornaments. The chalcedony of which these are formed must have fallen from some high mountain. Who knows how far away? It is beaten by the waves on the beach. Tourist visitors find them, and thus have the opportunity of carrying away with them an interesting remembrance of Santa Catalina. I remained there more than twenty-four hours. The island belongs to a rich man, who refused to sell it for five million dollars. He has made it a holiday resort and a terrestrial paradise for tourists.

The perfect system of electric trains which connects Los Angeles with its suburbs, affords foreign visitors the opportunity of a beautiful pleasure trip, which I was able to avail myself of through the kindness of friends. In less than four hours after leaving the shores of the Pacific, we reached the top of Mount Lowe, six thousand feet high. Leaving the beach, we ran through vineyards and fields which reveal the fruitfulness of the soil. There you have only to sow the seed and leave it to the care of the sun and rain, and in the Autumn you get an abundant crop. In less than half-an-hour, Los Angeles appeared like a majestic queen with her beautiful white palaces scattered through the perennial green of the surrounding hills. Then, between new hills, we reached the aristocratic city of Pasadena, where the millionaires of the United States pass the winter. In the midst of green carpets dotted with flowers and amidst the perfume of orange trees, we reached the foot of Sierra Madre. To the inhabitants of California, the word "foothill" suggests all that one can imagine as good, beautiful and healthy. There, orange and lemon blossom and ripen without danger of frost, and there one gathers even in winter the most delicate vegetables. There also the sick recover their health.

From Altadena, which is at the foot of the mountain, you can ascend in a railway to a height of five thousand feet. At this height begins the most attractive part of the sight, because when once there you immediately enjoy the splendid panorama of the open valleys and plains. An electric railway, constructed by the characteristic boldness of the Americans, spreads its lines from peak to peak, suspended over dizzy abysses below, and then climbs the rocks of granite, which seem inaccessible, to such a height of six thousand feet. And so one enjoys the whole beauty of the mountains without being an alpinist. I spent several hours contemplating the splendid sight that one enjoys up there, and stretched my vision as far as the ocean, which one can see on clear days.

But I must return to Los Angeles. Already our Sisters are well settled, and have begun their work, not only in behalf of the Italians but also for the poor Mexicans who are numerous here and in great need of help. Priests are so few here that the heretics have already sown their cockle in this beautiful country. I've never seen a country in which there was a greater number of sects, and of the most ridiculous kind. Returning home one evening at six p.m., I had to pass through one of the principal streets, when my attention was drawn to a group of women and men prostrate on the ground at the corner of the street, crying and beating their breasts, whilst one of them preached in a loud voice that they should be sorry for their sins. I was told to wait a minute if I wished to see a funny sight.

Then, quite suddenly, they all stood up and clapped their hands and jumped and danced very joyfully. The preacher assured they jumped with joy. This practice of theirs has given them that the sins they had wept over were pardoned, and so the name of the "Holy Jumpers." There are also the Nazarenes who profess to live without eating or drinking. Christian Science holds sway everywhere. Right in the center of the town these people have a big tent, where there are written in big letters the words of Holy Scripture referring to the miracle performed by Saint Peter at the door of the Temple, and there they perform their miracles, carefully prepared beforehand, of course. There the lame walk and the blind see, in the presence of those foolish enough to allow themselves to be deceived. But a poor lame man who, in good faith, went in the hope of being cured, was badly treated on one occasion. The spirit invoked was unwilling to perform the miracle. The minister shouted, "Lord, listen to us because we are holy and innocent, and come immediately after you." But it was of no use. The poor man could not walk, and the minister was so displeased and enraged, that had the man not left the tent in a hurry, it would have gone ill with him.

Some of our poor Italians fall into the net set to catch them. If a good knowledge of our Faith is necessary everywhere, it is more necessary still in these Protestant countries.

And this shows us how necessary it is to study the Catechism well. How can a poor emigrant be faithful to the truth he does not know? How can he practice what he ignores? The small Catechism contains the greatest doctrines of our Holy Faith. In it the cultured, who, like the eagle, penetrate the Divine Mysteries, find food, whilst the simple, not so anxious to speculate, are contented to find the road which leads to Eternal Life. Take religion away from man, and nothing remains in this life but illusion, trials and afflictions without number. Where can he find the strength to resign himself to trials and misfortune, if he has not the comforting thoughts which religion suggests? Whence do rebellions and seditions arise, if not from a lack of religion? We are greatly mistaken if, desirous as each one is in her own sphere to contribute to the greatness of our country, we do not base our hopes on that cornerstone which is Christ and His Church.

Very fortunate you are, my dear daughters, that whilst you attend to the acquisition of that culture which is necessary for yourselves, you do not neglect the study of that highest science, religion. You are still more blessed in the fact that you know how to draw fruit from this study. Therefore, yours is not vain science that puffs up, but that which reforms manners, educates the heart and forms character. Blessed are you in becoming worthy instruments in the hands of God. The Church and Society expect great things from you, because your presence alone, your virtues and your teachings create a salutary atmosphere, and from you emanates a beneficent influence, educative in the full sense of the word, and immense will be the good you will do,

Having finished my work in Los Angeles, I returned to Chicago, where I found the Hospital progressing very nicely. In the past twelve months, nine hundred patients have been treated and three hundred and fifty operations performed with splendid results.

When I arrived, the famous Doctor Murphy, president of the hospital, asked me what I thought of my children–alluding to the many doctors that work there night and day. I answered that I was delighted. It was not question of children, but of physicians and surgeons, some of whom are already famous in the medical world; yet, you should see how humbly they submit to the regulations I dictated, after having studied carefully the local conditions. If discipline is necessary in a school, it is essential in an institution of this kind, where great are the dangers of abuses. If I am now able to leave Chicago with a tranquil mind, it is because I know my instructions are carefully observed.

Regulations are helpful not only to Religious but to everyone, for human nature is prone to tire, relax and change according to events. To persevere in our good resolutions, in spite of difficulties and aversions, strengthens the character and assures happy success to individuals and institutions.

And now, my good daughters, after having tired your patience, I greet you dearly, with the consoling anticipation of seeing you soon, while I implore for you the choicest blessings of the Sacred Heart.

Yours most affectionately in Corde Jesu,

Mother Frances Xavier Cabrini

"The Kingdom of God has no
limits; its limits are those of the
globe itself. Come, and let your
glory be the glory of your
celestial spouse, the working
out of that celestial talent —
the sublime vocation of
cooperating with Christ
for the salvation of souls."

Epilogue: Mother Cabrini and Her Work
Catholic News — New York, January 5, 1918

When on December 22 Mother Cabrini, the founder of the Missionary Sisters of the Sacred Heart, died at Columbus Hospital, one of her foundations in Chicago, a really great woman departed out of a world that needs her and her kind very much. She was one of those great women organizers who accomplish so much, and yet do it so quietly that only those who are intimately acquainted with her work know of it. There are a great many people who seem to think that the days of the saints of old, who accomplished so much in great social work for mankind, are gone never to return. Some of them even hint that the Church has lost its power to produce such wonderful workers, but a little knowledge of the lives of such wonderful women as Mother Frances Xavier Cabrini would disillusion them.

There is almost no woman of our time, and this is said very deliberately, who has accomplished so much for charity and social service in the higher sense of that term as Mother Cabrini. The emigration of the Italians from their home country to this country brought together a great many of them in various American cities under circumstances where they needed care and where in case of accident or sickness they could not be cared for in their poor homes. All of us have had the experience of how pitiable it was to have to deal with ailing or injured Italians, whose language no one could speak, and of whom only a few fragmentary words could be understood. The loneliness of it all was grief compelling. Mother Cabrini came to this country about twenty-five years ago and proceeded to found a series of hospitals, schools and academies for the Italians, and in spite of discouraging conditions of all kinds, succeeded in making a wonderful success of her work.

As the result of this great, good woman's initiative there are now hospitals for the Italians in New York, Chicago, Denver and Seattle. Her work is extended clear across the continent and she gathered around her a group of the most zealous women, intent only on their task and the care of others, to accomplish what was needed. There are schools for the Italians in New York, New Jersey, Pennsylvania, California, Louisiana, Colorado and Washington, so that North and South, East and West, everywhere the fruit of her efforts is to he seen. She was only a little past thirty when she came to this country, and she has spent three decades laboring for us though not all of that time was spent here, and see the result. Must it not be confessed that the Church is still capable of producing wonderful saintly persons to accomplish the seemingly impossible?

But what has been done here is not all. The order founded by her in 1880, thirty-seven years ago, and approved by the Holy See less than thirty years ago, has some scores of centers of activity in Italy, nearly a dozen in South America, two in Spain, one in England and one in France. Pope Leo XIII suggested to Mother Cabrini in 1889 the extension of her work to America, North and South, in order to bring aid and cheer and the consolations of religion to the Italian immigrants who had come to North and South America.

His Holiness knew her well, for she had been called to Rome to take charge of the Pontifical school there in 1887, and two years was quite enough to show her wonderful spirit of broad Catholicity and wide-open charity.

Mother Cabrini was born in Lodi, Italy, July 15, 1850. She was, therefore, when she died only sixty-seven, not full of years as so many of the founders of religious Orders are, but undoubtedly she covered a long space in a short time. The order was founded in Codogno, Italy, and originally was to have been a teaching order, but she very soon recognized the need, however, of social service in orphan asylums and hospitals, especially after coming to America, so these were founded. The hospital system established by her proved to have a great field for usefulness, and so was rapidly extended. Columbus Hospital, New York, was founded in 1892; Columbus Hospital, Chicago, in 1905; Columbus Sanitarium, Seattle, only a few years ago. In Chicago besides Columbus Hospital, Columbus Hospital Extension at Lytle and Polk Streets was founded for the poor.

It is marvelous to think that one woman can accomplish so much and assume so much responsibility, but, of course, the great reason why it could be accomplished was because Mother Cabrini won all hearts to herself and made them share something of her own enthusiasm in working for others. The public is likely to hear little of her. Many a woman of wealth who has done not a tithe of what Mother Cabrini has done gets an immense amount of publicity. She avoided publicity and even now, after her death her friends would respect her attitude in the matter, but for the fact that the story of it will itself do so much good for her work now that she is gone. Not only will her daughters in religion mourn her, but there are countless little children under her care who will miss her visits. She has left behind her a wonderful monument in her work which will live for future generations.

The Requiem Mass was held in the chapel of Columbus Hospital, New York City, on Monday, Dec. 31, at half-past nine. His Excellency the Most Rev. John Bonzano, D. D. Apostolic Delegate, presided. The celebrant of the Mass was the Right Rev. Bishop Hayes assisted by the Right Rev. Monsignor Mooney, the Right Rev. Monsignor Lavelle, the Right Rev. Monsignor Edwards, the Rev. V. Yanuzzi, the Rev. E. Coppo and Father Dineen, the Bishop's secretary.

"You lost your cross? Then you
are the most unhappy person in
the world because the one who
has no cross is not a follower of
Jesus Christ; so I wish you a
very long and very large cross
full of thorns, which you will
carry as a precious jewel with a
smile on your lips."

Prayers from the Retreat Notes of St. Frances Cabrini

For Discernment

My Jesus, I have not always recognized your loving plans for me. Every day, with the help of your light I learn more of you loving care. Continue to increase my awareness of the gentleness of your loving plans. I want to follow the purpose for which I was created. See, I am in your hands. Help me to choose the best way to serve you. Walk with me, Jesus. Stay by my side and guide me! Amen.

For Anxiety

Jesus, fortify me with the grace of your Holy Spirit and give your peace to my soul that I may be free of all needless anxiety, solicitude, and worry. Help me to desire always that which is pleasing and acceptable to you so that your will may be my own. Amen.

Surrender to Jesus

My loving Jesus, I enclose myself in you and surrender myself completely in your loving Heart. Enlighten my mind with a ray of your light, move my heart and soul and make me do whatever pleases you and is for your greater glory. Jesus, I love you so much...but I am so weak that in my ignorance and sinfulness I still do not know how to correspond, even partially, to all the special graces and loving tenderness with which you surround me. I will think of you and rest in you, my beloved Jesus. Behold your servant—do with me whatever you want! Amen.

Novena to St. Frances Cabrini

Day One

November 4/December 13

Opening Prayer

Most Sacred Heart of Jesus, thank you for the gift of life and for your servant, Saint Frances Cabrini. Fill us with the fire of your love and root in us the same spirit that animated Mother Cabrini. Renew our hearts so that we may live as she did, faithful and open to your will. Amen.

Meditation

The source of Mother Cabrini's energy, motivation, and inspiration was her burning love for the Sacred Heart of Jesus. Utterly confident that she was loved by God, her gratitude propelled her to reach out to each person she met and draw them into a relationship with Christ. Mother Cabrini wrote: "Jesus... How I wish I could enflame everyone with your holy love!" Today let us meditate upon the depth of the love Christ has for us. Pause to consider how to can return that love by sharing it with others in word and deed.

"See what great love the Father has lavished on us, that we should be called children of God! And that is what we are!"

1 John 3:1

Closing Prayer

St. Frances Cabrini, pray that I may grasp how deeply Jesus loves me, and that I may strive to return his love through service to others. Amen.

Day Two

November 5/December 14

Opening Prayer

Most Sacred Heart of Jesus, thank you for the gift of life and for your servant, Saint Frances Cabrini. Fill us with the fire of your love and root in us the same spirit that animated Mother Cabrini. Renew our hearts so that we may live as she did, faithful and open to your will. Amen.

Meditation

On the 50th anniversary of Mother Cabrini's canonization, Pope John Paul II referred to her as a missionary of the New Evangelization. He said she brought "new ardor, new methods and new expressions" in carrying the Gospel to all those she encountered. Mother Cabrini's energy for evangelization arose from her complete surrender to the will of God. She wrote: "My Jesus, help me! I surrender myself totally to you, to serve you faithfully and to attract many souls to your holy love." Today let us meditate upon what we need to surrender to God so that our hearts are open to doing whatever he asks of us.

> "For whoever would save his life will lose it,
> but whoever loses his life for my sake will find it."
> *Matthew 16:25*

Closing Prayer

St. Frances Cabrini, pray that I learn to trust Jesus as fully as you did. Help me understand what it means to lose my life for his sake. Amen.

Day Three

November 6/December 15

Opening Prayer

Most Sacred Heart of Jesus, thank you for the gift of life and for your servant, Saint Frances Cabrini. Fill us with the fire of your love and root in us the same spirit that animated Mother Cabrini. Renew our hearts so that we may live as she did, faithful and open to your will. Amen.

Meditation

St. Frances Cabrini did not shy away from difficult problems, nor from difficult people. With generosity of spirit she found creative solutions to complex issues. Her dedication to serving others arose from her deep desire to imitate Christ. She prayed constantly to do his will and to be his hands on earth. In her retreat journal she wrote, "Jesus, strengthen my fidelity and make me great-hearted in generosity." Today let us consider what it means to be generous in the eyes of God. In what ways can we better imitate St. Frances Cabrini's focus on the needs of others?

"In all things I have shown you that by working hard in this way we must help the weak and remember the words of the Lord Jesus, how he himself said, 'It is more blessed to give than to receive'"

Acts 20:35

Closing Prayer

St. Frances Cabrini, pray that my heart may grow as wide as the universe. Intercede for me so I may be given the grace to grow in perseverance in generosity. Amen.

Day Four

November 7/December 16

Opening Prayer

Most Sacred Heart of Jesus, thank you for the gift of life and for your servant, Saint Frances Cabrini. Fill us with the fire of your love. Root in us the same spirit that animated Mother Cabrini, that we may be, like her, your hands on earth. Renew us so we may live as she did, faithful and open to your will. Amen.

Meditation

Mother Cabrini had an enormous desire to hear God's Word. This led her to cultivate a profound ability to listen for His will. One of her favorite Bible verses was "Speak Lord, your servant is listening" (1 Samuel 3:10). Renowned as a woman of action, St. Frances Cabrini was foremost a woman of prayer. She saw every project she undertook as simply the carrying out of God's will. She took no credit for any of it and wrote, "God has done it all: I have only been a spectator of God's work." This was only possible because she listened so closely in prayer. Let us contemplate what interferes with our ability to hear God's will.

"My God, I have always loved your Word from the depths of my being."
Psalm 40:8

Closing Prayer

St. Frances Cabrini, pray that I may listen better and know clearly what God wants of me. Amen.

Day Five

November 8/December 17

Opening Prayer

Most Sacred Heart of Jesus, thank you for the gift of life and for your servant, Saint Frances Cabrini. Fill us with the fire of your love. Root in us the same spirit that animated Mother Cabrini, that we may be, like her, your hands on earth. Renew us so we may live as she did, faithful and open to your will. Amen.

Meditation

It was inconceivable to Mother Cabrini to put anything other than Jesus first in her life. "I have been created for God and must live only for him—in whatever way he wants me," she wrote. Mother Cabrini never faltered because she never doubted she was doing God's work. In her retreat journal she noted, "During every hour and every moment I must desire what God wants from me—nothing more, nothing less." Today let us consider how much of our daily life is centered on ourselves and our own desires. Let us consider, too, how we can center our days more fully in Jesus.

> "Fan into flame the gift I gave you: not a cowardly spirit,
> but one that makes you strong, loving and wise."
> *2 Timothy 1:7*

Closing Prayer

St. Frances Cabrini, pray that I may learn to place my heart entirely within the Sacred Heart of Jesus. Amen.

Day Six

November 9/December 18

Opening Prayer

Most Sacred Heart of Jesus, thank you for the gift of life and for your servant, Saint Frances Cabrini. Fill us with the fire of your love. Root in us the same spirit that animated Mother Cabrini, that we may be, like her, your hands on earth. Renew us so we may live as she did, faithful and open to your will. Amen.

Meditation

Mother Cabrini had keen empathy for those who faced difficulty in finding work at just wages, decent housing, or who struggled to access education and health care for their families. Her practical nature demanded that she and the Sisters do something about the oppressive conditions of poverty. Enterprising, tireless, creative, and industrious, Mother Cabrini provides an example for how we are to act on behalf of the poor. She wrote, "We must love one another and be gently compassionate to all." Let us consider how God is calling us personally to care for the poor. Let us seek opportunities to serve them effectively, both in prayer and in deed.

> "Jesus Christ was rich but he became poor,
> to make you rich out of his poverty. "
> *2 Corinthians 8:9*

Closing Prayer

St. Frances Cabrini, pray that I may become a true friend of the poor. Amen.

Day Seven

November 10/December 19

Opening Prayer

Most Sacred Heart of Jesus, thank you for the gift of life and for your servant, Saint Frances Cabrini. Fill us with the fire of your love. Root in us the same spirit that animated Mother Cabrini, that we may be, like her, your hands on earth. Renew us so we may live as she did, faithful and open to your will. Amen.

Meditation

The letters of Mother Cabrini to the Missionary Sisters are filled with advice on growing in humility. She once wrote that she could do great things with three humble souls, but would ruin the missions with a hundred proud ones. "Humble yourselves and often confess your pride, your secret pretension to be held of some account as a recompense for all your work," she wrote, "The devil is evil and wise but you will be wiser than he only when you have learned humility." Let us meditate today on how attached we are to our desires, so that we may let go of them and cling wholly to whatever Jesus desires for us.

> "Take my yoke upon you and learn from me,
> for I am gentle and humble in heart."
> *Matthew 11:29*

Closing Prayer

St. Frances Cabrini, pray that I may grow in humility so that I may grow to be more like Christ.

Day Eight

November 11/December 20

Opening Prayer
Most Sacred Heart of Jesus, thank you for the gift of life and for your servant, Saint Frances Cabrini. Fill us with the fire of your love. Root in us the same spirit that animated Mother Cabrini, that we may be, like her, your hands on earth. Renew us so we may live as she did, faithful and open to your will. Amen.

Meditation
St. Frances Cabrini considered reaching out to the suffering as Jesus did to be the highest form of charity. Whether a person's need was physical or spiritual, Mother Cabrini's charity was practical, down-to-earth and concrete. She wrote to the Missionary Sisters, "Know how to alleviate pain, dress wounds, console the troubled, strengthen the weak, with the precious balm of the love of Jesus' Heart." Her view was that a missionary had to be prepared to do whatever was needed. There was to be no hesitation. Let us contemplate how we can equip ourselves better to care for the neediest in our communities. How we can offer compassion and care in effective ways, both close to home and around the world?

> "Sell your possessions and give to the poor.
> Provide purses for yourselves that will not wear out, a treasure in heaven
> that will never fail, where no thief comes near and no moth destroys."
> *Luke 12:33*

Closing Prayer
St. Frances Cabrini, pray that I may be given the grace to respond in love to those who suffer.

Day Nine

November 12/December 21

Opening Prayer

Most Sacred Heart of Jesus, thank you for the gift of life and for your servant, Saint Frances Cabrini. Fill us with the fire of your love. Root in us the same spirit that animated Mother Cabrini, that we may be, like her, your hands on earth. Renew us so we may live as she did, faithful and open to your will. Amen.

Meditation

Mother Cabrini was an unusual woman, especially for her time. She was well-informed on cultural, social and political subjects, an astute businessperson, able to speak with the simplest person on the street and the most esteemed national leader. She was also a woman of contemplation, humility and hospitality. Her holiness integrated virtue with action, and courage with compassion. She took no credit for the 67 schools, hospitals, and orphanages she founded, saying simply, "God has done it all; I have only been the spectator of His work." On this Feast of St. Frances Cabrini, let us remember the many qualities which made her such an extraordinary witness of God's love. We pray that we, like her, may take as our motto the words of Philippians 4:13:

"I can do all things through him who strengthens me."

Closing Prayer

St. Frances Cabrini, pray that I may grow in love of God and serve him as wholeheartedly as you did.

Litany of the Sacred Heart of Jesus
by Pope Leo XIII

℣: Lord, have mercy on us.

℟: Christ, have mercy on us.

℣: Lord, have mercy on us. Jesus, hear us.

℟: Jesus, graciously hear us.

℣: God the Father of Heaven,

℟: Have mercy on us.

℣: God the Son, Redeemer of the world,

℟: Have mercy on us.

℣: God the Holy Spirit,

℟: Have mercy on us.

℣: Holy Trinity, one God,

℟: Have mercy on us.

℣: Heart of Jesus, Son of the Eternal Father,

℟: Have mercy on us.

℣: Heart of Jesus, formed by the Holy Spirit in the womb of the Virgin Mother, ℟:

℣: Heart of Jesus, substantially united to the Word of God, ℟:

℣: Heart of Jesus, of Infinite Majesty, ℟:

℣: Heart of Jesus, Sacred Temple of God, ℟:

℣: Heart of Jesus, Tabernacle of the Most High, ℟:

℣: Heart of Jesus, House of God and Gate of Heaven, ℟:

℣: Heart of Jesus, burning furnace of charity, ℟:

℣: Heart of Jesus, abode of justice and love, ℟:

℣: Heart of Jesus, full of goodness and love, ℟:

℣: Heart of Jesus, abyss of all virtues, ℟:

℣: Heart of Jesus, most worthy of all praise, ℟:

℣: Heart of Jesus, king and center of all hearts, ℟:

℣: Heart of Jesus, in whom are all treasures of wisdom and knowledge, ℟:

℣: Heart of Jesus, in whom dwells the fullness of divinity, ℟:

℣: Heart of Jesus, in whom the Father was well pleased, ℟:

℣: Heart of Jesus, of whose fullness we have all received, ℟:

℣: Heart of Jesus, desire of the everlasting hills, ℟:

℣: Heart of Jesus, patient and most merciful, ℟:

℣: Heart of Jesus, enriching all who invoke Thee, ℟:

℣: Heart of Jesus, fountain of life and holiness, ℟:

℣: Heart of Jesus, propitiation for our sins, ℟:

℣: Heart of Jesus, loaded down with opprobrium, ℟:

℣: Heart of Jesus, bruised for our offenses, ℟:

℣: Heart of Jesus, obedient to death, ℟:

℣: Heart of Jesus, pierced with a lance, ℟:

℣: Heart of Jesus, source of all consolation, ℟:

℣: Heart of Jesus, our life and resurrection, ℟:

℣: Heart of Jesus, our peace and our reconciliation, ℟:

℣: Heart of Jesus, victim for our sins, ℟:

℣: Heart of Jesus, salvation of those who trust in Thee, ℟:

℣: Heart of Jesus, hope of those who die in Thee, ℟:

℣: Heart of Jesus, delight of all the Saints, ℟:

℣: Lamb of God, who takest away the sins of the world,
℟: **Have mercy on us, Lord.**

℣: Lamb of God, who takest away the sins of the world,
℟: **Graciously hear us, Lord.**

℣: Lamb of God, who takest away the sins of the world,
℟: **Have mercy on us, Lord.**

Amen.

The most important thing we do in life is to die well.

For those who are suffering, dying, as well as those who attend to them, this is a time that can be very difficult.

Beautifully designed and thoughtfully curated, *Passing Time* is a treasury of over 300 pages of classical Catholic texts to help people who are going through this time of life. It has catechesis, meditations, and prayers on suffering, the hour of death, mourning and burial, and Purgatory and remembrance.

www.catholictreehouse.com/passing-time

Enflame your love for the Sacred Heart of Jesus

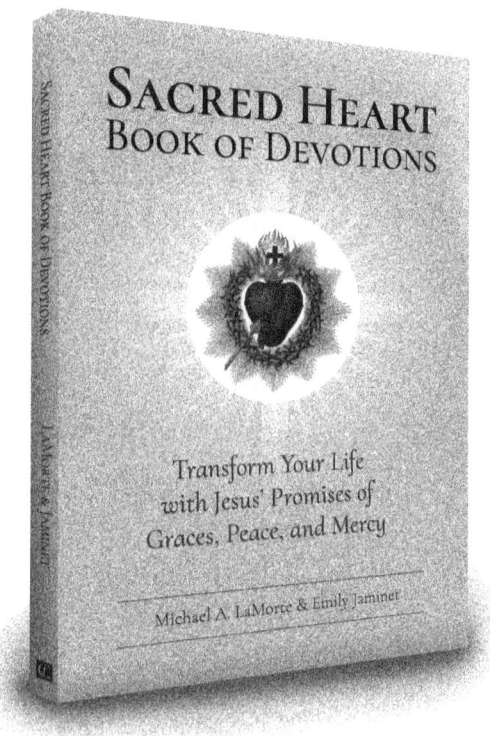

Perhaps the most comprehensive Sacred Heart devotional to date, the *Sacred Heart Book of Devotions* is a timeless collection of essential resources. Full of history, timeless prayers and novenas, classical sacred art, hymns, and more, this is an incredible resource for anyone who has or wants to develop a devotion to the Sacred Heart.

---

www.catholictreehouse.com/sacred-heart

Put your faith into action by letting the saints show you the way.

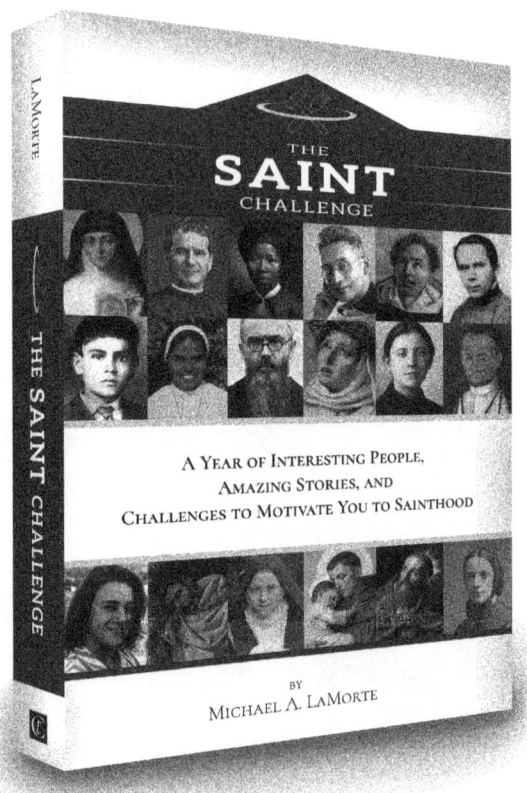

The Saint Challenge is a daily devotional that brings the saints alive and puts your faith to work inspired by their example. Designed to be used over and over, *The Saint Challenge* offers you a unique opportunity to delve into the captivating lives of the saints to find wisdom and inspiration for your own journey of faith. Over 450 pages of stories, challenges, and resources that turn the witness of their lives into inspiration for your personal growth in holiness.

www.thesaintchallenge.com

www.ingramcontent.com/pod-product-compliance
Lightning Source LLC
Chambersburg PA
CBHW020431130626
46549CB00001B/79